Copyright © 2023 Church of God by Faith, Inc.

All rights reserved. No portion of this book may be reproduced in any form or by any electronic or mechanical means, including information storage and retrieval systems, without written permission from the publisher or author, except as permitted by U.S. copyright law.

All Scripture quotations, unless otherwise indicated, are taken from the Authorized King James Version.

Other versions used are:
Scripture quotations marked (NLT) are taken from the *Holy Bible*, New Living Translation, copyright ©1996, 2004, 2015 by Tyndale House Foundation. Used by permission of Tyndale House Publishers, Carol Stream, Illinois 60188. All rights reserved.

Scripture quotations marked MSG are taken from *The Message*, copyright © 1993, 2002, 2018 by Eugene H. Peterson. Used by permission of NavPress. All rights reserved. Represented by Tyndale House Publishers.

Scripture quotations taken from the (NASB®) New American Standard Bible®, Copyright © 1960, 1971, 1977, 1995, 2020 by The Lockman Foundation. Used by permission. All rights reserved. lockman.org

Scripture taken from the New King James Version®. Copyright © 1982 by Thomas Nelson. Used by permission. All rights reserved.

NIV - THE HOLY BIBLE, NEW INTERNATIONAL VERSION
NIV Copyright 1973, 1978, 1984, 2011 by Biblica, Inc. Used by permission. All rights reserved.

The inside devotional pages have been designed using assets from Freepik.com (Image by pikisuperstar on Freepik)

Published by:
BE Books
A Division of Becoming Engaged Enterprises, Inc.
2810 NE 13th Street * Gainesville, FL 32609

ISBN: 978-0-9797717-6-7

# MORNING GLORY

## A Devotional for Walking by Faith

A Production of the COGBF National Board of
Christian Education

# PREFACE

Spending time with God is such a wonderful and cherished experience. It is a time when we can connect, share as well as receive. During this time, we embrace the fact that God has our attention, and we have His. We appreciate the moment that we are in the presence of the almighty God and that is an experience like none other. We hope that this devotional will give you the experience of being in God's presence. Being in communion with God is delightful and enjoyable. *Morning Glory: A Devotional for Walking by Faith* is designed to bring you into God's presence.

This devotional was a compilation effort by the National Board of Christian Education to give you an opportunity to spend time with God. We hope that the content of this book will bring joy, peace, encouragement, and hope as you take the journey with us.

About five years ago, the idea of having a devotional emanated with me and was presented to the National Board of Christian Education. The devotional idea was received with excitement. Upon receiving the blessing from our illustrious leader, Bishop James E. McKnight, Jr., we launched the project with the late Elder Calvin McDonald taking the lead. Due to the passing of Elder McDonald, Deacon James Thomas assumed the lead in continuing the project.

We are indeed grateful for the efforts of Deacon Thomas, his dedication and commitment to the devotional project has been outstanding. We are thankful for the authors who shared their inspiration so that others are blessed and encouraged. The contributing authors have been diligent in writing to bring this inspiration. We hope that the devotional will encourage you to spend time with God in an intimate manner. God wants His children to engage in worship and prayer.

Many thanks to the editorial staff who spent countless hours ensuring the quality of the devotional. The National Editorial Team consisting of Lady Myrtice Landers and Sister Carolyn Cowan, is commended for faithfulness in assisting us in the editorial process. We are indeed grateful for your profound efforts.

Blessings as you journey with us,

Min. Dr. Deloris Y. McBride, NBCE Director

# DEDICATION

When asked who would lead the efforts of this project, the late Elder Calvin McDonald graciously accepted. Until his departure, he worked faithfully with his team to begin the process ensuring we valued the vision and the guidelines. We dedicate this edition to Elder Calvin McDonald in appreciation for his service. Rest in God, our brother.

Dedicated to
Elder Calvin McDonald

## DAY 1

# TROUBLED TIMES

> *Therefore, we will not fear, though the earth give way and the mountains fall into the heart of the sea, though its waters roar and foam and the mountains quake with their surging. Psalm 46:1-3*

Tragedy knows no bounds, it can strike at any moment and can happen to anyone without regard to the trail it leaves behind. An accident, a natural disaster, and a disconcerting doctor's report can be devastating. Where do you turn? How do you face it?

The Psalmist reminds us that, "*God is our refuge and strength,* an ever present help in trouble." *Therefore, we will not fear, though the earth give way and the mountains fall into the heart of the sea, though its waters roar and the foam and the mountains quake with their surging*" (Psalm 46:1-3).

Dawson Trotman, founder of the Navigators, drowned tragically at age 50. The bitter news of his drowning swept like cold wind across Schroon Lake to the shoreline. When Lila Trotman, Dawson's widow walked upon the scene, a close friend shouted, "Oh, Lila ...Dawson's gone!" To that, she replied in calm assurance to the words of Psalm 115:3 "*But our God is in the heavens; He does whatever He pleases.*" All the anguish that normally consumes and cripples those who survive, did not invade her heart. Instead, she leaned upon her sovereign Lord, who had once again done what He pleased.

**Bishop James E. McKnight, Jr.**

# DAY 2

# FAITH AND OBEDIENCE

> *Now faith is the substance of things hoped for, the evidence of things not seen. Hebrews 11:1*

Shelby Turner defines faith in the Dictionary of Bible Themes as, "*A constant outlook of trust towards God, whereby human beings abandon all reliance on their own efforts and put their full confidence in him, his word, and his promises.*" How is this kind faith developed? The Apostle Paul said, "*So, then faith cometh by hearing, and hearing by the word of God*" (Rom. 10:17).

I learned to have faith in God as a young child by observing my father and mother exercising their faith and walking in obedience to God's word. Through them I learned how to trust God for healing, for provisions, and for guidance in everyday decisions.

They also demonstrated that faith and obedience are linked together. You can't hold to one and neglect the other". James said, "*For as the body without the spirit is dead, so faith without works is dead*" (James 2:26). As we hear God's word, we must act in obedience, regardless the cost.

Dr. B.J. Miller said, "It is a great deal easier to do that which God gives us to do, no matter how hard it is, than to face the responsibilities of not doing it."

**Leading Lady Delois T. McKnight**

## DAY 3

# A GOOD GOD

> *For I know the plans I have for you, says the Lord. They are plans for good and not for disaster, to give you a future and a hope.*
> Jeremiah 29:11 NLT

Many people think of God in the wrong way. They think God is always ready to punish and destroy, but the opposite is true. The word of God declares that it is His will that none should perish, but that all should come unto repentance. It is God's desire that we prosper and be in good health. Sickness and poverty are not His will for us.

Yes, there will be times of pain and suffering, but through all of them the Lord promised to be with us. He will be a strong Tower for us during our challenges in life. If we persevere, he will help us to bring our hopes and dreams to pass. Yes, in the midst of it all, He will see us through.

**P.S. He knows and He cares enough to bring it to pass.**

**Ruling Elder H. N. Turner**

## DAY 4

# CONTENTMENT

> *Contentment Godliness with contentment is great gain.*
> *1 Timothy 6:6*

Many people live their whole life without ever being content. When we do not have a relationship with our creator, which is essential in a Christian's life, we do not find peace and contentment. We may find ourselves being a complainer. When we grumble at one another, nothing happens, but, when we take our concerns and complaints to God, He can do something about our situation.

I am often reminded when Jesus said, "For without me you can do nothing." The key to spiritual growth and personal fulfillment is contentment. We should be content with what God is doing in our lives. When we understand the importance of our relationship with God, then our purpose in life becomes clearer and more meaningful. Then, our contentment will be complete.

**Lady "Precious" Turner**

## DAY 5

# MASTER, DO YOU CARE?

> *And he was in the hinder part of the ship, asleep on a pillow: and they awake him, and say unto him, Master, care thou not that we perish? Mark 4:38*

The disciples were obeying Jesus' command, "Let Us Cross over to the Other Side" when the storm came upon them. Obedience does not save us from the storms of life; but when we obey His word, He is with us to see us through. Sometimes He delivers us from difficulties. Sometimes He gives us grace to pass through them. Sometimes we are at our wits' end but not our faith's end. We should not measure His care and love for us by the storms we encounter in life.

It is possible to feel that God is ignoring our plight. That He really doesn't care. The Scripture tells us to cast all of our cares on Him, "because he cares" for us. When you go through deep waters, I will be with you. When you go through rivers of difficulty, you will not drown. When you walk through the fire of oppression, you will not be burned up; the flame will not consume you, for I am your God.

**Ruling Elder James E. Williams**

## DAY 6

# A PEARL FOUND IN A LILY

> *But Jesus looked at them and said to them, with men this is impossible, but with God All things are possible. Matthew 19:26*

Now, we know Pearls don't grow in lilies, but if you can believe, all things are possible to him who believes. I was lost in a world of sin, and couldn't find much comfort, or peace within. I searched all over, but couldn't find anyone to love me the way I desired to be loved. I prayed and prayed until one day, the pearl was found. One hot and humid day, the lily came alive producing a beautiful pearl.

The relationship was for real, untouched, with no blemish, the waiting was over. I didn't have to doubt the love; it was genuine from the beginning. You can't buy it because the price is too high. You can't give it away because it was made only for you. The pearl is special and to be cherished by only you. It was hidden in the heart for a lifetime of happiness, joy, peace, and loves to be embraced. With men, there may be doubt, that what seems to be impossible, but with God All things are possible, to them that can believe.

**Leading Lady Lillie Pearl Williams**

## DAY 7

# BEAUTY PAINS

> *He cuts off every branch in me that bears no fruit, while every branch that does bear fruit he prunes so that it will be even more fruitful. John 15:2*

Pain is beauty. This is something we all know, especially women. Though beauty is eye appealing, we understand that comfort is on a different side of beauty. For example, you have a deep desire to wear your favorite pair of shoes, however, they are uncomfortable, but they are appealing to the eye. Even though the experience is uncomfortable, it's necessary to complete the task of being presentable.

Beautification is all about preparation. It's the process of removing or covering any flaws that would oppose your desired look. This process is what God does to us. He prunes us so that we can bear more fruit. The fruit is what makes the tree attractive. The fruit brings eye-catching colors and intense smells. We must remember that holiness has a beauty that we have yet to tap into. This beauty takes away all the attributes that are not like God. It allows you to shine so that men could see who God really is.

**Reflection:** What is God asking you to strip away so that you can experience true spiritual beauty?

**Leading Lady Gwendolyn Ware**

## DAY 8

# THE FRUIT OF THE SPIRIT

> *Jesus says, By this my Father is glorified, that you bear much fruit and so prove to be my disciples. John 15:8*

When you think of the word fruit, you probably think of something like an apple or a banana. However, when Paul talks about the "fruit of the Spirit" he is not referring to a piece of fruit you eat but a fruit that is displayed through the character of a believer filled with the Holy Spirit. When we are filled with the Holy Spirit, the fruit of love, joy, peace, patience, kindness, goodness, faithfulness, gentleness, and self-control is given to us as a whole package that is beautiful to the eye and transforming to the soul.

The fruit of the Spirit emanates the Spirit of God and reveals what God is like. In other words, their works demonstrate the change of sanctification that is at work in our hearts. God has given us a basket of fruit that is perfect through the Spirit, therefore we have a responsibility to display the character of God in our daily walk. We must consistently display a fruit basket that honors God and advances His Kingdom. As we abide in Him, we will bear much fruit that's eye-catching and soul-reaching.

**Think About it:** Can we see your fruit basket?

Ruling Elder Reginald L. Daymon

## DAY 9

# YOU ARE NEEDED

> *The harvest is plentiful, but the workers are few. Matthew 9:37*

It is a NOW TIME, and YOU ARE NEEDED! In the wake of worldwide turmoil, we have an open door to speak truth and life. The call to come, serve, work, and witness together is urgent. Every time you see the faces of other human beings, you see souls that are so loved by God that He sent His Son to die for his redemption. They matter deeply to God, so they must matter deeply to us as well!

So, reaching them with the Good News of salvation is a mission assigned to you and me. We are missionaries commissioned to carry out the plan of salvation for those who are lost, it may be our neighbor, our family, our friend, and our co-worker. The Kingdom of God needs laborers to reap the harvest, people to pray, and those willing to go out and reach souls who are hurting, burdened, and in need of a savior. There is a window of time to reach the harvest! Let's go!

**Think About It:** Will you join us today?

**Leading Lady Veronica Daymon**

# DAY 10

# A SATANIC DECEPTION

> *For this, you know with certainty, that no immoral or impure person or covetous man, who is an idolater, has an inheritance in the kingdom of Christ and God. Let no one deceive you with empty words, for because of these things the wrath of God comes upon the sons of disobedience. Ephesians 5:5-6.*

The world has normalized all types of perversion and sexual sins. Sadly, many of these perversions are being embraced in today's Christian church and it isn't new. The Apostle Paul wrote to the saints in Ephesus, "*For this, you know with certainty, that no immoral or impure person or covetous man, who is an idolater, has an inheritance in the kingdom of Christ and God. Let no one deceive you with empty words, for because of these things the wrath of God comes upon the sons of disobedience.* Eph.5:5-6.

MacArthur said, "*No Christian will be sinless in this present life, but it is dangerously deceptive for Christians to offer assurance of salvation to a professing believer whose life is characterized by persistent sin and who shows no shame for that sin or hunger for the holy and pure things of God.* The scripture exalts us to, "*Run from sexual sin! No other sin so clearly affects the body as this one does. For sexual immorality is a sin against your own body*" (1 Corinthians 6:18).

**Bishop James E. McKnight, Jr.**

# DAY 11

# FOLLOWING CHRIST

What does it mean to follow Christ and how do I encourage others to do so?

> *I love them that love me; And those that seek me early shall find me. Proverbs 8:17*

First, it is important to have a personal, intimate relationship with Christ and that is developed by regularly spending one-on-one time with Him. It has been most productive for me to start early in the mornings reading, praying, meditating in His word, and spending quality time with the Lord. This is a time of quietness and stillness in which I can surrender my mind to the Lord and prepare my heart for whatever He has ordered for my day. The scripture declares "I love them that love me; And those that seek me early shall find me" (Prov.8:17).

This is a promise that we can lay hold of, whether we are in a cooperate or private setting. We can bring our personal request to the Lord and what a privilege it is to talk to Him about our struggles, our weaknesses, and seek Him for guidance. This is also a time when I confirm my love toward the Lord and give Him thanks and praises for the things that He has already done.

*"If I am to wholly follow the Lord Jesus Christ,*
*I must forsake everything that is contrary to Him" ~ A.W. Tozer*

**Leading Lady Delois T. McKnight**

# DAY 12

# LOVE YOUR ENEMIES

> *Ye have heard that it hath been said; Thou shalt love thy neighbor and hate thine enemy. But I say unto you, love your enemies, bless them that curse you, do good to them that hate you, and pray for them which despitefully use you, and persecute you.*
> Matthew 5:43-44

We may struggle with the teaching of Jesus concerning love your enemies on whether it is possible considering my enemies. We are not to analyze but obey His word.

Two kinds of love flow from the same fountain of goodwill to all humankind. One is that feeling by which we approve of the conduct of another person, commonly called the love of complacency; the other is by which we wish well to the person, although we cannot approve of their conduct.

It is impossible to love the conduct of a person who does not regard the word of God. We may disapprove of their conduct, yet we must wish the person well; we may not approve of their behavior; we are to still speak kindly of them, and to them; we cannot return evil for evil; we are to seek to do him good. In this way, you will make him feel guilty and ashamed, and the LORD will reward you.

**Ruling Elder James E. Williams**

# DAY 13

## SPIRITUAL GIFTS

> *But, the fruit of the spirit is love, joy, peace, long-suffering, gentleness, goodness, faith, meekness, temperance.*
> *Galatians 5: 22-23*

During the festive time of the year, we tend to think of giving out fruit baskets for Thanksgiving and fruitcakes for Christmas. But there is something better and more rewarding than fruity gifts. You can't beat giving out the fruit of the Spirit, with the greatest of these being LOVE. We don't even need to wait for the festive time of the year. These gifts can be done daily, or year-round. They bring joy to the receiver, peace where there might be confusion, long-suffering where one might feel like giving up, gentleness in the midst of despair, goodness where hope is lost, faith to believe it's already done, meekness in knowing someone cares, and temperance holding on, never to let go. Most of all, love to say I care.

Our children need to see more of these gifts displayed in the homes, oftentimes; our words may not come out as they need to, especially after a long trying day. We might get upset and say things we don't mean to say, but allow love to be exemplified by saying, I am sorry.

**Leading Lady Lillie Williams**

## DAY 14

# WHAT'S YOUR RESPONSE?

*Let your light so shine before men, that they may see your good works, and glorify your Father which is in heaven. Matthew 5:16*

Imagine visiting your favorite restaurant. You order a dish you've desired for some time. You are detailed in reference to your order to ensure it is prepared just right. You're patiently awaiting the meal and the waiter brings your meal out. After a long wait it is completely wrong! The intense hunger pains have kicked in and the meal that you desired is not up to par. There is a restaurant full of people and they're in the vicinity in which they can see your reaction. Your natural human feelings and emotions have kicked in at the moment. What's your response?

As Christians, character development is key. As Christ's representatives, we must strive to emulate His character daily. It is our duty and responsibility to ensure that God's light shines through us. It's essential that when we respond to conflicting or emotionally driven situations that we remember it's God that we are representing. As children we were taught not to embarrass our parents. We must be the same way about God, intentional about not embarrassing Him.

**Think about it:** What's your response when things don't go your way?

**Leading Lady Gwendolyn Ware**

## DAY 15

# OBEDIENCE IS AN ACT OF LOVE

> *He that hath my commandments, and keepeth them, he it is that loveth me: and he that loveth me shall be loved of my Father, and I will love him, and will manifest myself to him. John 14:21*

Perhaps you are struggling to obey God completely in your life and you are wondering how to overcome. Sometimes, we partially obey His commandments and believe that we are being obedient. However, to God partial obedience is not good enough and is counted as disobedience, Brothers, and sisters we must completely obey God and trust him to act on our behalf.

One thing we must understand is that obedience requires love for God and faith in God. As Abraham stood the test of faith through obedience by offering his son as a sacrifice, we will encounter the same. One might obey God somehow religiously, but absolute obedience always emerges from absolute faith in God alone.

Many times, obedience means sacrifice; sometimes obedience can be painful. Sometimes it can mean stretching ourselves outside our comfort Zone. On our own, we may not be able to do it. We therefore need God's help through the Holy Spirit to help us. Obedience therefore is borne not out of fear but out of faith and love. We obey Him not just because it is our obligation as Christians, but because He called us to obey Him and we listened. Every act of obedience accumulates confidence for the next obedience. And with every act of obedience, one discovers inner fulfillment and happiness

**Think About it:** Do you love God enough to obey him completely?

**Ruling Elder Reginald L. Daymon**

## DAY 16

# MAKE THEM SEE

> *Then again He laid His hands on his eyes, and he looked intently and was restored, and began to see everything clearly. Mark 8:25*

At our 99th General Assembly, I am reminded of the message given during the Ordination Service by Ruling Elder James Ware. It was a message filled with hope to inspire us to diligently approach others to encourage them to see Jesus Christ as a loving Savior. While individuals are blinded by the cares of this life, despaired on every hand, and inattentive to God's desires for them, we must open their eyes to see clearly.

As Christians, it is important to be mindful of everyone's state of being. For example, one might not be attired according to our specifications or behave with dignity. One's focus and intentions are often ungodly and unholy. There might be tendencies to project unrighteousness in every possible manner. But it is imperative that ministers of God position themselves to "Make Them See". We are challenged by God to love and reach out to individuals who are not walking or living a godly life and "Make Them See" that God has an overwhelming love for them and wants to acknowledge them as His children. We must "Make Them See" how much our Savior loves them, how much our Savior desires to surround them with blessings, hope, joy, and peace. We must reflect God's image of holiness and righteousness and in doing so, we provide a reflection that can transcend everything and thus give hope to a dying world. We must declare the Word of God. This is the Beauty of Holiness.

**Dr. Deloris Y. McBride**

# DAY 17

# POWER OUTAGES

> *For who is God, save the LORD? and who is a rock, save our God. God is my strength and power: and he maketh my way perfect. He maketh my feet like hinds' feet: and setteth me upon my high places.*
> *II Samuel 22:32-34*

For residents living in Florida, hurricane season is an annual occurrence accompanied by frequent electrical power outages, catastrophic winds, and water damage. I experienced a recent power outage on a day that was filled with bright sunshine, and a 15-minute downpour resulting in a one-hour outage. During this brief period, I had forgotten that there was a power disconnect. I proceeded to flip the light switch with no results. I flipped it again and again with no results. My daughter, observing my futile efforts, reminded me by saying, "Daddy, the power is off."

Power outages are often caused by storm winds that blow trees and limbs across power lines creating a source disconnect and interrupting current continuity-black outs. In other cases, it is simply a failure of the power company to maintain their lines by periodically clearing away trees and limbs that have the potential to fall in high winds. In retrospect, the utility companies usually restore our power in several days or weeks. However, God can restore our power connection within minutes when there is a repentant heart of confession.

When was the last time you checked your power line for potential hazards?

**Lord, I thank you for sharing your strength and power with me and making my days perfect.**

**James Thomas**

## DAY 18

# HOMESICK FOR HEAVEN

> *God will wipe away all tears from our eyes; and there shall be no more death, neither sorrow, nor crying, neither shall there be any more pain: for the former things are passed away. Revelation 21:4*

Have you ever had an opportunity to observe a kindergarten or pre-kindergarten classroom on the first day of school? Children who have never been away from their parents will do all in their *little power* to escape and reunite with their parents. Occasionally, some do escape and will have to be cornered and brought back into the classroom. With tears streaming and ear-piercing squeals, they continue their relentless attempts until they fall asleep. When the parents return, there is a burst of excitement! Little feet sprint toward the parent(s) with incredible speed. Some leap into the arms of their waiting parents. Instead of *squeals of fear and sadness*, they squeal with joy and gladness. They get to go home!

As we observe our world today, we see many catastrophes. Death and dying are all around. Some parents have lost their children. Some children have lost their parents. Some seniors have lost all of their family members. Consequently, many spend hours each day with tears streaming down their cheeks and hearts squealing in pain. Many just want to go home to be with the Lord where they will be reunited with family, friends, and loved ones. On that day there will be no more sadness, no more death, no more "good-byes"… Nothing that we experience on earth will cause sorrow in heaven. There will be eternal joy. Oh, what a *going home* that will be!

As you look at the world around you, are you becoming homesick for heaven? How many tears have you shed recently? Have you buried your face in your pillow and wept bitterly? If so, remember that Jesus will return! We will be able to run into his arms and go home!

*Abba Father, I'm feeling homesick. Tears are streaming. My heart is squealing! Lord, comfort and strengthen me! Please let me lay my head into the bosom of your LOVE until you return.*
*In Jesus' name, I pray. Amen.*

**Geraldine Russell**

## DAY 19

# WHAT RULES YOUR HEART?

> *And let the peace of God rule in your hearts, to the which also ye are called in one body; and be ye thankful. Colossians 3:15*

Think back to your elementary school days. You learned that a ruler is a mathematical tool used to measure the length of an object in either inches, centimeters, or in some cases, millimeters. As you grew older and entered junior high, you may have begun to talk in more abstract terms of what a ruler is and discussed the fact that a ruler could also be the leader of any one person or a group of people. Believe it or not, these two descriptions of a ruler are not that distant from each other because a leader of people may not be made out of wood like a physical ruler, but he or she is still the measuring tool the people use to examine their own lives. For instance, Queen Elizabeth was the leader of the citizens of England, and she was the one who generally made the decisions that govern their actions and dictated how they lived from day to day. If they need to know what the law says about a certain situation, they would look to her. That's the mark of a great ruler: to become the representative example of how the people should live.

With that description of a ruler in mind, consider what Paul encouraged the church at Colosse to do in Colossians 3:15. The verse says, *"And let the peace of God rule in your hearts, to the which also ye are called in one body; and be ye thankful."* Besides the rulers we physically have, there is one ruler that is most important in our hearts and that is the peace of God! The peace that God gives allows us to face each day and each situation with the assurance that He is in control and whatever happens only happens because He allows it. How kind of God to give us His peace in exchange for our issues! If we allow that peace to be the ruler of our hearts, when stressful situations arise, we will find ourselves going in whatever direction will lead us back to that peace. If we admit it, there are times when we let stress, depression, or sadness rule our hearts and our actions prove it, but continuing in that way will destroy us. Eventually, we will begin to realize that God, the faithful ruler of peace, will always lead us back to the Presence of the Lord. There, and only there, will our hearts be able to experience true rest and that, too, will be evident in our daily walk.

**Think About It:** Who or what is ruling your heart today?

**Domonique Brunson**

## DAY 20

# WORKS OF LOVE

> *My little children let us not love in word, neither in tongue, but deed and in truth. 1 John 3:18*

When misunderstanding arises, Love covers. When you are mistreated and falsely accused, Love endures, is kind, and never strikes back. When one has done you wrong, and is in need, Love reaches out and does them a good deed.

Love always draws and never drives. The speech of Love is always with grace, seasoned good with SALT.

LOVE never stirs up strife, but always works for PEACE. Love for God is obedience to him in all his commandments.

**Evangelist Nathaniel Scippio, Edited writing**

## DAY 21

# NO GREATER LOVE

> *For God so loved the world, that he gave his only begotten Son, that whosoever believeth in him should not perish, but have everlasting life. John 3:16*

People may find it hard to believe that God loves them because of the sins that they have committed. They may find it difficult to believe that they can be truly forgiven of their crime and may even feel undeserving of God's gracious tender love. They may even ask the question, "How can God love a person like me?"

Proof that God loves you, despite your sins, is in the Bible which is the living Word of God almighty. *We all have sinned and come short of the glory of God, but God demonstrated His love toward us, in that while we were yet sinners, Christ died for us all.*

For God so loved the world that He gave His only son, Christ Jesus, that whosoever believes in Him shall not perish, but obtain eternal life with Him in heaven (St. John 3:16). Jesus loves us so much that He gave His life as a ransom for humanity to redeem us back to the Father, our God.

Through the death and resurrection of Jesus Christ, we now can have an everlasting relationship with God the Father. No greater love hath no man than this, that a man lay down his life for a friend (John 15:13).

**Dr. Leticia Hardy**

# DAY 22

# SPIRITUAL SEEDS

> *And when much people were gathered together, and were come to him out of every city, he spake by a parable: A sower went out to sow his seed: and as he sowed, some fell by the wayside; and it was trodden down, and the fowls of the air devoured it. Luke 8:4-5*

Early in Jesus' ministry, he used parables as an example to bring light to what heaven and spirituality would be like for his followers. A parable is a story, or an anecdote relating to godly matters and gives a lesson to assist us in living within the earth. The story in Luke chapter 8 tells of how individuals respond to the gospel message through the Word of God.

A farmer went out to sow seeds. Some seeds fell by the wayside, were trampled on and eaten by birds. Some seeds fell on rocks and withered away; and still, other seeds fell on thorns. The thorns grew with it and dried up the seeds due to hard and dry soil. After several failed attempts, the farmer's (Sower's) seeds fell on good, fertile soil and grew into a large crop yielding a great harvest; one hundred times more than what was planted!

The "seed" Jesus was referring to is the Word of God and the "soil" is a person's heart. When an individual hears the gospel, "Good News," reads the Bible, and communes with likeminded people of faith, one of three things will happen.

They will reject the Word by hardening their hearts, so the seed won't grow.

They will believe for a while, but when trouble or difficulty arises, they forfeit their faith/commitment.

They will hear God's Word, do what it says, and believe by following Jesus'

**Instructions.** So, what will your response be when you get the opportunity to receive God's Word? Take a moment and reflect on your life and see what it would be like with or without Christ. Personally, I choose the third one and I think you should too.

**Jessica Lucas**

## DAY 23

# HELP IS ON THE WAY!

> *Let your conversation be without covetousness; and be content with such things as ye have: for he hath said, I will never leave thee, nor forsake thee. So that we may boldly say, The Lord is my helper, and I will not fear what man shall do unto me. Hebrews 13:1-6*

Trouble comes in all shapes and sizes. It is unpleasant and sometimes becomes unsettled and without an answer or solution. Job said days are full of trouble. But, there is a promise to the believer, that when trouble comes, our helper will never leave or forsake us. Our helper is Jesus Christ.

**Prayer: Lord, when trouble comes and my personal storms begin to rise, help me to hold on and stretch out my faith on your promises, while being fully persuaded, that whatever you have promised, that you are able to perform it. I know that nothing is impossible with you, and that you will perfect that which concerns me and my household. Thank you, Jesus, for your grace!**

Elder Garry Shelton

## DAY 24

# WHAT DO YOU HAVE?

> *Then Peter said, "Silver and gold have I none; but such as I have give I thee: In the name of Jesus Christ of Nazareth rise up and walk." Acts 3:6*

I have said to myself so many times, if I had thousands of dollars, I would give to organizations that help people, to those who are homeless, sick, hurting and without resources to make their life more comfortable. If we wait on the abundance of finances, we will never help anyone.

Money is not always the answer to help those who are in need. Sometimes they may need a companion, someone to encourage them when they are troubled, to prepare a meal, to be a friend, or offer a helping hand. Search your heart. You can send a card to encourage them or write a letter. There are so many things we can do if we only pray and ask God how we can be a blessing to someone in the time of trouble.

**Heavenly Father, help me to use what I have to help others in need. In Jesus' name, Amen.**

Mary Calhoun

# DAY 25

## WORK YOUR FAITH

> *Now faith is the substance of things hoped for, the evidence of things not seen. Hebrews 11:1*

As a child, I was always fascinated with magic. Magicians are known for making things disappear into thin air. Now you see it, now you don't. The quick and easy solution to solving problems. It seemed so much easier to me than having to exercise my faith to get things to happen in life. One thing I have learned on my Christian journey is this; it's not necessarily our faith that makes things happen, but our faith in God's WORD that moves God. He never promised us that our faith would not fail, but that HIS WORD would not fail!

While exercising my faith, I have discovered that more powerful than magic is this…the God I serve is known for making things APPEAR out of thin air, right before our very eyes. No curtains, doors, or hocus pocus needed!!! Work your FAITH people work it!

**Lesley Thomas**

## DAY 26

# HE CARES FOR YOU

> *I will lift up mine eyes unto the hills, from whence cometh my help. Psalm 121:1*

Those things that seem impossible are possible with God. Those things that seem unbearable are bearable with God. For the Lord thy God is Sovereign. He knows exactly what we are going through; and not only does He know, but He also promised to take care of us. He told us to cast all our cares upon him, for indeed he does care.

Even when it seems like we are all alone, he's right there. His right hand will uphold us, His spirit will sustain us. It's almost a magical occurrence when we call on his name. Even now He knows what we are going through, He knows the pain we feel. We will find comfort in knowing there is no sorrow that heaven can't heal.

With each passing day, the burden will get lighter. The tears will be fewer for the Lord says: "Blessed are they that mourn, for I will comfort you." So, when we don't know where to turn, when we don't know what to do, we need to lift our eyes to the hills from whence cometh our help for our help comes from the Lord (Psalm 121:1). Jesus does care for us.

**Felicia C. Parker**

## DAY 27

# LEARNING TO BE CONTENT

> *Not that I speak in respect of want: for I have learned, in whatsoever state I am, therewith to be content.*
> *Philippians 4:11*

Paul writes how he learned to be content during times of lack and times of abundance. Paul was an incredible man. It is difficult to imagine, but Paul was writing about being content while in prison. Contentment can be defined as a state of happiness or satisfaction. We can learn as Paul did the secret of contentment. It is not about us having perfect circumstances in our lives. Contentment comes from putting our hope in the Lord who will never leave us or forsake us. We have come to understand that God alone can provide peace, joy, and happiness in our lives.

**Heavenly Father, thank you for providing the secret to contentment. We are content with what we have in our lives – possessions, status, or situation. We will continue to pursue, and practice being content with you alone.
In Jesus' name. Amen.**

**Venetta Law**

# DAY 28

## REGISTER TO SERVE

> *I beseech you therefore, brethren, by the mercies of God, that ye present your bodies a living sacrifice, holy, acceptable unto God, which is your reasonable service. Romans 12: 1*

For many years, the United States of America required each young man to register to serve our country at the age of eighteen. However, the loving Lord requires each of us to register by believing on Him the moment we hear His voice, (Rev. 3:20) to serve in "His army". Then we are to *present our bodies as a living sacrifice, holy, acceptable unto God, which is our reasonable service* (Romans 12:1). What a wonderful thought as we begin each day by registering to serve a God who can keep our body and soul safe in his arms. Let us go forth today serving God by serving others with His light shining brightly through us in this dark and sinful world.

Inasmuch, as the United States of America needs men, the Lord needs men, women, boys, and girls to serve in His army.

**Mary Smith**

# DAY 29

# THE THREE THINGS THAT MOVE GOD:

### Prayer, Praise and Faith

> *Now faith is the substance of things hoped for, and the evidence of things not seen. Hebrews 11:1*

Prayer is a two-way conversation with God asking Him of our heart's desires. He will then answer with a **"Yes," "Not Now,"** or **"Not at All."** It is in those moments of waiting that we must not lose heart. We must continue strong in our faith knowing and trusting God will answer right on time.

God inhabits the praises of His people. He delights and loves when we offer our praise unto Him. Praise can bring instant healing, it can calm the storm, and it can ignite a fire within someone's soul. Praise can also cause the tears to flow—tears of joy.

Faith is the essence of things hoped for, the evidence of things we cannot see. It is our faith that moves mountains. Faith also moves God to do a mighty work and activates the Holy Spirit to perform wonderful acts within the earth.

These are the most important elements of a believer's life and should be used daily. Prayer, praise, and faith literally keep Christians afloat every day as we maneuver through our own personal journey in life. We have to ensure these three things are full, ready, and active at any given moment.

**Cheryl L. Thomas**

# DAY 30

# ARE YOU ALL IN?

> *And he returned back from him, and took a yoke of oxen, and slew them, and boiled their flesh with the instruments of the oxen, and gave unto the people, and they did eat. Then he arose, and went after Elijah, and ministered unto him. I King 19:21*

I heard a wonderful message during our 99th General Assembly in December 2019. The message was given by Ruling Elder James Williams. The Message was entitled, "Are You All In?" The challenge to us comes with a commitment to commit. One must be willing to leave hindrances and those things that circumvent our desire and purpose to fulfill our mission to serve with impact.

Elisha, the son of Shaphat, was plowing with others and was approached by the prophet Elijah. Elijah was told by God to find his replacement and Elisha would be that replacement. Elijah approached Elisha and placed his mantle on him which symbolizes the bestowing of power and succession. Elisha later took his oxen and killed them and served a meal to many people. What Elisha did with his oxen was definitive of his attitude and commitment to serve. This act indicated that he was "all in" and that he was fully committed to the task and work at hand. Elisha had nothing to go back to and therefore could fully serve God and assist Elijah in providing a service to the people of Israel. Elisha was totally committed to his service. As Elisha was committed to serving God, we too must surrender anything that prevents us from giving God our total dedication.

**Dr. Deloris Y. McBride**

## DAY 31

# WISHFUL THINKING

> *Yea, a man may say, Thou hast faith, and I have works: shew me thy faith without thy works, and I will shew thee my faith by my works. James 2:18*

In the life of the believer, fate and destiny are two factors that we will have to contend with in becoming the best that we can become. "If fate means that you lose, give him a good fight anyhow" (William McAfee).

"Destiny is not a matter of chance, it is a matter of choice; it is not a thing to be waited for, it is a thing to be achieved" (William Jennings Bryan). Wishful thinking is the formation of a belief based on what might be pleasing but is not based on reality; some would refer to this as daydreaming.

Listening to the prayers and testimonies of some believers, it seems as though they are expecting God to do all the hard work and they wait to collect the prize. The harder you work, the more blessed you will become. In our prayers, we often ask God to go into the hospitals and heal the sick. James tells us that faith without works or accompanying activity is dead.

If there is no struggle, there is no progress. "Those who profess to favor freedom and yet depreciate agitation, are men who want crops without plowing up the ground; they want the ocean without the roar of its mighty waters" (Fredrick Douglas).

Every good gift and every perfect gift is from above, and cometh down from the Father of lights, with whom is no variableness, neither shadow of turning. James 1:17

**James Thomas**

# DAY 32

# SPIRITUAL OBESITY AND FAMISHED FAITHFULNESS

> *All therefore whatsoever they bid you observe, that observe and do; but do not ye after their works: for they say, and do not.*
> Matthew 23:3

Throughout Jesus' earthly ministry, he had to reprimand the Scribes and Pharisees often. They were obese with spirituality. They looked pious. They carried the law with them wherever they went. They memorized the law to generate recognition and prestige from the people. They prayed several times a day. They withdrew themselves from anything that would cause them to feel unclean. They went into the temple or synagogue often. They loved teaching the congregants their version of the *truth*. When Jesus confronted them, they ignored the Ten Commandments and pledged to rid the community of his new teachings. They were famished in faith because they refused to believe that Jesus was the Son of God, their promised Messiah. The Law proved Jesus' identity. His work confirmed his Sonship. However, they chose spiritual obesity over faith to believe. In the end, they had to face "Truth".

Before Jesus ascended, he warned his followers that in the last days, the spirit of the scribes and Pharisees would continue to increase. He told them to beware of their power to influence believers. Leaders were admonished to guard the flock faithfully.

Over 2000 years later, we see evidence that spiritual obesity is still infiltrating churches around the world. People are more concerned about their public image than about their faithfulness to the call of God upon their lives. They spend many hours trying to figure out what they can do to go viral on social media, while churches and families are fighting for survival.

Are you spiritually obese with formality, or, spiritually obese with faithfulness to the call of God upon your life? It's time to assess!

**Heavenly Father, increase the motivation of my heart to become more faithful to You in all I do for the kingdom of heaven. In Jesus' name. Amen.**

Geraldine Russell

# DAY 33

# LOOKING FOR A PLACE TO SHINE

> *Let your light so shine before men, that they may see your good works, and glorify your Father which is in heaven. Matthew 5:16*

As I walked out of my front door and started to my car, I realized immediately that the day would be another scorcher. Not only was the temperature high, but so was the humidity. And not only was the humidity high, but the sun was absolutely beaming! It seemed that even if I tried to walk on the shady side of the street, the sun kept finding ways to peek through the branches and leaves, no matter how thick the foliage. When I finally arrived at my car, I hurriedly jumped in and sighed in relief. It only took me a few seconds to notice that the sun was even beaming into the car! I tried everything to block it. I pulled down my sun visor and even extended it, but the sun was still shining through. I sat up straighter so the rearview mirror could block the beams, but the sun was still shining around it. I even put on my own shades, but still the sun was right there.

At that moment, the Holy Spirit began to reveal to me why He had just taken me through that experience. If you recall, I had just tried to dodge the sun every chance I got, but there always seemed to be at least one place where light was shining through. Once I got settled in the car, it seemed that I had found a place of shade, but even with the rearview mirror and the visors there, sunbeams were still reaching around them both. So, the verse in Matthew 5:16 came to mind and it states, *"Let your light so shine before men, that they may see your good works, and glorify your Father which is in heaven."* Ultimately, our Father's intention is to get the glory out of our lives. The only way

He can do that is for us to allow His light to shine through us, just as the sunbeams kept finding me. No matter how far you think you have drifted from God or how coy you may be, just know that the SON is always looking for a place to shine through YOU! There is no need to try to hide it because somebody's life depends on your light to shine. Don't be discouraged if your spirit has been battered and bruised because that brokenness only provides more places for the SON to beam through. So, let Him shine!

**Think About It:** In what ways will you allow the Lord to shine through you today?

**Domonique Brunson**

## DAY 34

# HOW TO BE STRONG IN THE LORD!

> *Finally, my brethren, be strong in the Lord, and the power of his might. Ephesians 6:10*

Blessed is the one who does not always have to have the last word. Let us live every day without speaking a critical thought of anyone. We should always think of others, and not ourselves. We should praise God continuously from the depths of our hearts, and always be mindful of how we entertain strangers. Never get angry, or resentful at any time.

ALWAYS BE SWEET, LOVING, AND KIND. Never be jealous of anyone, only to improve ourselves. We should stand for the right, regardless of what the accusation might be. Always have a smile for everyone, children, or adults.

Never gossip, backbite, fuss or fight. Never criticize or be rude to anyone. Never complain or find fault anywhere. Always search yourselves and see what we have done.

**Evangelist Nathaniel Scippio, Edited writings**

# DAY 35

# UNITY AMONG BELIEVERS

> *Behold, how good and how pleasant it is for brethren to dwell together in unity! Psalm 133:1*

How often have we heard this quote, "Where there is unity, there is strength?" As believers, we all must work and operate together as one unit and one body in the Holy Spirit and recognize Jesus as our head. The need for unity, through the operation of the fruit of the Spirit, is so critical in the lives of believers (Galatians 5:22-23).

There is a dire need for the Saints of God to stand fast in the liberty wherewith Christ Jesus has set us free. This unity comes by loving one another and our neighbor as ourselves. Unity among the believers can only be accomplished by walking in God's Spirit.

The fruit of the Spirit, which is love, joy, peace, longsuffering, gentleness, goodness, faith, meekness, and temperance is the unified law that gives us God's liberty to bestow upon each other. As we encounter the suffering, hurting, and wounding hearts of our brethren, God challenges us by the Word to express the fruit of the Spirit in aiding them.

There may be a believer in your church that could use encouraging words of faith and hope. Do you know someone that needs godly peace, joy, and love? Are you willing to support your fellowman through acts of kindness, gentleness, and goodness?

Our prayer is for the Father, our God, to strengthen the unity of His Spirit within us that we may serve one another in pure and righteous Fruit of His Holy Spirit.

**Dr. Leticia Hardy**

## DAY 36

# WHAT ARE YOU SAYING?

> *Death and life are in the power of the tongue: And they that love it shall eat the fruit thereof. Proverbs 18:21*

Our words are powerful. The things we say can make or break a situation, or can completely bring a miraculous healing. It's all in what we say and believe to be true according to the Word of God. The power of life and death are in our tongues and our mindset sets the pace for what does or does not happen in our lives.

Back in the Spring of 2017, I was attending a chapel service at my daughter's school. The speaker for that morning was having an altar call and he called me up for prayer and spoke things over my life that only a few select people knew about. He also spoke about a ministry that I would have for children. Well, let's fast forward to 2020.

In October of that year, I published my autobiography and in December, I began JL Lucas Enterprises which focuses on children who are talented in the visual arts. So, of course I had NO IDEA that God was going to birth these things inside of me. I kept praying and asking God for direction and he approved everything in a short amount of time. I said that to say this, "What are YOU SAYING?"

**Jessica Lucas**

## DAY 37

# LEMONADE

> *But as for you, ye thought evil against me; but God meant it unto good, to bring to pass, as it is this day to save much, people alive.*
> Genesis 50:20

The enemy's plan is to steal, kill, and destroy. His goal is to destroy you the moment you were conceived in your mother's womb. Therefore, babies are being aborted; the enemy has deceived the woman and she believes that she has the right to kill her unborn child. God can take a ruined, distraught person, an unplanned pregnancy to change situations, turn them around, and enhance one's life to become productive and prosperous.

Do not look back and do not give up. *"Forget the former things; do not dwell on the past, See, I am doing a new thing! Now it springs up; do you not perceive it? I am making a way in the desert and streams in the waste land* (Isaiah 43:18-19)". God can provide streams of blessings in dry places. When you are told no, do not give up. When you do not see a way out, trust God. He has an open door; He can let rivers of blessings flow on your behalf. Believe God, trust Him, and the sour, bitter lemon can become sweet lemonade.

**Mary Calhoun**

## DAY 38

# A FAMILY PRAYER

> *I exhort therefore, that, first of all, supplication, prayers, intercession, and giving of thanks, be made for all men; for Kings and for all that are in authority; that we may lead a quiet and peaceable life in all godliness and honesty. I Timothy 2:1-2*

Father, I thank you for another opportunity to come to you in prayer. I pray that You would bless our families in our health, wealth, peace, and relationships with You and one another. I thank you Father that we acknowledge You as the Lord and Savior of our lives. Father, in the name of Jesus, we receive your love for us, and we know that we have been made the righteousness of God through Christ Jesus.

Help us to exemplify your love and grace in the earth as You have prayed. We thank you for manifesting your wisdom, healing, prosperity, and power in us daily. We decree and declare it done in your son Jesus' name, AMEN!

**Lesley Thomas**

# DAY 39

## LEARNING TO WALK

> *I taught Ephraim also to go, taking them by their arms; but they knew not that I healed them. Hosea 11:3*

I heard the old saying for years, "You have to crawl before you walk." Like a baby, we must learn how to crawl first; but if we never get on the floor, we will never learn. We won't learn how to pull ourselves up to start taking a tentative step or two. When babies start taking steps, we encourage them to go on by holding them up by their hands. Sometimes we praise their every effort and keep encouraging every attempt they make to walk. We never get discouraged nor do we give up until they learn how to walk.

In Hosea 11:3, our heavenly Father taught Israel to walk. He took his children by their arms and drew them with gentle cords and with bands of love (verse 3-4). The Father picks us up when we fall. He is never discouraged with our progress, nor will He ever give up. The more difficult we find the process, the more care and kindness He extends. God consistently provides for us, and we refuse to see what He has done. God will take our hand and show us how to walk with Him.

He guides our footsteps all the way and continues to do so every day. We don't have to keep standing in the same old place. We must keep on walking regardless of what comes our way; for God sees, knows, and understands.

**Felicia C. Parker**

# DAY 40

# GOD OF ANOTHER CHANCE

> *And the word of the Lord came unto Jonah the second time, saying, Arise, go unto Nineveh, that great city, and preach unto it the preaching that I bid thee. Jonah 3:1-2*

God called Jonah to preach to Nineveh because the people were wicked. But Jonah wanted nothing to do with this assignment from God. Instead, Jonah decided to run away from God. He got himself into a desperate situation and prayed to God for help. The Lord came to Jonah a second time and told him to preach to Nineveh. Jonah was obedient to do as God had asked. I recalled times in my life I did not follow what God would have me to do, but it did not take long to know I needed God's help. I did like Jonah and asked God for forgiveness and was willing to do what was right.

**Prayer: God, you are gracious and merciful. A God who hears our prayers. A God who forgives, redeems, and restores. God delights in giving us another chance. In Jesus' name. Amen**

**Venetta Law**

## DAY 41

# WALKING IN THE SPIRIT

> *If we live in the Spirit, let us also walk in the Spirit. Galatians 5:25*

As I was walking early one morning, I heard a voice saying, "Look up and around you". I raised my head toward the sky and I saw the beautiful stars, moon, and the whole element as I had never seen them before. I began praising God silently and soon I was praying for every household I passed as I walked. The prayer continued and I was praying for my co-workers, children at school, and everything about that day. I experienced an overshadowing of the Spirit that particular morning that I had never felt before.

Then, I remembered the Apostle Paul's scripture, "Walk in the Spirit." The Holy Spirit used my physical condition to grow me in "Grace and knowledge "of His word. (II Peter 3:18)

God loves us and He will use things to heal us and focus us on other needs. "If we live in the Spirit, let us also walk in the Spirit" (Gal. 5:25). Having a hunger for living in the Spirit and walking in the Spirit will become a way of life for us on this earth.

**Mary Smith**

# DAY 42

# BETWEEN SUNDAYS

> *Therefore, my beloved brethren, be ye steadfast, unmovable, always abounding in the work of the Lord, forasmuch as ye know that your labor is not in vain in the Lord. 1 Corinthians 15:58*

As Christians, we tend to think our service to Christ begins and ends in worship service. We enter our sanctuaries on Sunday, offer up a few hours of worship, and walk out of the church into the world. For most, we've sowed two-to-three hours once a week.

But what happens in between Sundays? Does your worship stop here? Could it be possible that worship is not a moment in time, but a lifestyle? Our greatest worship is how we live our lives daily.

Could your worship be treating others well? Could it be making the most of the awesome gift of life and living it well? Our Savior suffered, bled, and died so that we could have life.

Our worship doesn't begin and end on Sunday. It must extend into our homes, place of employment, and extracurricular life. No matter where we are or what we are doing, the world should be able to see the glory of the Lord in us daily. It is that light that will draw the world directly to Him. We have six days in between Sundays. We must make sure those days reflect Him as well!

**Life Application:** *Would someone know you're a Christian if they never saw you in church? Ask five people who do not know you're a Christian, their thoughts about you. If you're not pleased with their responses, adjust your behavior.*

**Cheryl L. Thomas**

## DAY 43

# 2020 V.I.S.I.O.N.
### (Victoriously Inspiring Someone in Opportunities Now)

> *But charge Joshua, and encourage him, and strengthen him: for he shall go over before this people, and he shall cause them to inherit the land which thou shalt see. Deuteronomy 3:28*

After reading this passage of Moses' encounter with God, three words stand out, **command, encourage,** and **strengthen.** I realized that God desires us to inspire others on their journey even when our journey is complete. Moses was not allowed to cross over into the Promised Land because of earlier misconduct.

Specifically, God told him to speak to the Rock but instead, he struck the Rock. Because of this act of disobedience, Moses would have to suffer the consequences of not physically experiencing the Promise Land. His journey would continue through the life of someone else, Joshua. Moses was instructed to prepare his successor. God told him to **command** (Give specific instructions), **encourage** (make sure Joshua is on top of things), and **strengthen** (ensure his commitment).

We too must share God's instruction – the **WORD,** ensuring individuals understand and accept the **WORD** of God and **Jesus Christ** as Lord and Savior. We must see through the eyes of God. When we do, we will always have perfect VISION and direction to instruct, encourage, and strengthen others on their journey.

Dr. Deloris Y. McBride

## DAY 44

# RETURN TO SENDER

> *When they fast, I will not hear their cry; and when they offer burnt offering and an oblation, I will not accept them: but I will consume them by the sword, and by the famine, and by the pestilence.*
> *Jeremiah 14:12*

Have you ever felt like your prayers were not being heard in heaven, that maybe they were being sent to God's voice mail? I am sure that most people will never confess to such doubts. This is what King David had to say when he was in distress, "But as for me, when they were sick, my clothing was sackcloth. I humbled my soul with fasting; and my prayer returned into my bosom" (Psalm 35:13).

Elvis Presley recorded a song that made it to the top of the billboard charts containing the lyrics: "I gave a letter to the postman, he put it in his sack, bright in early next morning, he brought my letter back - She wrote upon it Return to Sender, address unknown, no such number, no such zone…" This song was the story of a love relationship gone bad without hope of reconciliation. Jeremiah shares from God's upper story of His love relationship with His people, the nation of Judah, who had been unfaithful. God said that because of their disobedience and rebellion, He would not hear them when they called. Unlike the unforgiving lover, He says to them, "I have loved thee with an everlasting love."

"Behold, the Lord's hand is not shortened, that it cannot save; neither is his ears heavy, that he cannot hear" (Isaiah 59:1-2).

**James Thomas**

## DAY 45

# A LESSON FROM AN EAGLE

> *But they that wait upon the LORD shall renew their strength; they shall mount up with wings as eagles; they shall run, and not be weary; and they shall walk, and not faint. Isaiah 40:31*

God created an eagle with amazing attributes. They can soar at altitudes as high as 20,000 feet above sea level. That's over three miles! Their eyesight is 3 to 4 times keener than the average human being. They can swoop down upon prey with amazing speeds. Some have wingspans over six feet that help them escape predators. What lesson can believers learn from an eagle?

When an eagle senses or sees a storm approaching, it uses the rising updrafts created by the colliding air masses to glide above the storm. It expends little energy flapping its wings. It rides on the moving air just above the storm. In addition, it uses its keen eyesight to see if the object moving below is food or dangerous.

Like the eagle, believers should learn how to rise above the storms that continue to "brew" in these last days. Storms will come. However, believers don't have to be injured or destroyed by the colliding forces. When a storm approaches, just allow your mind to glide above the trouble. How? By rehearsing and meditating on the promises found in the word of God. Once the storm subsides, believers can use a little energy to return to the scene. Mature believers can assess the damage and assist in rebuilding the fellowship if needed. Sometimes, storms cause fellowships to fortify and become stronger. Like the keen eye of an eagle, they can see if what's moving below is beneficial or dangerous to the fellowship.

Believers, storms are brewing all around. Let's use our keen insight and our unique abilities to soar above the cares and troubles of this world. Each storm will eventually subside. Until then, let's continue to mount up on the spiritual wings of faith and glide!

**Heavenly Father,** teach me how to glide above the storms that will come in my life because I am a believer in the "finished work" of Jesus Christ. Teach me how to see the benefits and/ or the dangers in each one. Teach me how to assess and rebuild effectively through love. In Jesus' name, I pray. Amen.

**Geraldine Russell**

# DAY 46

# GRACE FOR THE RACE

> *And of his fulness have all we received, and grace for grace. For the law was given by Moses, but grace and truth came by Jesus Christ.*
> *John 1:16-17*

It takes a special type of person to be a member of a track and field team. You may find that comical, but I am serious! The amount of strength, endurance, conditioning, skill, and dedication required to excel at that particular sport is truly something amazing. Running has never been my favorite activity, but these team members do it for enjoyment! Once their feet hit the track and the whistle blows, they are flying in the wind, legs carrying them the needed distance till they reach the finish line. It could be a sprint or a marathon, but they always give it their all. When they finish, they may be breathing heavily and they may be sweating profusely, but they are proud of their accomplishment because whether they won first place or not, they still crossed the finish line. I am sure they could all tell you there was a point where they felt like giving up during the race, but God gave them the grace to finish.

Maybe you were a member of a team like this when you were in school or maybe you run marathons currently. Maybe you are like me and only enjoy watching and rooting from the sidelines. No matter which category you fall into, we are all a part of one race called LIFE. As soon as we are born into this world, the race begins. Early on, we will see that there are times in life when we feel like quitting just like those runners. It is a given that we won't always have a clue what hurdles or obstacles we will encounter from day to day, but we keep running and we keep living because there is a reward at the finish line. Maybe a loved one dies, and you have to overcome the obstacle of grief. Maybe you lose a job, or a car and you have to jump over the hurdle of financial hardship. Maybe you decided to go back to school, and you have to face a difficult final exam. These are some of the uphill parts of the race that require endurance. However, no matter what you have to experience, there is grace for you to continue the race. John 1:17 tells us that *"...grace and truth came by Jesus Christ"* and I am so glad that I can say I know this Jesus! It is all because of Him that we do not have to "run" this race of life all alone. His grace carries us. So, as you continue throughout your day and you feel yourself getting tired, take a break in God's Presence and remember that His grace will be there to help you finish your race. Press on!

**Think About It: In what areas of your life do you feel you need God's grace most?**

Domonique Brunson

## DAY 47

# GOD'S REFLECTION IN MAN

God is our Father and He is reflected in all of His children. You will know them without hearing their testimony. The true idea of God seems almost lost and forgotten, Man is God's reflection, needing no cultivation, but ever beautiful and complete, all worldly decorations are not necessary. It may be worthwhile to remark here that, if any man is in Christ Jesus, he reflects Him and not the devil.

No man looks in a mirror to see himself, and sees another, as the mirror only reflects the one who stands before it. The reflections of God are **Love, Joy, Peace, Long-suffering, Gentleness, Goodness, Faith, Meekness, and Temperance (Galatians 6:22-23, KJV)**. Daniel felt safe in the Lion's Den, for he was the reflection of God, and God has power over all Lions.

**Excerpts from the writings of Evangelist Nathaniel Scippio**

## DAY 48

# FAITH OVER FEAR

> *Ask, and it shall be given you; seek, and ye shall find; knock, and it shall be opened unto you: Matthew 7:7*

One Thursday morning, I received a phone call from a dear sister who was in distress. She was informed that her son-in-law's sister was in the hospital. The doctors revealed to the family that she had cancer. My dear sister asked me if I would accompany her to the hospital to pray for the young lady. I immediately replied, "Yes, I would love to." After the call ended, I began to seek God's message to deliver to this young lady.

I prayed throughout the night and rose up early Friday morning. As I began searching the scriptures, the Holy Spirit led me to Exodus 15:26 and St. Matthew 7:7-8. The Holy Spirit began to minister these words to me, "So many people have forgotten how great God is. They have neglected to see Him as the sovereign God. They have overlooked the true Healer of all diseases and placed their hope in man."

When I entered the hospital room, the Lord directed me to lead the young lady into the sinner's prayer before ministering His Word to her. She was told that if she confesses her sins and believes on the Lord Jesus Christ she would be saved. She was further instructed to accept Him into her heart as her Lord and Savior and to live for Him from this day forward. By doing so, God will honor her request. She did this willingly and wholeheartedly.

After ministering to her that God honors faith regardless of the doctor's report, God wants her to cast her fear and focus on Him. Furthermore, God directed me to tell her to read His Living Word daily. His Word states, "I am the Lord that healeth thee" (Exodus 15:26). In addition to that, follow the instructions of Matthew 7:7-8, "Ask and it shall be given you; seek, and ye shall find; knock and it shall be opened unto you."

Miracles are still happening if you only believe!

**Dr. Leticia Hardy**

# DAY 49

## THE NEW YOU

> *Therefore if any man be in Christ, he is a new creature: old things are passed away; behold, all things are become new.*
> II Corinthians 5:17

Leading up to the New Year, we normally make resolutions to work on our physical appearance by making promises to eat healthier, exercise more to shed unwanted pounds, etc. The business endeavor, the book, closing on the house and similar things are all met with great expectation and zeal. Soon after January 1, comes March, we have fallen off of the beaten path. Why don't we as believers take the same tenacity concerning our spiritual well-being? The following commentary comes from a good friend of mine in the ministry, Prophetess Sheila Davis.

"God is setting up new beginnings in ways [we can] reach the lost. One way to reach people who are in need is to witness by sharing our testimony of how God has transformed us into new creatures. In your circle of influence, you may know a single mother who doesn't know how she's going to provide for her children." Or, you may know of a family of eight who is only living off of one income. We have all seen hard times in our lives, but God is a sustainer and has carried us through each of our difficulties. There are several stories in scripture that can attest to this statement. Our modern-day trials are echoed in the Old and New Testaments, but the good news is, Christ has delivered us out of each single hardship. He is worthy for just being our Deliverer, our God, and our King!!!

**Jessica Lucas, and Contributing Author: Prophetess Sheila Davis**

# DAY 50

# LISTENING

> *Wherefore my beloved brethren, let every man be swift to hear, slow to speak, slow to wrath. James 1:19*

I had a bad habit of interrupting my adult children before they finished their sentence. When my son talks to me about something, I would interrupt the conversation thinking that I knew which direction the conversation would be going. This would make my son so angry, and he would yell at me, "Mom, please let me finish. I would be quiet and then become offended.

Listening is an art. I am learning to listen and keep my thoughts to myself and allow the Holy Spirit to guide me before I speak. I remember during my husband's lifetime, when asked a question, he was slow to speak. Sometimes I thought that he took too long before giving an answer. I can see him now dropping his head as if he was thinking; then, he would raise his head with words of wisdom.

The Apostle James admonishes us to be slow to speak and swift to hear. If we adhere to his words, the Holy Spirit will direct us, and we can avoid unwanted wrath.

**Lord, help me to be slow to speak and swift to hear.**

Mary Calhoun

## DAY 51

# FROM GLORY TO GLORY

> *And I will restore to you the years that the locust hath eaten, the canker worm, and the caterpillar, and the palmerworm, my great army which I sent among you. Joel 2:25*

On my route home there is a piece of property that sat tucked away and went virtually unnoticed as I have driven by almost every day for several years. Recently, the property was purchased by a new owner, and they began to work on the small house and land that sits there. Slowly, day by day, a very noticeable change began to take place. Overgrown plants and shrubs were cut back, old windows were replaced, and new fencing was put up. The grass was mowed, and old dead trees were cut down. Soon, before my very eyes, that piece of property was transformed into a small "Ponderosa" and now stands out and cannot be missed by those that drive by.

With a few changes and some dedicated attention, what was virtually a wasteland became something of great value. This is what happens when we begin to seek God and use His word in areas of our lives that lie dormant and stagnated. His word brings life and renewal to the dead things that may have overshadowed the gifts and talents that lie within us. Stir up the gifts that lie within and watch God bring new life!

**Lesley Thomas**

# DAY 52

# THE KNOCK AT THE DOOR

> *Behold, I stand at the door, and knock: if any man hear my voice, and open the door, I will come in to him, and will sup with him, and he with me. Revelation 3:20-22*

Jesus knocks at the door of our hearts because He wants to save us and fellowship with us. Jesus is patient and persistent in trying to get through to us. He will not break in and enter, but He will knock. Jesus allows us to decide whether or not to open our lives to Him. I know this because I felt unsatisfied with myself when I didn't have Christ's presence within me. I did not realize He was knocking at the door of my heart because I was too busy enjoying worldly pleasures. I did not know the pleasures of the world like money, security, and material possessions could be dangerous. During those times I didn't realize I was only experiencing temporary satisfaction. But God offers everlasting satisfaction.

We need to leave the door constantly open to our hearts and to God because only then will we not worry about hearing His knock. Letting Him in is our only hope for lasting fulfillment. I know there are so many things we would like to tell God, but we don't know how because we are afraid. Through all our ups and downs, we still need to remember to choose Him first even though the faith we have in Him sometimes is minimized.

There are times when it seems like God doesn't mean that much to us because we are still lost and don't really know Him. But one day, He will and we will know Him. We will be able to talk with Him without being afraid.

"Amazing grace! how sweet the sound, that saved a wretch; like me! I once was lost, but now I am found, was blind, but now I see. 'Twas grace that taught my heart to fear, and grace, my fears were relieved; How precious did that grace appear the hour I first believed (John Newton)!"

**Felicia C. Parker**

## DAY 53

# THE UNLIKELY KING

> *But the Lord said to Samuel, do not look at his appearance or at his physical stature, because I have refused him. For the Lord does not see as man sees; for man looks at the outward appearance, but the Lord looks at the heart. I Samuel 16:7 NKJV*

God instructed Samuel to anoint one of the sons of Jesse as king. Have you felt overlooked or undervalued? It is interesting that David's father, Jesse, completely left him out of the family's gathering. He did not even feel David was worth considering. But the Lord made it clear to Samuel that He rejected Eliab, the oldest son, the tall handsome warrior. But God anointed David as king because he had a heart for God.

**Father, we are humbled and awestruck by your amazing ways. May we continue to focus on our moral and spiritual qualities. We pause to say thank you for your mercy and grace. In Jesus' name, we pray. Amen.**

**Venetta Law**

# DAY 54

# WHAT LOVE!

> *For God so loved the world that He gave His only begotten Son, that whosoever believeth in Him should not perish, but have everlasting life. John 3:16*

We live in a world today with a count of over 7.9 billion people. Just think, all these souls are loved by one Father, God. He loves us so much that He gave His only Son to die for our sins (John 3:16). However, John says that he saw a number around the throne of God that no man could number (Rev. 7:9). What a mighty God we serve! Today, we bow in humility as Apostle Paul did to the all-knowing and all-loving God of this universe.

**Lord, grant us according to the riches of Your glory that we are strengthened with might by Your spirit in the inner man. It is our hope that Christ who died for us will dwell in our hearts by faith and we will be rooted and grounded in the love of our Father, God (Ephesians 3: 14-19).**

Mary Smith

## DAY 55

# EXPECTED END

> *For I know the thoughts that I think towards you, saith the Lord, thoughts of peace, and not of evil, to give you an expected end.*
> Jeremiah 29:11

A good friend shared this story with me. "From elementary to high school, everything was a breeze. I received numerous awards for my academics, but when I started college in 1999, everything changed." I experienced culture shock for the first time in my life. I moved away from home and had newfound freedom that caused me to lose sight of what was important. As a result, my grades started to slip and there were many times I felt like giving up. My friend was at a place where he was lost in trying to find answers to questions of uncertainty; it seemed graduation would never come. Fast forward five years later, my good friend graduated with honors. Now, that is something to really celebrate!

Life can be similar to the illustration above. Sometimes it seems like everything is running smoothly in accordance with our outlined plans and goals. Conversely, other times are the exact opposite as we face various trials. In this life, many days cause us to wish we could throw in the towel. During those days, I often reflect and find comfort in the words of the Prophet Jeremiah. *God desires to give us an expected end.* Once we regain our focus on him, life's trials will be much more bearable, knowing that the LORD will eventually bless us richly in all areas of our lives.

*Food for Thought: What are you troubled about today? What areas of your life do you find difficult to remind yourself of God's expected end?*

**Cheryl L. Thomas**

# DAY 56

## SOFT BOOT

> *And Jesus answered and said unto her, Martha, Martha, thou art careful and troubled about many things: Luke 10:41*

We struggle with various opportunities that cause us difficulties because we tend to have many tasks going simultaneously. These things can become overbearing and may cause us to slow our pace or reduce our effectiveness. Like a computer that has many tasks open at the same time, information may not be able to process properly. There may be a lag in completing various tasks, so a soft boot may be necessary to continue to work efficiently. We press the Control/Alt/Delete keys at the same time to get to the Task Manager. The Task Manager then enables us to determine which activity we need to close and which activity to continue. It may be necessary to close several activities in order to process the activity that takes precedence. Like Martha, we can have too many things that we are concerned about. However, what is most important is spending time with Jesus, fulfilling His purpose and plan for us for the moment.

Now in this Christian journey, we must prioritize and understand what we need to do first and what is most important to be effective. We must pause and control our behavior and ensure that what we are doing is reflective of Kingdom work and the will of God. Sometimes, we have to delete items from our plate or end a task to be effective. The scripture that comes to mind is Ecclesiastes 4:6 – "Better is an handful with quietness, than both the hands full with travail and vexation of spirit." Control our behavior, alter mindsets, and delete those things that interfere and prevent us from serving our God given purpose. Let the Task Manager, JESUS, operate in you.

Thank you Lord for the opportunities to serve You. Help us to always be mindful that You are directing our paths for Your glory and purpose.

Dr. Deloris Y. McBride

# DAY 57

# MOTIVATION

> *Go to the ant, thou sluggard; Consider her ways, and be wise:*
> *Proverbs 6:6*

To reach the height of our God-ordained talents, motivation is a key ingredient in our lives. Motivation is that inner drive that refuses to take a day off. It is the mindset of not giving in to how I feel today or what has been put in my way. I will survive.

I remember watching my mother use the power of **thirteen walnuts** as a driving force for her daily exercise routine. While in her early nineties, she was living alone and desiring to maintain her independent lifestyle. Her thinking was that if I am to keep moving, I will need to keep moving. So, she established an exercise routine of placing thirteen walnuts on her front porch as her motivators. Each morning she would place thirteen individual walnuts on her front porch. The routine was to hand carry a single walnut to be placed on her back porch and make return trips until all thirteen walnuts were on the front porch.

During the afternoon, the routine was repeated until all thirteen walnuts were on the front porch again. She did not let the challenges of old age stop her from her goal of mobility and independent living. She refused to give in to her hurting knees. I believe that with her motivation and perseverance, she remained mobile and independent until she died at 96 years old.

**James Thomas**

## DAY 58

# DON'T GIVE UP!

> *Yea, and all that will live godly in Christ Jesus shall suffer persecution. II Timothy 3:12*
> *… he that endureth to the end shall be saved. Matthew 10:22b*

Despite years of unimaginable childhood abuse, some people rose above hopeless situations and became famous around the world. They resolved that nothing would stop them from achieving their God-given talents and goals in life. They used their pain to push them to a level of expertise that few have been able to accomplish. Many set records that will take another lifetime to match. Their intrinsic drives motivated them to press onward. When one goal was achieved, they set another one. They continued to achieve higher goals until the nature of "aging" limited their success. Many of them went on to train other generations in their techniques and skills. Some are still being recognized for their achievements years after their deaths. They never gave up!

Believers, times are becoming more challenging. Stumbling blocks are being hurled into the pathway of believers worldwide. Illnesses and diseases are taking their toll. "Nest eggs" are being depleted. Hatred is walking boldly through neighborhoods armed with AK-15s. Fear is mounting. Many are becoming discouraged. Sometimes it seems like training the next generation is too exhaustive. However, you can't give up! Persevering is the only way to ensure that "faith" will be passed on from one generation to another. Continue to use your gifts and talents to the glory and honor of God so that when this mortal takes on immortality, the legacy left behind will be remembered for generations. Cheer up and never, ever give up! You are building a great legacy. Press on!

*Lord, help me to press onward through heartaches, pains, and mounting sorrows as each day presents its challenges. Help me to build a legacy that will impact generations to come. Amen.*

**Geraldine Russell**

## DAY 59

# HERE A DOUBT, THERE A DOUBT

> *Wherefore, if God so clothe the grass of the field, which today is, and tomorrow is cast into the oven, shall he not much more clothe you, O ye of little faith? Matthew 6:30*

I love when Spring arrives! It feels like everything is waking up around me. The leaves on the trees begin to sprout, the flowers begin to bloom, the birds begin to sing, and the world feels just a little bit more alive. I even start to feel a little more energized because the sun is out just a little while longer. As the season progresses, I especially love seeing open fields covered in brilliantly colored flowers stretching as far as the eye can see. Each time I ride past one, I am immediately awed again by a God who could create such majestic beauty right here on earth. And I think to myself that as beautiful as they are, we have never heard of a flower doubting that in each season of its existence, whether it be spring, summer, fall, or winter, God will protect and cover it simply because He is its Creator.

I think we can take our cue from this flower. What an awesome way to walk through life! To be able to live each day knowing that you are covered, protected, clothed, fed, and all of your needs are met is such a blessing. That should be the outlook of the child of God. However, to be honest, there are days when I allow a little doubt to creep into my heart. I know intuitively that God will take care of me and supply my every need, but when He does not work according to MY time clock, sometimes my faith wavers and that is exactly what the devil wants. When I share these doubts and feelings with the Father, though, He takes me to verses like Matthew 6:30 which says, *"Wherefore, if God so clothe the grass of the field, which today is, and tomorrow is cast into the oven, shall he not much more clothe you, O ye of little faith?"* How encouraging it is to know that if God never stops taking care of each blade of grass and each flower in the field, neither of which are made in His image, then there should be no room for doubt in my heart that He will take care of ME. So, the next time you find yourself wondering IF God will work things out for you, kick doubt to the curb and let your faith remind you that the question is not IF He will do it, but WHEN will He do it. The answer will always be "right on time"!

**Think About It:** When is the last time you doubted your doubts?

**Domonique Brunson**

## DAY 60

# REPLACE FEAR WITH FAITH IN YOUR LIFE

> *There is no fear in love; but perfect love casteth out fear: because fear hath torment. He that feareth is not made perfect in love.*
> *1 John 4:18*

There are so many Christians that live in a constant state of fear. You are afraid that you will not be able to hold out until the end. Some of you are afraid that the little place on your face will become a cancer. Others stay upon their beds, and think they are having a heart attack. It is probably only a case of indigestion, caused by overeating.

The devil will say that your heart is going to stop beating, you will breakout in a cold sweat, you will think I never knew that I had heart trouble before, but the devil convinces you that you do, and you live in fear.

**Excerpts from the writings of Evangelist Nathaniel Scippio**

# DAY 61

## WILL HOPE IN GOD

> *But those who hope in the Lord will renew their strength. They will soar on wings like eagles; they will run and not grow weary; they will walk and not be faint. Isaiah 40:31*

We know that we are living in an age of uncertainty, conflict, civil unrest, and life's challenges. Oftentimes, our heart weighs down in a sinking well of heaviness, and the dark spirits of anxiety and hopelessness creep into our inner soul to try to overtake us. Regardless of how the enemy tries to paint an image of hopelessness in our minds, or plant seeds of despair in our hearts, always remember the words of our Lord found in Isaiah 40:31 which states, "But those who hope in the Lord will renew their strength. They will soar on wings like eagles; they will run and not grow weary; they will walk and not be faint."

According to Hebrews 13:6, the Lord commanded us to open our mouths and boldly say, "The Lord is my helper, and I will not fear any man." Today, no matter what kind of weapon has formed against you, it shall not prosper. The Lord promised to watch over us and keep us from all harm. He promised to bless our present state as well as our future outcome.

Our prayer is that you will cast all your cares and burdens upon Christ Jesus. He cares about His people. He is our hope of glory that shineth His light into our heart, mind, soul, and body. He will give us rest from all worries, and peace from all our fears.

**Dr. Leticia Hardy**

# DAY 62

# TAKING YOUR LEAP OF FAITH

> *Commit thy way unto the LORD; Trust also in him; And he shall bring it to pass. Psalm 37:5*

Business owners are always taking risks that can profit or break their aspirations. For people who are just starting, such as myself, I have learned not to heed the advice from everyone, but to pray and listen to the Holy Spirit's leading. We can save a lot of difficulty and hardship if we are obedient to the Lord the first time because delayed obedience is disobedience in His eyes.

Earlier today, I had a conversation with a business consultant who is a Christian and lives her life through prayer and following the Holy Spirit. As I was taking my leap of faith with our conversation, the Holy Spirit spoke to her about the steps I needed to take concerning my business endeavors, transactions, models, strategies and partners. She informed me I had to first deal with the strongholds that were hindering me from moving forward in my kingdom work. I am new to the business sector and have never heard of the marketplace belonging to Christians in business.

For those individuals who are Christian business owners, we have to realize the enemy does not want us to succeed or prosper. It's his job to defeat us and to discourage us from being successful. He does not want us to thrive within our respective areas of expertise. The Lord, on the other hand, wants us to be on top and on the winning side. In order to do this, "We must jump when God says jump," she said. We must go when He says go and not follow our own desires. We should be totally influenced by the power of the Holy Spirit to make Godly, purposeful decisions that will positively affect our businesses in its totality.

**Jessica Lucas**

## DAY 63

# CHOOSE TO FORGIVE

> *A brother offended is harder to be won than a strong city; and their contentions are like bars of a castle. Proverbs 18:19*

Someone told me many years ago that "offense can only be taken; it cannot be given." In life we will have many opportunities to take offense or become offended because of the actions of others. When we choose to TAKE offense and it lingers, it wounds the soul. We should move swiftly to forgive. It is then that GRACE, like a flood will rush in and cover us all. Choose to forgive!

Father, we thank you for the grace that you give us each day. Help us to remember your forgiving heart and help us to not take your mercy and love for granted. Help us to choose forgiveness when we face life's challenging circumstances.

**Lesley Thomas**

## DAY 64

# FOOD FOR THOUGHT

> *I am Alpha and Omega, the beginning and the ending, saith the Lord, which is, and which was, and which is to come, the Almighty.*
> *Revelation 1:8*

He can calm the troubled waters when you walk in deep despair. There is hope when you feel helpless knowing that the Lord is there. Sharing in your sunshine moments or in valleys deep and wide, He will never, ever leave you. He is always by your side. There's no other friend so faithful through the sunshine and the rain, through the teardrops and the laughter in your joy and in your pain.

We could never, ever thank Him for His love He gives so free, never changing, never ending throughout all eternity. Oh, the wonder of all wonders as we live from day to day knowing that we have a Father who is with us all the way.

God is a father that will walk with us each step and every mile. He promises to never leave us nor forsake us. He can do anything far more than you could ever imagine or guess or request in your wildest dreams. God can do anything, Jehovah, Messiah the reason why I sing. He's Alpha and Omega, the Beginning, and the End. He's my Savior and Redeemer and my closest friend.

**Felicia C. Parker**

# DAY 65

# TIMIDITY AND BOLDNESS

> *For God hath not given us the spirit of fear, but of power, and of love, and of a sound mind. II Timothy 1:7*

Paul encourages Timothy to allow his spiritual gift to dominate his natural reluctance to speak and act timidly. Paul reminds Timothy he can overcome fear with the power of God. Can you relate to Timothy's reluctance to speak? Public speaking is ranked as the number one fear. I, too, have dreaded speaking in public. I overcame my public speaking fear with prayer and meditating on God's word. I was able to triumph over public speaking when God revealed fear is the opposite of faith. I also was allowing pride to hinder me. I was self-conscious and did not want to be embarrassed. Instead of avoiding public speaking, I started to embrace opportunities to speak. I now do my best and trust God to do the rest.

**Heavenly Father, thank you for providing us with the Holy Spirit, our comforter, and the power to overcome our fears. We thank you for removing fear from our lives. We pray for holy boldness In Jesus' name, Amen.**

Venetta Law

## DAY 66

# CLAY IN HIS HAND

> *The word which came to Jeremiah from the LORD, saying, Arise, and go down to the potter's house, and there I will cause thee to hear my words. Then I went down to the potter's house, and, behold, he wrought a work on the wheels. And the vessel that he made of clay was marred in the hand of the potter: so he made it again another vessel, as seemed good to the potter to make it.*
> *Jeremiah 18:1-4*

Jeremiah went down to the Potter's house and watched him using his hands to make vessels of clay on the wheel. He noticed that the Potter would mar a vessel and then he would make another vessel.

Today, we understand that we are made over again as we present our "bodies a living sacrifice, holy, acceptable to God" (Romans 12:1). Then day-by-day, we can grow in the image of His likeness. We use the gifts that He gives us to bring Him glory and add others into the Kingdom of God.

What an honor it is to be clay in God's hands because He is the Potter, and we are the clay in His hands glorifying His name daily.

**Mary Smith**

## DAY 67

# THE FINAL UNVEILING

> *For precept must be upon precept, precept upon precept; line upon line, line upon line; here a little, and there a little. Isaiah 28:10*

*"Little by little, He is changing me.*
*Line by line, 'til I agree*
*Precept by precept, He's changing me. Jesus is changing me."*

This is a short refrain from a song I love that speaks volumes. It tells the true picture of how change often happens... little by little. Sometimes we make the awful mistake of throwing people away because they don't quickly transform into our wishes or dreams of how we think they should be. We also don't leave much room for the Holy Spirit to do His job of regeneration. I am afraid that we often miss the awesome pleasure and privilege of seeing the final picture of the changes God orchestrates in the lives of His children because we are often not patient and loving enough to stay around for the final unveiling.

We all have the metamorphosis that we are going through. God is smoothing corners and sanding out the rough spots in our personality, burning out impurities in our character, and refining His treasure... little by little.

So, if the change you desire to see, even in yourself, isn't happening as quickly as you want, relax, and let the Master Carpenter, the Author, and FINISHER of our faith complete the work He has begun in you... and in those around you.

Remember, works of art take time!

**Cheryl L. Thomas**

# DAY 68

# TRANSFORMATION

> *Thy kingdom come. Thy will be done in earth, as it is in heaven.*
> Matthew 6:10

When we were very young, the moment we started putting words into sentences, we were taught the Lord's Prayer. Every Christian home, all around the world, made sure that family members knew and recited the Lord's Prayer. One part of the prayer states, "Thy Kingdom come and Thy will be done, on earth as it is in heaven." Before we can enter Heaven, we must become a part of His earthly Kingdom. A kingdom is a place where a king reigns; the Kingdom of God is where God reigns. When we accept Jesus as Lord and Savior, He comes into our lives in the form of the Holy Spirit.

When God's Kingdom comes into our lives, He transforms us to become citizens of His Kingdom by clothing us in the righteousness of His Son, Jesus. When we accept Jesus as Lord and Savior, we have rights and privileges that are wonderful and special to members of the Kingdom. A question one might ask is, "How can I enter the Kingdom?" We enter the Kingdom of God through His Son, Jesus Christ. Jesus died so that we might live. When He returned to Heaven, He made His Holy Spirit available to all of us. We must allow the Holy Spirit to live within us and transform us from unrighteousness to righteousness.

The Holy Spirit is our Comforter and Guide. He enables us to communicate with God and enables us to live according to God's Plan. Jesus came so we could have abundance and eternal life. Will you let Jesus transform you to become a child of God?

Father, I acknowledge my sins and ask your forgiveness. Please come into my life and transform me. I accept your gift, the Holy Spirit. Amen.

Dr. Deloris McBride

## DAY 69

# END OF THE RAINBOW

> *I do set my bow in the cloud, and it shall be for a token of a covenant between me and the earth... And the bow shall be in the cloud; and I will look upon it, that I may remember the everlasting covenant between God and every living creature of all flesh that is upon the earth. Genesis 9:13-16*

When I was a little boy, I can remember hearing the story of the rainbow in the sky. I was told that if one could follow it to the end, there would be a pot of gold. How exciting this was to my childlike imagination! I would chase the rainbow in my mind and take hold of that pot of gold and imagine all my little troubles away.

Something is amazing about suddenly seeing this phenomenal sight appear out of nowhere in the sunlit skies of a summer afternoon. The reality is that I became an adult and heard the real biblical account. There never was a pot of gold, but something far better at the end of the rainbow. God had put it there as a sign and a promise to never again destroy the earth by flood. It became His signature in the sky as a periodic reminder to Himself and man.

What then can I expect to find at the end of the proverbial rainbow? God offers mankind a new covenant filled with grace and mercy. It is a life filled with peace and abundance now, and in the world to come, life eternal.

Never abandon the chase for your visions and dreams because they are the substance of which success becomes a reality.

**James Thomas**

# DAY 70

# A HEALING DOSE

> *Is there no balm in Gilead; is there no physician there? Why then is not the health of the daughter of my people recovered? Jeremiah 8:22*

The world is becoming increasingly dependent upon medical stimulants and experimental drugs to keep advancing from one day to another; meds to rise; meds to sleep; meds to just make it through the day. Although there are many underlying factors for the deteriorating health of society, one causation rises far above others. It's "a famine for the word of God." Too many of God's people have lost their "appetite for the word." Contrary to life a few decades ago, believers' morning coffee is being accompanied by the latest happenings on social media. Meditating on the word of God has been insidiously infiltrated by never-ending distractions. Our "holy offspring" are being caught up and swept away by the rip currents of our time. Many of them have been lost at sea. The cares of life have enveloped many. Sickness, diseases, and infirmities have taken their toll upon humanity.

Pharmaceutical giants are raking in billions of dollars because of physical and psychological illnesses.

What's the answer to the world's mounting crisis? Is it to continue to inundate society with legalized drug addictions with no healing components? What's the lasting solution? A mass migration back to the word of God! In the word of God is where believers find life-saving prescriptions for all of life's needs. Take a good dose of God's life-giving word daily. It produces healing with no immediate or lasting side effects.

**Lord, increase our appetite for consuming more of your word. It is our "Healing Balm". Amen.**

**Geraldine Russell**

# DAY 71

# FINDING TREASURE IN THE TRIAL

> *Beloved, think it not strange concerning the fiery trial, which is to try you, as though some strange thing happened unto you: But rejoice, inasmuch as ye are partakers of Christ's sufferings; that, when his glory shall be revealed, ye may be glad also with exceeding joy. 1 Peter 4:12-13*

When the movie Titanic blasted onto the scene, it was quite a different story from what I was expecting, but I absolutely loved it! I had always read about the tragic demise of this "unsinkable" ship as well as the terrible trials and untimely deaths of so many in those frigid waters. I always saw it as one of those moments in history I hoped would NOT be repeated. However, when I saw the movie, it left me with a completely different outlook on the entire situation. Rose, the main character, was telling the story from her point of view after surviving the ordeal many years before. She did not focus mainly on the iceberg that sank the ship, but on the opportunity she had during the voyage to experience a love like she had never known before or since. It was an experience she still treasured in her heart, and it seemed as if she remembered the love far more than she remembered all that she and her partner went through trying to survive, even at the expense of his death. Rose realized that the love she walked away with had changed her and made her forever better.

I pondered that experience for quite a while after watching the film because I knew there was something the Holy Spirit was trying to show me, and it floored me when I realized what it was. As children of God, there is ALWAYS a treasure that can be found in any trial we face. God often allows us to go through a trial because either He is trying to build our character, or He is trying to strip us of another layer of our "old man" and add something new, or there is a lesson there to be learned for us or for someone else. 1 Peter 4:12 tells us not to think it's strange when we come up against these "fiery trials". They WILL come. I have even experienced a couple of "Titanic" situations in my life that made me feel like I was drowning in sorrow and pain, but…I SURVIVED. Not only did I come out of each situation with more strength and more wisdom than I had previously, but I found myself having drawn closer to God. I unearthed gifts I did not even know I possessed. My prayer life is now deeper than ever and for all of these, I am grateful to the TRIAL. If it had not been for those trials, I would never have discovered the TREASURES God buried within them just for me. 1 Peter 4:13 tells us to rejoice and I can definitely say in my rejoicing that the treasure is worth the trial!

**Think About It:** What treasures can you find through your trials today?

**Domonique Brunson**

## DAY 72

# HURRY, HURRY, HURRY!

> *Seek ye the Lord while he may be found, call ye upon him while he is near. Isaiah 55:6*

The entire world is in such a hurry, and rush that everyone seems to be confused. So many of you get out of bed in the morning and have no time to pray. You say I have got so much to do; I must fix the lunches and get the kids off to school and do the washing. People are so busy that they do not have time to serve God; suddenly they wake one morning to discover that they have a cancer, tumor, or heart trouble, then they find time, and plenty of time to serve God!

One of my friends, a minister, had a cerebral hemorrhage; He had gotten so busy that he did not have time to worship God. My friend told me that "I just went in such a rush all the time, that I was busy from morning until night, but when you get flat on your back, you will begin to think. I thought I had so many bills and owed so much that I just had to keep going. I realized how utterly insignificant those bills were. I also realized that everything could operate without me."

**Evangelist Nathaniel Scippio, Edited writings**

# DAY 73

# DO NOT LOSE YOUR SPIRITUAL APPETITE!

> *According to their pasture, so were they filled; they were filled, and their heart was exalted; therefore, have they forgotten me. Hosea 13:6*

Since COVID-19, so many Christians have acquired the spirit of apathy. Although this pandemic may have caused major disruptions of church attendance and routines, it is not solely responsible for believers falling into a sense of apathetic stupor, and a lack of concern for the things of God and the cares of the soul. Christians who were once diligent in personal prayer, Bible study, and church services are now numb toward Jesus and his mission in the world. It's not that these Christians are ignorant to the truth, they know what honors God. They know how to pray, read the scriptures, sing, and serve. In spite of this knowledge, this numbness prevails. The concern for the things that matter to God has dried up. They have lost their **Spiritual appetite**.

Spiritual apathy is deadly for the soul of the believer. According to Hosea 13:6, "But when they grazed, they became full, they were filled. And their heart was lifted up, therefore they forgot me." During the pandemic, God blessed us to receive financial blessings, assistance, and resources. This alone should cause us to serve God for all His benefits that He has bestowed upon us.

It is God's desire that believers gird up the loins of their minds, lift their heads, open the doors of their hearts, and allow the King of Glory to come in. The Lord wants to reignite the heart, mind, body, and soul of every believer with His fervent power to spread the good news of salvation to all humanity.

Our prayer is for God to send us a fresh wind and a new fire!

**Dr. Leticia Hardy**

## DAY 74

# FAITH OVER FEAR

> *For God has not given us a spirit of fear and timidity, but of power, love, and self- discipline II Timothy 1:7 NLT*

This scripture literally became a reality on Friday, April 9, 2022. My family was attending the viewing of a relative who had transitioned to be with the Lord. He was a believer in Christ and loved people and served his country.

As we were getting out of the car to head into the sanctuary, my daughter and I were hand in hand, while my husband had our son, or so I thought. Towards the end of the service, no one could find our 4-year-old son anywhere. My husband, daughter, and I were frantically searching different areas in the church to see if we could find him, but to no avail. We asked different family members and friends, but no one knew where our little boy was. Fear had set in, and my faith was definitely tested.

As a result, I began to pray with tears in my eyes asking God to protect my son wherever he was. The Lord reassured me that my faith had to activate over the fear I was feeling. I knew he was going to be alright. Come to find out, he was wandering in the parking lot by himself and a relative brought him inside. He was found kneeling on the ground near the front pew playing a game. Whew!!! Gratefulness and praise flooded my soul as the Lord once again came through.

**Jessica Lucas**

# DAY 75

## THE TROUBLING OF THE WATER

> *For the angel, went down at a certain season into the pool, and troubled the water; whosoever then first after the troubling of the water stepped in was made whole of whatsoever disease he had. John 5:4*

It may not be your season of fruitfulness now, but God will sustain you. Every person, family, marriage, and church will experience a season of drought. The question is, are you preparing for the return of the rain, the troubling of the water…IT'S COMING! Be not weary in doing well, for in due season you will reap if you faint not.

Father, we thank you that you have promised to keep us and to never forsake us. Help us to remember that your promises are sure even in those times when we may be full of doubt and discouragement. Your word says that you will supply our needs according to your riches in glory by Christ Jesus.

**Lesley Thomas**

## DAY 76

# R-E-S-P-E-C-T IN MARRIAGE

> *The wife hath not power of her own body, but the husband: and likewise also the husband hath not power of his own body, but the wife. Proverbs 31:11*

The popular "Respect" song written and produced by the late Aretha Franklin rings true. Respect is something that is earned and not automatically given. In marriage and other purposeful relationships, what does respect look like? Is it someone being overbearing with a list of dos and don'ts? Is it the wife being totally and absolutely submissive to her husband, no matter what? Or is respect a cohesive part of a Godly relationship that holds a high degree of holiness as we are all representatives of Christ?

In terms of the aforementioned questions, I think the last one fits quite well. As a wife myself, I initially had a hard time respecting the authority of my husband. In my mind, I believed the husband and the wife should both be submissive to each other. We both should strive in respecting the other person without hesitation or reservation. We do need to set boundaries as to what we will and will not tolerate in the relationship, but for the most part, I was very selfish in the way I was thinking.

Biblically, I had some issues with the wives submitting to your husband's scripture, etc. Now, after almost 15 years of being together, I have learned to cherish and respect his leadership, his accomplishments, his name, and his masculinity as a man. Respect goes both ways, and in a Christian relationship, we are held to a higher standard due to biblical and spiritual principles that we follow each day.

**Felicia C. Parker**

# DAY 77

# DO NOT LOOK BACK

> *But his wife looked back from behind him, and she became a pillar of salt. Genesis 19:26*

The angels of God warned Lot and his family of the impending destruction of Sodom. What could have been so luring in Sodom that was worth Lot's wife's life? Are we still looking back on our former life or our future with Christ? What are the desires of our hearts? God has promised the faithful a great gift of eternal life.

We no longer just desire to eat, drink, and the comforts of this world. God is warning his people today of a time of great destruction. This world is fading away and we want to be ready. Decide what it will take for you to strengthen your spiritual self. Let us focus on having a heart for God. Let us work on what is eternal and everlasting.

**Heavenly Father, we ask you to examine our hearts as we seek to do your will. Lord, we no longer desire our past lives. On this day we reaffirm our love for you. And look forward with anticipation to the coming of the Lord. Amen.**

**Venetta Law**

## DAY 78

# GROW AND GROW

> *But speaking the truth in love, may grow up into him in all things, which is the head, even Christ: from whom the whole body fitly joined together and compacted by that which every joint supplieth, according to the effectual working in the measure of every part, maketh increase of the body unto the edifying of itself in love.*
> *Ephesians 4:15-16*

Growing up on a farm in my early years, I watched my mother plant vegetables in her garden. As I played nearby the garden each day, I watched the vegetables grow. I asked my mother what caused them to grow. She said, "The Lord, baby." She loved to share the vegetables with her neighbors.

As Christians, we are planted in "God's Garden" to grow and receive nourishment from Him. The Bible, the Word of God, is our nourishment to eat daily. We must practice *speaking the truth in love, that we may grow up in all things into Him who is the head. Christ, from whom the whole body is joined and knitted together by what every joint supplies, according to the effective working…causes growth of the body for the edifying of itself in love* (Eph 4:15-16).

**Mary Smith**

## DAY 79

# THE THREE LETTER WORD

> *Proving what is acceptable unto the Lord. Ephesians 5:10*

When we hear the phrase, "Three and four-letter words," we typically think of words that are offensive and ones that should never come out of a Christian's mouth. We think of expletives. Words bleeped out in television shows which are signs of frustration and anguish. But we as Christians are all too familiar with a three-letter word most of us do not find comforting... **NOW!**

In a time when personal success is defined by tangible signs such as money, houses, yachts, or any of many outward signs of wealth, we often shun "now" because we see all of the things we have not accomplished and the pinnacles we have yet to reach.

You may not be where you want to be. It doesn't really matter where you are right now because it's only the launching pad for where God is taking you. It doesn't have to be an endpoint if you don't want it to be.

What great blessing could you be overlooking now as you try to race into your future? Take inventory of those things today. List them all. It may take hours, days, or weeks; but I believe it would take forever. Take at least 30 minutes every day this week and write every blessing that comes to your mind. You'll find yourself becoming more thankful and aware of daily blessings you often overlook. Remember, getting to the next thing requires being thankful for **new** things!

**Cheryl L. Thomas**

## DAY 80

# THE POWERFUL GIFT THAT CONTINUES

> *Honour the LORD with thy substance, and with the first fruits of all thine increase: So shall thy barns be filled with plenty, and thy presses shall burst out with new wine. Proverbs 3:9-10*

Giving is a wonderful way to Honor the Almighty God! When we give according to God's plan, we make an eternal investment. Giving to God's work is investing for eternity. The giver is blessed (… "He will reward each person according to what he has done" Mat. 16:27) and when someone is saved as a result of your financial contribution, the receiver is blessed with eternal life. What a powerful gift! We should always be willing to give to support our church and the Kingdom of God (See Luke 6:38 and Matthew 13:44–46).

The Bible teaches us to give cheerfully and generously. Proverbs 3:9 states, "Honor the LORD with your wealth, with the first fruits of all your crops; then your barns will be filled to overflowing, and your vats will brim over with new wine." Giving establishes and positions us for a great return on investment.

**Thank you, Lord, for blessing us to be a blessing. We are grateful that you love us so much and have given us the prime example to follow.**

Dr. Deloris Y. McBride

# DAY 81

# FORBIDDEN FRUIT

> *And when the woman saw that the tree was good for food, and pleasant to the eyes; and a tree to be desired to make one wise, she took of the fruit thereof, and did eat, and gave also unto her husband with her, and he did eat. Genesis 3:6*

It is amazing to me that throughout the ages, mankind has come to view the grass on the other side of the fence as greener. I am reminded of an incident in my childhood experience when our neighbor, Mr. Andrew, had a farm with various kinds of fruit trees (peaches, plums, pears, grapes, etc.) He was a kind and gentle man who allowed the neighborhood boys to come and help with farm chores. Our temptation came during the plum season. We asked him if we could have some plums.

There were two sections of his farm that had plum trees. In one section the plums were normal size, a variety of red and yellow, extremely sweet, and exceptionally good. In the other section, the plums were golf ball size, a variety of red and yellow, extremely sweet, and delicious. He agreed to give us our request, but with specific instructions not to go into the other plum section. Those were his choice plum for special people and for sale, I assumed. We all replied, "Yes sir." However, as soon as his back was turned, we made a beeline to the forbidden section. We just could not resist the temptation - bad, bad boys!!

**Lord, help us to resist the temptation and patiently wait on our due season.**

**James Thomas**

# DAY 82

# MAGNIFYING FAITH

> *For he looked for a city which hath foundations, whose builder and maker is God. Hebrews 11:10*

When Abraham, Isaac, Jacob, and Moses drew nearer to the end of their earthly pilgrimage, their eyes began to wax dim to the world around them. Their eyes were fixed on the promises of God. Their faith enlarged like a magnifier as the world around them grew dimmer.

People all around are drawing nearer to the end of life. Death and dying fill headlines every day. Prophecy is being fulfilled before our eyes. Perilous days have come, and greater peril is on the horizon. Hearts are troubled on every side. Still, there is a continual struggle for power among those in authority. That struggle has caused a distinctive fault line and intense polarization of the nation. Like earth's tectonic plates, the nation is being shifted and pulled apart with a deep and widening crater of opposing "values". Millions of people are walking blindly into those craters because of deception, as plainly stated in the Word of God. "Many shall be deceived" (Matthew 24:5); therefore, it warns believers to take a closer look into the Word of God so that they will be better equipped to understand the implications of world events.

May the Word of God be magnified in all believers so that we may see clearly how God's prophetic promises are being fulfilled before our dimming eyes. May His Holy Word be magnified and become our life-long guide.

**Lord, help us to magnify your word above all earthly powers and authority. May we see your precious promises more clearly as the world around us grows dimmer. In Jesus' name. Amen.**

**Geraldine Russell**

# DAY 83

# TOTAL PRAISE

> *I will praise thee, O LORD, with my whole heart; I will shew forth all thy marvelous works. Psalm 9:1*

Each week in our world, there are a number of live sporting events, music concerts, or theater productions and they all have one thing in common. They will all have hundreds or even thousands of fans who will leave all of their love and devotion right there at that event. They give the person of the hour their full love and support while they are there, and they leave full of excitement, enthusiasm, and inspiration.

That is exactly the height and magnitude that our worship of God should reach. We should be giving God our *total* praise. The word "total" implies that we are not just giving Him pieces of praise, but we are giving Him every praise with our whole hearts. We are giving Him our complete dedication and surrender. We are telling Him that He alone deserves all the glory and the credit for everything we've been through. We're telling Him that He is our Source and our Shield and that we will praise Him for everything that He is. We love to sing *about* giving God total praise, but the time has come for us to be about giving Him our *all*!

**Think About It: Have you dedicated yourself to giving God total praise in every area?**

**Domonique Brunson**

## DAY 84

# ADAM AND EVE OPENED THE GATE!

> *But of the fruit of the tree, which is in the midst of the garden, God hath said, ye shall not eat of it, neither shall ye touch it, lest ye die. Genesis 3:3*

When Adam and Eve submitted to the temptation of the devil in the garden of Eden, they opened the floodgate of sin and sickness upon mankind. The second Adam, Jesus Christ, came to deliver you through his death and sufferings. If you will take those sicknesses to the second Adam, who is without sin, you are entitled to deliverance from them just as you are from sin.

You have a right to claim perfect health. Do not let the devil put thoughts in your mind to deceive you. If you like to go to church, love the children of God, and enjoy reading your Bible, he will tell you that you are demon possessed. The devil and the Lord cannot abide in the same house. A spring cannot produce sweet water and bitter, neither does a tree bring forth good and evil fruit.

**Evangelist Nathaniel Scippio, Edited writings**

# DAY 85

# TRUSTING GOD IN THE MIDST OF GRIEF

> *God causes all things to work together for good to those who love God, to those who are called according to His purpose. Romans 8:28*

Sometimes it is difficult to understand why unexpected situations, circumstances, and death happen in our lives. We sometimes come to a crossroad where we find it hard to trust God's decision. We keep asking, "Why? Why? Why, Lord?" Why did this happen? The pain of grief continues to grip, squeeze, and pound the heart like a sledgehammer. The will to live another day seems hopeless. The ability to whisper a prayer feels fruitless. The weight of the mind is like the burden of heavy tons of steel. The constant stream of hot flowing tears never ceases to stop.

It is okay to question God, when you know that you have lived according to His precepts and examples. When you faithfully serve him willingly and joyfully, God grants you the right to seek answers from Him.

In my time of sorrow, I've learned to trust God's decision, even though I don't fully understand it. I realized that I must trust God in all things. It is not an easy task. It is truly challenging to ask God to give me this day my daily bread.

Robert Stanley once quoted, "God will work through everything that touches your life for your benefit." Eventually, you will see how God has worked out every detail of the next chapter of your life to bless you. This life as a Christian is truly a Faith Walk with God.

The key to maintaining your faith in the midst of adversity is to trust our sovereign God, knowing that something good is coming from this adversity.

**Dr. Leticia Hardy**

# DAY 86

## YOUR MEASURE OF FAITH

> *For I say, through the grace given to me, to everyone who is among you, not to think of himself more highly than he ought to think, but to think soberly, as God has dealt to each one a measure of faith.*
> Romans 12:3

"Daddy, thank you for trusting me." My 4-year-old son said these words to my husband a few weeks ago. We both were amazed at his understanding of trust. When we think about it, our children trust us as parents for everything. From their education, to clothing, food, and shelter, every little thing is taken care of. It is the same with our Heavenly Father. As His children, each of us is given a measure of faith to ensure our rights as his sons and daughters.

What is your measure of faith? Is your faith strong and secure when trouble and doubt arise, or do you fold in fear when the enemy throws his treacherous darts? I have experienced the highs and lows of faith. I am a missionary and early in the ministry, my faith was solid as a rock. Nothing could deter me from what I knew God could do. As I got older, my faith in the Lord became a little unsteady. There were times when I didn't know how our bills were to be paid, or if the lights were to be turned off. Now, I literally have to put my faith in God for ALL THINGS. From simply getting out of bed to shopping for groceries, my life depends on the grace and mercy of our Father, and I believe you should trust Him too.

**Jessica Lucas**

## DAY 87

# HE FOUGHT THE BATTLE

> *These things I have spoken to you, that in me ye might have peace. In the world ye shall have tribulation: but be of good cheer; I have overcome the world. John 16:33*

Wake up each day with the expectation that the devil will try to fight you with all that he has. You must also wake up each day knowing that Jesus FOUGHT FOR YOU and gave you everything you need to win. Listen carefully to His voice because the fight is FIXED. Your victory is guaranteed!

**Lesley Thomas**

## DAY 88

# RECEIVED PEACE IN THE STORM

> *Thou wilt keep him in perfect peace, whose mind is stayed on thee: because he trusteth in thee. Isaiah 26:3*

Life can seem unbearable at times with physical pain, difficult decisions, financial hardships, the death of a loved one. When the enemy comes in like a storm to shatter our dreams and threatens to engulf us, we become fearful, perplexed, and plagued by doubts. We may even find it difficult to pray. While the blowing winds of trials are sweeping over us, we can experience peace of mind and calmness of spirit when we keep our minds on God. In fierce storms, we must put our soul in one position, keep it there, and remain steadfast.

When thunder, lighting, falling rocks, winds, waves, turbulent seas, and roaring breakers come, we will be able to hold fast to our confidence in God. His love is everlasting in Christ Jesus. We will receive perfect peace even in the storm as we focus our mind on His word.

We will become steady and stable supported by God's unchanging love and mighty power.

Do you feel overwhelmed by your storm? If so, fix your mind on the Lord and ask for His help. Trust Him to give you peace in the midst of your storm.

**Felicia C. Parker**

# DAY 89

# FAITH IN THE UNSEEN

> *Now faith is the substance of things hoped for, the evidence of things not seen. Hebrews 11:1*

God's arrangement is for us to have faith in him. We base our faith on the unseen. We live in a world that seeks science and technology for answers in our lives. The most powerful first step for unbelievers was to have faith in the existence of God. We came to know this world did not come into existence spontaneously, but God created the world. As Christians, we decided to walk in faith and not by sight. This required complete trust in the Lord.

And how do we acquire this sustaining faith? Reading the Bible and the various accounts of faithful Christians are great sources of inspiration. Also recalling how God has always been faithful to us can keep us encouraged that God will continue to demonstrate his love for us. We can be confident God is able and willing to continue to do the ordinary as well as the impossible for those who love him.

**Lord, help us to be faithful in our trust in you. We pray our faith will not be merely words but also show itself with our obedience. Lord, let us continue to have faith in the unseen because You have always been faithful to us. Amen.**

Venetta Law

# DAY 90

# A DAY'S JOURNEY

> *But do not overlook this fact beloved that with the Lord one day is as a thousand years, and a thousand years as one day. II Peter 3:8*

As Jesus walked this earth over two thousand years ago, they referred to His walking a day as a "Day's Journey." But today, God has allowed man's knowledge to increase so that he is building planes that can journey around the world in a day. Yet, Peter says, "That with the Lord one day is as a thousand years, and a thousand years as one day" (II Peter 3:8). Just think, according to man's record it has been over two thousand years since Jesus walked on this earth; but with our Lord, it has just been two days plus. Oh, what a "Great God we serve! Let us glorify Him each day that we are on the earth. "For the earth is the Lord's, and the fullness thereof, the world and those who dwell therein..."( Psalm 24: 1). Our day's journey could be over in one day.

**Abba Father, thank You for this day that You are allowing us to enjoy. Help us show Your kindness according to Your word. In Jesus' name, we pray. Amen.**

Mary Smith

## DAY 91

# IN SYNC

> *Blessed be the Lord, who daily loadeth us with benefits, even the God of our salvation. Selah. Psalm 68.19*

We live in a computer-driven, technologically advanced society. Every day you're likely to hear about the latest, greatest laptop, mobile phone, or smartwatch. Technology companies and data service providers are always in competition seeking to be the first company to enter the market with the newest, groundbreaking device or service they want us to believe will revolutionize our lives. Technology has become so advanced that you can even connect most of these devices and "sync" all of your information so that even sounds, documents, notes, e-mail, applications, photos, and contacts are on all of the devices you own. If it is on your computer, it can be on your phone. If it is on your phone, it can be on your smartwatch. Designed as a productivity and convenience feature, "syncing" allows an individual to be able to access all the data they need - no matter where they are in the world.

Hence, the question is, how many Christians "sync" daily? I'm not asking if your electronic devices are synced, but is your life in sync with God? You see, God has also provided us with devices so that we can access Him. They are reading His Word daily, daily prayer, and meditation.

For the Christian that "syncs" to God through these vehicles, daily access is granted God's presence and power no matter where life takes you. When was the last time you synced your life with God? Do it today.

**Cheryl L. Thomas**

## DAY 92

# HONOR GOD WITH YOUR BEST

> *Honor the Lord with your wealth, with the firstfruits of all your crops. Proverbs 3:9*

One of the ways we honor our Lord is through giving our best and first, tithing. What is tithing? Tithing is giving the first 10 percent of our earnings, which is the Biblical way. This percentage belongs to God. If we keep it, we are robbing HIM (Mal. 3:18), and who dare rob God? As good stewards, we are good managers. God gave us 100 percent and only asked for the first 10 percent.

Don't spend your Tithes. God has a special plan for them. Tithes are used to facilitate the furthering of the Gospel, enabling the lost to attain Kingdom status.

Tithing is a part of our stewardship and is an important aspect of living as disciples. It is a way of thanking God for how He has blessed us. Tithing is a sacred part of worship because as disciples we have been entrusted to care for others and to assist in His work. God wants us to give to Him first, cheerfully, and consistently.

**Thank you, Lord, for giving us opportunities to share in the Kingdom.**

*Dr. Deloris Y. McBride*

# DAY 93

# A LYING TONGUE!

> *The lips of truth shall be established forever: but a lying tongue is but for a moment. Proverbs 12: 19*

A lying tongue is listed as one of the six things that God hates. The tongue can be dangerous if left uncontrolled. There is a saying that says, "Loose lips sink ships." The various passages in the Bible warn us about the power of the tongue. The tongue is said to be desperately wicked, full of deadly poison and an unruly evil that no man can tame. A lying tongue should not be on the Christian's menu of activities. If we know that it is one of the things God hates, what should be the position of the Christian regarding it?

Some will say that a little lie won't hurt you, but it offends God! It matters to Him. It appears to me that in our world today, a lying tongue is pandemic, global in scope. It's like a virus, highly contagious and everyone is susceptible. The good news is that there is an antidote and spiritual vaccine. It may need a periodic booster shot. The vaccine has been available for thousands of years to whosoever will receive it. It has an eternal shelf-life and is kept in the hands of the Creator. It is marketed under the label, <u>HOLY SPIRIT</u>. It is freely given to all who believe.

**"Truth crushed to earth shall rise again"
(William Cullen Bryant).**

**James Thomas**

# DAY 94

# SING UNTO THE LORD!

> *He put a new song in my mouth, a hymn of praise to our God.*
> *Many will see and fear the LORD and put their trust in him.*
> *Psalm 40:3*

When the dark clouds of sorrow hover above, *sing unto the Lord a new song*. When thunder from the world's never-ending clashes rumbles through, sing unto the Lord a new song. Like the barnyard sparrows at the dawning of a new day singing merrily upon rooftops and in trees, sing unto the Lord a new song. The lyrics and melody will be fine-tuned when the new song flows from a heart of thanksgiving - morning, night, and noon. When you are weary, sing! When you feel yourself drifting away into the land of heaviness, sing unto the Lord a new song. When your heart is filled with joy, sing unto the Lord! Sing unto the Lord every day, no matter what comes your way. Like the barnyard sparrows that sing above, sing of the wonders of God's unfailing love.

**Lord, put a new song in my heart. Help me to sing of your wondrous love that you send from heaven above. Help me to sing as day gives way tonight. Help me to sing of your wondrous love when tears of sorrow dim my sight. Help me to sing a new song every day as I continue to stroll down the believer's narrow way. Lord, help me to sing a new song today! Amen.**

*He cares for the sparrow. He will surely care for you!*
*Sing unto the Lord! Amen!*

**Geraldine Russell**

## DAY 95

# THE GIFT OF FAVOR

> *Let the favor of the Lord our God be upon us, and establish the work of our hands upon us; yes, establish the work of our hands!*
> Psalm 90:17

Imagine that you apply for a higher job position for which there were hundreds of other applicants. Somehow, your application is approved for the first interview. Then you find yourself in the smaller pool of second interviewees. Next, it comes down to the top three candidates and you are one of them! You go in unsure of how you got to this point but praying and hoping to make it to the top. Wonder of wonders, you win the position!

People in various careers have this very testimony and most will tell you that they are only in their position because of the favor of God! They may not have the exact qualifications, they may not have the necessary connections, and they may not even have the experience the position calls for, but the one thing they do have that triumphs over all of the others is the GIFT OF GOD'S FAVOR. Many times, it may not look like the desires of your heart could possibly come to pass. But, the favor of God is truly a gift! So, as God showers His favor upon you, walk through your day confident that His favor has gone before you to establish all of your works.

**Think About It:** Where do you see God's favor at work in your life today?

**Domonique Brunson**

## DAY 96

# GOD'S SUSTAINING PROMISES

> *The LORD our God be with us, as he was with our fathers: let him not leave us, nor forsake us: 1 Kings 8:57*

Issues of life can sometimes bring such heartache and pain. The amount of effort you put into prioritizing your future has now been driven off course by some cruel unexpected circumstances. You once knew your purpose in life, but suddenly that purpose is warring against you. Now you feel as if your life is a train wreck.

You may not feel as though you are in control of your life right now. That is where God wants you. Now, he is ready to fill your life with his life sustaining promises. God has given us His great and precious promises that give us hope, peace, and strength. God promised never to leave us (Deuteronomy 31:6). God promised to meet all our needs according to His riches (Philippians 4:19). God is going to make you the head and not the tail (Deuteronomy 28:16). He will deliver you from every trap set by the enemy and protect you from every weapon formed to bring you destruction. God is faithful and will keep His promises concerning you (Joshua 21:45).

God's light of gladness is available to all that put their trust in Him. On this day, rejoice in the Lord who is the hope of our salvation. Rest assured that His promises will prevail.

**Dr. Leticia Hardy**

## DAY 97

# WHAT'S YOUR STORY?

> *And they overcame him by the blood of the Lamb and by the word of their testimony...Revelation 12:11*

Every time I meet someone new, or I am introduced to a person for the first time, I ask them "What's your story"? I oftentimes would like to know their background, family history, hobbies, interests, likes, and dislikes to see if we have anything in common. During an anniversary dinner of a community group that I belong to, I was awarded the opportunity to share my testimony with approximately 15 women. This was the first time outside of the church that I shared God's abundance in my life. Needless to say, I was shaking like a leaf the entire time. The Holy Spirit reassured me that I would do just fine.

There was a point in the ceremonial dinner where we had to "Get to Know Your Neighbor." We had to ask questions about the person we were sitting next to. Come to find out, I was sitting next to a professional make-up artist who is a Christian and loves the Lord. She has an almost 2-year-old daughter who is just too adorable for words. Growing up, the young lady went to a Christian school in New York, and she told me that her experience there literally saved her life. She became more intimate with God and was more concerned with His will for her life.

I urge everyone to share their testimony and see what God can do to enhance His Kingdom for His Glory.

**Jessica Lucas**

## DAY 98

# REJOICE

> *Rejoice in hope, patient in tribulation, continuing instant in prayer.*
> *Romans 12:12*

There is a reason scripture tells us to guard our hearts and renew our minds. Stress, anger, fear, and disappointment will come, and it does not do a body good! Life will sometimes throw us things that will cause us to question the very existence of God! But He promised us that he would never leave or forsake us.

He already promised to provide for our EVERY need. We have got to start trusting His word when it does not look like we win! Even in tough times His word never fails! In the darkest night we must remember that if God did it before He will do it again.

**Lesley Thomas**

# DAY 99

# WAITING ON GOD

> *But they that wait upon the LORD shall renew their strength; they shall mount up with wings as eagles; they shall run, and not be weary; and they shall walk, and not faint. Isaiah 40:31*

Waiting on God to help me was not easy. So, I waited patiently. I cried many days, mornings, and nights. I didn't know what to do. When I started praying, God heard my cry. He lifted me out of the pit of despair, out of the mud, and the mire. He set my feet on solid ground and steadied me as I walked along. He gave me a new song to sing, a hymn of praise to His Holy Name. I am hoping many will see and hear what He has done for me and be astounded, and they too can put their trust in God who is powerful and has true love for everyone.

In the Bible, I read how David received four benefits from waiting on God. (1) God lifted him out of despair. (2) set his feet on solid ground, (3) steadied him as he walked, and (4) put a new song of praise in his mouth. Often blessings cannot be received unless we go through the trial of waiting. There are some who do not want to wait on God. They want a microwave, quick fix, not knowing that the true blessings come by waiting, trusting, and having faith in God. It might not seem easy but wait on God because the end results are the best results. Wait on God.

**Felicia C. Parker**

# DAY 100

# IMMERSE YOURSELF

> *Practice these things, immerse yourself in them, [a] so that all may see your progress. Keep a close watch on yourself and on the teaching. Persist in this, for by so doing you will save both yourself and your hearers. 1 Timothy 4:15-16*

Paul counseled Timothy to continue to meditate on the word of God. This advice is also relevant for us. Have you considered the benefit of meditating on God's word for yourself? I recognize the importance of knowing the scripture for myself. The more I divulge into God's word the greater I have desired to know him more. I have a changed heart and have greater faith in the power of God.

Do you have the desire to meditate on God's Word but seem to lack the time? I have had this experience.

My life was hectic with my primary focus on my career. My life lacked balance. But I continued to have the desire and sought the Lord for ways to devote time to him. God revealed times I could carve out to devote to him. I would listen to the Bible by audio on my way to work. I also sought ways to streamline my life for God. The more I read God's Word the more I grew spiritually. I had greater love, faith, and obedience. I had a changed heart and had greater faith in the power of God.

**Abba Father, continue to help me to meditate on the word of God as I go throughout the day. In Jesus' name. Amen.**

**Venetta Law**

## DAY 101

# NEARER TO THEE

> *Let us draw near with a true heart in full assurance of faith...*
> *Hebrews 10:22a*

Spring is such a beautiful time of year in the country. The wildflowers are blooming and the farmers' crops are green. The early morning sun reflects who is in charge of the universe. For as I walk "our Father's" presence seems nearer. What a Great God who spoke this world into being over six thousand years ago! And He is still lovingly drawing us nearer to Him.

As we seek God with a true heart each day to draw nearer to Him, He renews and refills us with His spirit of righteousness. Therefore, let us walk showing an inner man of beauty, shining, and blooming like the flowers that God has created.

**Abba Father, help us this day to express beauty in everything we do and say in Your Name we pray. Amen.**

**Mary Smith**

## DAY 102

# GOOD DISTRACTIONS

> *Finally, brethren, whatsoever things are true, whatsoever things are honest, whatsoever things are just, whatsoever things are pure, whatsoever things are lovely, whatsoever things are of good report; if there be any virtue, and if there be any praise, think on these things.*
> Philippians 4:8

Distractions. These are the little things that come along to divert your attention when you're on your way to purpose and destiny. They keep you from getting the "traction" necessary to act on your purpose or goal.

What most people fail to realize, however, is that not all distractions are bad. I've encountered times when I was moving full throttle towards a goal, that someone suggested an idea, proposal, or plan that didn't quite fit the purpose of my life. It was a great idea that would reap awesome benefits; however, it would deter or impede progress and forward movement toward my current goal. I knew if I took advantage and participated in this idea, my focus would slowly dissipate, and my initial goal would be temporarily abandoned.

When you're on the road to destiny, one has to be very purposeful. Your mindset has to be that if it doesn't accomplish your God-ordained purpose, it's not something for which you have the time, energy, or resources to participate. So, instead of simply looking out for those "bad" distractions, also, be on the lookout for those good distractions that are disguised as great ideas. Refuse to be sidetracked and keep moving toward your purpose.

**Cheryl L. Thomas**

# DAY 103

## WIFI (WHILE I'M FAVORED, I)

*Surely, LORD, you bless the righteous; you surround them with your favor as with a shield. Psalm 5:12*

As born-again Christians, we are connected to God. With this connection, we have possessions that enable us to fulfill His purpose for us as we journey through life. We are connected to His favor. The psalmist states, "God blesses the righteous and surrounds us with favor." God's favor is powerful, encompassing, protective, and wonderful, and moves us to satisfy Him in every aspect. Because of this abundance of favor, While I'm Favored I (WIFI) will bless the Lord at all times and others.

While I'm favored, I will reach those who are suffering discomforts and who don't have a relationship with God to proclaim the Name of Jesus. While I am favored, I will love my neighbor as I love myself. While I am favored, I will support leadership and be an enhancer and influencer for the body of Christ. While I am Favored, I will declare and decree the goodness of the Lord and command the blessings of the Almighty God.

May the joys of God's favor give you peace and hope as you inspire others to develop a relationship with God.

**Dr. Deloris Y. McBride**

# DAY 104

# A WOUNDED SPIRIT!

> *The spirit of a man will sustain his infirmity; but, a wounded spirit who can bear? Proverbs 4:18*

The Bible says that the spirit (or the mind or the heart) will sustain (nourish or provide sustenance) his infirmity (sickness). Bad things do happen to good people because it is the common fate of all human families. They should not be viewed as God's punishment for sin. Job, when responding to his wife's advice to curse God and die, says to her "what? Shall we receive good at the hand of God and not evil?"

A steady diet of the Word of Faith is essential for those who minister to the wounded, depressed, or the weak. Job was at an exceptionally low point in his suffering when his three friends came to comfort him. After listening to his complaining and cursing the day that he was born, Eliphaz says, "Now, let me speak." He tells Job how much good he has done in helping lift up the weak knees of others and now trouble has come to his door, and he is fainting. Here comes the chastisement! "Remember, I pray thee, whoever perished, being innocent? They that plow iniquity, and sow wickedness, reap the same" (Job 4: 7-8).

**Father, help us that seek to encourage and lift those that are wounded in spirit, grant us the grace to speak kind words of faith, praying that every word will have healing virtue.**

**James Thomas**

# DAY 105

# ANCHORED!

> *Which hope we have as an anchor of the soul, both sure and steadfast, and which entereth into that within the veil... Hebrews 6:19*

Storms of life will come. Winds of life will blow. Sea billows-of-life will roll into our lives. However, being anchored in the Word of God brings comfort and stability during those times that all believers experience. Your earthly vessels may bob up and down and may seem to topple into the sea of life, but the anchor of God's Word renews your courage and calms your fears. Therefore, when the storms-of-life rage, praise Him for being anchored. When dark clouds shadow the brightness of your day, praise Him for being anchored. When waves of sickness come crashing into your lives, praise Him for being anchored. Keeping praise in your mouth, hope in your heart, and daily dives into the Word of God anchors your earthly vessel.

Like the nation, the world continues to rock and reel from one crisis to another, we find hope, peace, and an anchor for our souls in the Word of God. His Word is settled in heaven forever! That's our assurance when storms-of-life rage. Believers are anchored forever!

**Heavenly Father, when storms in my life arise, help me to rest soundly in your promise to anchor my soul.
In Jesus' name. Amen.**

**Geraldine Russell**

# DAY 106

# HOW ARE YOUR REFLEXES?

> *And he spake a parable unto them to this end, that men ought always to pray, and not to faint. Luke 18:1*

In my opinion, going to the doctor for a checkup is not the most fun event in the world. However, there are some parts that I remember enjoying while growing up. One of those parts was when the doctor would use the triangular tool to hit my knee and my knee would fly up into the air. It was a pretty funny feeling and always made me laugh in amazement at how the human body was created. My knee, though, demonstrated that my reflexes (reactions) were on point and functioning the way God intended.

Spiritually speaking, just like my knee, there are some "reflexes" that should become part of our very nature such as prayer, Bible study, and running to God because He is the strong tower where our strength, peace, and hope lie. The Bible tells us that we should ALWAYS pray and not get tired of praying, no matter how tough it may seem to continue. Now, you may have fast natural reflexes like me, and I often consider the fact that as fast as my reflex is to kick my knee up, my reflex to pray at all times should be even quicker. Pray always for all things!

**Think About It:** Is prayer time with God a fast reflex for you?

**Domonique Brunson**

## DAY 107

# COMFORT FOR GOD'S PEOPLE

> *The Lord is my rock, my fortress, and my deliverer; my God is my rock, in whom I take refuge. He is my shield and the horn of my salvation, my stronghold. Psalm 18:2*

I am praying for you today. My prayer is that you will take comfort in knowing that God is your fortress; and that He will surround you with His loving care. Know that God is your deliverer, I pray that He will give you the victory over life's troubles.

I pray that God's shield of faith will continuously uphold you and protect you from the devices of the enemy. I pray that God's loving hands will be a stronghold that never gives away and never fails to lift you and comfort you.

I pray that God, in His generous, gracious, and abundant love will continue to shower your heart, soul, and spirit with His tender and everlasting mercies of joy and contentment. I pray that you will cast your burden upon the Lord, and that He will sustain you. I pray that the Lord will never suffer His servant to be moved. I pray that the Lord will fill your emptiness with His unconditional love and make you whole as you are comforted by His healing Spirit.

**Dr. Leticia Hardy**

# DAY 108

# MY SPIRITUAL JOURNEY

> *God, who got you started in this spiritual adventure, shares with us the life of his Son and our Master Jesus. He will never give up on you. Never forget that. 1 Corinthians 1:9*

My spiritual journey with the Lord began when I accepted Him into my heart and life in November of 1997. I was a 14-year-old freshman in high school who came from a Christian family. Growing up in church as children, we were taught to reverence God and respect our elders. On that Sunday morning, I was a young lady who needed a Savior. Prior to my spiritual birthday, I suffered from depression and anxiety. Everyone knew I was a "church girl," and when I got saved, it seemed the enemy was causing people to strip my self-esteem, identity, and image.

When I did surrender my life to Christ, I learned how to cast all of my cares on Jesus. My coping mechanism was to isolate myself and shut off from society. Now, Christ has allowed me to experience comfort, encouragement, inspiration and enlightenment from God's Word and His Holy Spirit.

As the Scripture states, God has been with us since day one and He will never give up on us because He has our best interest at heart. Never forget that He will always be with us until the end of time. As a result, we are reassured of His promise through Jesus that He surely cares for His children.

**Jessica Lucas**

# DAY 109

# NAKED AND AFRAID

> *But when they deliver you up, take no thought how or what ye shall speak: for it shall be given you in that same hour what ye shall speak.  Matthew 10:19*

There is a popular television show that I like to watch called Naked and Afraid. The premise of the show is that two strangers are stripped of their clothing and everything they own except one item of their choosing and dropped into the jungle with dangerous animals and predators to survive for 21 days. The one item that they can keep with them is one they think would be most helpful to their survival. During their time in the jungle, they are faced with many obstacles that they must try and conquer with only the knowledge and survival skills they have gained over the years.

This show reminds me of a time when I found myself in a fight or flight situation years ago and my faith was challenged. I was placed in a situation where I had to use the knowledge of God's word and my faith to overcome the immediate challenge. In the moment it seemed as though I did not have what I needed to defeat the enemy and I realized that I was naked and afraid. As I quickly said a prayer and assessed the situation, I realized the tools that I had were sufficient for my survival at that moment. They were my FAITH and the HOLY SPIRIT.

When times are tough and circumstances seem insurmountable, we must remember the measure of faith that we as children of God have been given. For when we use our faith, we can defeat all the evil tactics of the devil. We must remember that the Holy Spirit is ever present to lead and guide us at a moment's notice.

**Lesley Thomas**

## DAY 110

# HANGING ON EVERY WORD

> *And he taught daily in the temple. But the chief priests and the scribes and the chief of the people sought to destroy him, and could not find what they might do: for all the people were very attentive to hear him  Luke 19:47-48.*

People followed Jesus because His words were powerful. He had not been brainwashed by traditions. He made no false assumptions. He had no ulterior motives. Even from the earliest moments of Jesus' ministry people were "amazed at His teaching." People followed Him and listened to Him. He did not speak empty platitudes or culturally accepted clichés. In fact, they "were hanging on to every word He said." What power these words must have had! We can picture words being spoken by Jesus, one at a time, one phrase at a time. Men and women waited for each nugget of truth, almost holding their breath to take in what He said. As Jesus spoke, people tried to catch His words as they "fell," almost afraid that if they relaxed their attention, they might miss something. This required enormous concentration and complete submission. Today, we still can spend time in His Word. His Word is alive and active, sharper than any double-edged sword. But to get the full measure of His Word, we need to listen attentively.

God wants to reveal the depths of His Word to you. Read, think about the Word, meditate on it, and pray about it. Ask God to speak to you through His Word. It is still powerful, alive, and active. It will transform your life.

**Felicia C. Parker**

## DAY 111

# DRAWING SEASON

> *To everything, there is a season, a time for every purpose under heaven. Ecclesiastes 3:1*

Each season of the year, shop owners change their window displays to show items to shoppers for the new season. Their goal is to sell their inventory to make a living in this world. What a great example for a child of God! Plan each season of the year with ways to draw others into the "Kingdom of God." It may be wearing a seasonal colored dress, shirt, pants, or even a pair of shoes as a conversation starter to talk about Jesus. The point is that as we spend time in the word of God our inventory each season of the year will increase as we study ways to bring others to Christ. We are the shop owners on earth learning how to make a living in this world. We must use each season to plan to draw shoppers into the kingdom of God.

**Abba Father, please show us ways to draw others into Your kingdom each day. In Jesus' name, we pray, Amen.**

*Mary Smith*

## DAY 112

# HOW TO GET ANSWERS TO PRAYERS WHEN IT SEEMS IMPOSSIBLE

> *Now unto him that is able to do exceeding abundantly above all that we ask or think, according to the power that worketh in us.*
> Ephesians 3:20

**Today's Prayer: Dear Lord, please forgive me for thinking so small when You're such a GREAT BIG GOD! Help me to see as You see. I make the bold declaration that yesterday was the last day for thinking small things and praying small prayers.**

I know that You are able to do EXCEEDINGLY ABUNDANTLY above ALL that I could ever ask or think. So today, I think BIG thoughts and I believe that You'll bless me beyond measure. I pray IMPOSSIBLE prayers because I know You to be the God who makes the sun stand still, raging seas part, and dead things rise.

**I thank You because I am not just a talker, I am now a Water Walker!!! In the name of Jesus, I pray. Amen.**

Cheryl L. Thomas

# DAY 113

## GOOD TROUBLE

> *And they laid hands on them, and put them in hold unto the next day: for it was now eventide. Howbeit many of them which heard the word believed; and the number of the men was about five thousand. Acts 4:1-21*

For most of us in my generation, we have been taught by our parents to stay out of trouble at all costs. I would agree with you that this behavioral training is wise instruction.

The late Congressman John Lewis encouraged his followers and civil rights adherents to get into trouble, "good trouble, necessary trouble." His saying was "if you see something that is not right, say something, do something; to sit-in or sit-down is a way of standing up."

Dr. Martin Luther King said, "If a man has not found something that he is willing to die for, he is not fit to live." King David as a shepherd boy, after hearing the giant Goliath, defying the army of the living God said to his brothers, "Is there not a cause?"

Acts chapter 4 gives us a picture of how Peter and John chose to engage in good trouble as they were faced with the punishment of being jailed by religious authorities. Their response was "… Whether it be right in the sight of God to hearken unto you, more than unto God, judge ye. For we cannot but speak the things which we have seen and heard" (Acts 4:19-20). Even while hearing the threatening of the religious authorities, their prayer to God was to grant that with all boldness they may speak his word.

**James Thomas**

# DAY 114

# LIGHT UP THE WORLD!

> *Ye are the light of the world...Let your light so shine before men, that they may see your good works, and glorify your Father which is in heaven. Matthew 5:14a; 16*

The world is getting darker each day as world leaders compete for riches, power, and dominance. Many are blinded and being deceived by the cunning craftiness of the prince of the powers of the air. He has launched an all-out assault against "true worshippers". Persecution continues to steamroll across many nations. Laws continue to be instituted that will suppress believers' freedom to worship the only true and living God. Jesus warned his followers that persecution would be the norm until He returned to establish His kingdom. Today, the polarizing values of world leaders and the explosive power of technological advances have caused many believers to "shelter in place". Some have decided to lower their wattage to keep from drawing attention to the light of their eternal values. Many have been lured into the thin veil of "compromise". Consequently, masses are being deceived and led into the abyss of eternal separation from God.

How do believers counter this tragic reality? One subjective word... "LET". Despite the darkness, "Let" your light shine! Despite persecution, "Let" your light shine! Despite infirmity, "Let" your light shine". Despite opposition to eternal values, "Let" your light shine"! Believers have the answer to the darkness that is enveloping the minds of this unbelieving world. The answer: "LET your light shine before men so that they may SEE your good works and glorify God, our heavenly Father!" He still reigns over all earthly affairs; in darkness and light. Let's shine brighter, believers!

Heavenly Father, help me to LET my light shine brighter so that all I meet will see evidence of my love for You! Amen.

Geraldine Russell

# DAY 115

# RESIST...AND RESIST AGAIN

> *Submit yourselves therefore to God. Resist the devil, and he will flee from you. James 4:7*

Emails and social media are important to our everyday lives. When checking my email, I never know what will pop up in my inbox. On one particular day, I opened an email from one of my favorite trivia sites and the question referenced a certain celebrity and a lifestyle that did not represent the Kingdom of God.

I chose not to respond and deleted the email. The next day, as I was scrolling through my emails and answering my daily trivia questions, the same question popped up again! Once again, I deleted the email. This process continued for another two weeks until one day, I didn't see that question anymore. That result triggered a lightbulb moment in my heart. The Holy Spirit, being our Master Teacher, told me that is the same process we as believers should use on Satan.

When he presents a new temptation, resist him. When he changes the face and presents it again, resist him again. When he upgrades, changes the size, and presents it AGAIN, resist him AGAIN! You will notice that eventually, one day, just like my email, that season of temptation will pass. That does not mean Satan won't bring something else your way, because he will. However, the more you resist him through the strength of the Lord, the more he will run from you. As children of the Most High, Satan should be running from US, not the other way around. Be mindful of what James 4:7 states, "*Submit yourselves therefore to God. Resist the devil, and he will flee from you."* Be encouraged!

**Think About It:** In what areas of your life could you afford to resist and resist again?

**Domonique Brunson**

## DAY 116

# OBEDIENCE -THE COMPASS OF OUR SALVATION

> *And Samuel said, Hath the Lord as great delight in burnt offerings and sacrifices, as much as in obeying the voice of the Lord? Behold, to obey is better than sacrifice, and to hearken than the fat of rams.*
> *1 Samuel 15:22*

God has given every one of us the freedom of choice. We have the liberty to choose life over death and blessings over curses. God also gave us a living compass to lead and guide us in making the right choices and avoiding the wrong ones. That compass is called the Bible, the living Word of God. The Bible contains all the information needed to reap the benefits or the consequences of our choices. The Word of God clearly stated that we will surely reap the benefits or consequences of our sown seeds, whether good or evil.

Obedience will always be the key to our salvation. We have been granted the freedom to be led and directed by God's divine Word (the Bible) or we can choose to obey and follow the knowledge of our thoughts.

From Genesis to Revelation, you'll find that obedience to God will always lead man to salvation and prosperity. Disobedience to God's Word has caused many to lift their eyes in hell.

Choose this day whom you will serve.

**Dr. Leticia Hardy**

## DAY 117

# TRANSFORMATION BEGINS WITH YOU!

> *Don't become so well adjusted to your culture that you fit into it without even thinking. Instead, fix your attention on God. You'll be changed from the inside out... Romans 12:2 MSG*

Saturday, July 16, 2022, will be a day that I will never forget. My husband and I attended a session on the logistics of Transforming Cities and Places for the Kingdom of God. As I sat with my pen and notebook eagerly taking notes, I learned that transformation first begins with us transforming our families, homes, and neighborhoods. The presenters were Dr. Ed and Ruth Silvoso of Argentina. They spoke on how transformation first begins at home and revival is not only for the church, but for the nations.

I was shaking in excitement because I believe the Lord has called my husband and me to transform a generation for the Glory of God. I couldn't write fast enough. For two hours I was mesmerized by how they presented the gospel. Some of their points from the session were as follows...

God wants us to remember that the family is the basis of the church and the unity of the family begins at home.

Revival is not revival until it HEALS the LAND.

The first step towards change is always the most important and whatever we do or touch is a potential vehicle for transformation.

Being baptized in the Holy Spirit will allow us to receive the anointing for EXTRAORDINARY miracles.

Take heed to these points for they will utterly transform our world, but it first begins with YOU!!!

**Jessica Lucas**

## DAY 118

# RECALIBRATE - REFOCUS- REGROUP

> *Even them will I bring to my holy mountain and make them joyful in my house of prayer; their burnt offerings and sacrifices shall be accepted upon my altar; for my house shall be called a house of prayer for all people. Isaiah 56:7*

I was listening to a young lady talk recently. In her disillusionment, she declared that she would not be going back to church. She felt like her church had too many "life managers." She stated that she felt like there was too much attention paid to unnecessary things and not enough focus on God. In her despair I reminded her that sometimes we all must recalibrate, refocus, and regroup at times. Maybe she could change the way she interacted with her church and not leave.

The same applies to the "church." In an effort to keep up with the pressures of remaining relevant and being able to meet the needs of an ever-growing technology driven society, we have put a lot of emphasis on being prepared for the people and not preparing the people to meet God there. In this area the church may have fallen short. I encouraged her and I encouraged the church to do the same. There are times when we need to be sure that our focus remains on the One we are there to worship. The lights, singing and programs are all good, but we must remember to keep the main thing the main thing…Jesus and His love for us.

**Lesley Thomas**

## DAY 119

# FLOURISH LIKE A PALM TREE

> *And he shall be like a tree planted by the rivers of water, That bringeth forth his fruit in his season; His leaf also shall not wither; And whatsoever he doeth shall prosper. Psalm 1:3*

Have you ever seen a palm tree in the midst of a great storm? That tree may be bent so far over that it's almost touching the ground. When the wind finally stops, that palm tree bounces right back up. What's interesting is that while that palm tree is hunched over under the pressure of the storm, it is actually becoming stronger.

See, the reason God said we'd flourish like a palm tree is because He knows there would be difficult times. He knew things would come against us to try and steal our joy and victory. But God said, "You're" going be like a palm tree because when the storms of life blow, you are going to come right back up stronger than "before."

As you reflect on the events of your life, remember, the storms you have encountered have only made you stronger. You are wiser. You are more alive. You are headed for victory. Your brightest days are right out in front of you! Always remember that the secret to a flourishing life is our relationship with Jesus. In Him we find and draw the resources to flourish like the palm tree!

**Felicia C. Parker**

# DAY 120

## A LAKE CLASSROOM

> *Launch out into the deep and let down your nets for a catch... Luke 5:4b*

In educational classrooms, teachers are taught to include three "Learning Styles:" auditory, visual, and kinesthetic. For it has been proven that we understand individual learning in three learning styles. Auditory learners take in information through listening and speaking. Visual learners best absorb information when they see material being presented. Kinesthetic learners are "doers." They take the term "hands-on" literally so that no one is left out of the learning process. It is very important to teach all three learning styles in each classroom setting. So, how very exciting it is that our master teacher – Jesus has taught us this very important style of teaching in the word of God.

Jesus used the lake as a classroom as He taught Peter and others to fish. First, He sat in a boat on the lake to teach the word to them. Secondly, He directed Peter and others to "launch out into the deep and let down their nets for a catch." Thirdly, as the men obeyed directions, the nets were filled with a great number of fish, and they all worked together to bring them to shore. Thus, using all three styles of learning, (St. Luke 5:1 -11) let us go forth today in our classroom using our voice, character, and hands to draw others into God's Kingdom.

**Prayer: Father, thank You for the privilege today of working in Your classroom in this world, in Jesus' name we pray. Amen**

**Mary Smith**

# DAY 121

# HOW TO TAP INTO GOD'S ENDLESS SUPPLY

> *But my God shall supply all your need according to his riches in glory by Christ Jesus. Philippians 4:19*

Therefore, take no thought, saying, what shall we eat? Or, what shall we drink? Or, Wherewithal shall we be clothed? For after all these things do the Gentiles seek: for your heavenly Father knoweth that ye have need of all these things (Matthew 6:31-32).

Dear Lord, thank You for richly supplying everything that I will ever need. I never have to fear lack because Your supply is endless. When I become worried and anxious, help me remember Your promise. Whenever I am broke, help me to remember You are rich. When I am sick, depressed, or discouraged, help me remember You conquered death, hell, and the grave so that I could be alive and well. Increase my courage and faith so I will not be anxious and not worry because I know You, my heavenly Father, will always take care of me. In Jesus' name, Amen.

Cheryl L. Thomas

## DAY 122

# BODY WORKS!

> *What? Know ye not that your body is the temple of the Holy Ghost, which is in you, which ye have of God, and ye are not your own? For ye, are bought with a price: therefore, glorify God in your body and in your spirit, which are God's. I Corinthians 6:19-20*

Apostle Paul in his writings, reminds the believers that our bodies are a special place of dwelling for God's Holy Spirit. It is a sanctuary that is kept fit for His worship and habitation. It is not our own to misuse and abuse at will. He recommends that we glorify God with these bodies of ours. We are called to be caretakers of this devoted sanctuary.

We must take care to maintain our physical house by being diligent in our eating habits and physical exercise, so that our temple looks good both inside and outside. We should want our temple to be a statement of God's grace. Collectively, we are members of one body, fitly joined together where we care for one another. We help to mend the brokenhearted. We apply healing balm to those that are wounded by our thoughtless words and deeds. We fight the good fight to make sure the whole body is healthy.

**Father, I thank You for choosing to dwell daily in this earthen vessel of clay. Help me to keep fit for Your habitation so that I in no way intentionally defile this temple!**

**James Thomas**

# DAY 123

# REMEMBER THE TITANIC!

> *Be always on the watch, and pray that you may be able to escape all that is about to happen, and that you may be able to stand before the Son of Man. Luke 21:36, NIV*

Once described as the "unsinkable ship," the captain navigated the Titanic through the frigid waters of the arctic ice caps. With limited visibility and great confidence, the ship forged ahead unaware of the danger ahead. It sailed proudly through small, fragmented icebergs that had been separated from larger mountainous glaciers. Suddenly, the watchman saw the peril. The navigators scrambled to avoid the imminent danger. However, it was too late. The size of the ship prevented it from being maneuvered easily. Subsequently, it struck a huge iceberg that carved a hole in the bow of the ship. Ocean water flooded the massive ship from the boiler room to the captain's quarter. The unsinkable ship was sinking to the bottom of the Artic Ocean. Panic set in. Cries for help filled the radio waves. SOS flares were launched. When help finally arrived, only a few nearly frozen passengers had survived the tragic ordeal. Many lives were lost.

How could this magnificent maiden voyage end in such horrific tragedy? Only God can answer that question completely.

The scripture referenced above reminds believers to watch, pray, and obey the guidance of the Holy Spirit at all times. By doing so, they will be able to navigate around, or away from life's mountainous icebergs that suddenly appear in the lives of all believers. When our visibility is limited by the "fog of disobedience and unfaithfulness," we may find ourselves in imminent danger. The Holy Spirit is our Captain. He is the only One that can navigate believers through perilous times. Let's remember the Titanic by keeping a humble heart and an obedient spirit for the entire maiden voyage from earth to the pristine shores of heaven where eternal life awaits all believers.

**Heavenly Father, please help me to maintain my obedience to You, and become more fervent and consistent in my prayer life. In Jesus name. Amen.**

Geraldine Russell

# DAY 124

# JESUS IS THE ANSWER

> *And he is before all things, and by him all things consist.*
> *Colossians 1:17*

As I was preparing my high school students for a test one day, one of them asked me if I would mark their answer wrong if they answered the question with "Jesus" because He is the answer to all things. While laughing, I told them yes, I would mark it wrong because Jesus would have told them to study to put down the more specific answer to the question I was asking at the time. Such wise guys, right? Well, that conversation stuck with me for the rest of the day because where the real world is concerned, I would support my students 100% because Jesus is indeed the answer to *all* of life's problems!

Jesus left us a blueprint that includes all of His words and promises, and it is called the Bible. He expects that when we are facing any issue, big or small, we will turn to Him to bring us through it because He existed before the problem and already had a solution before it arose. We will *never* have all of the answers while we live here on earth, but there is someone who has answers to questions we have not even asked yet! That's just how omniscient He is. So, ask Him and expect Him to answer today!

**Think About It:** Have you been asking the Lord first for answers?

**Domonique Brunson**

# DAY 125

# GLORIFYING GOD WITH OUR GIFTS

> *Every good and perfect gift is from above, coming down from the Father of lights, with whom is no variableness, neither shadow of turning. James 1:17*

Imagine it's your birthday and your best friend presented you with a gift that you never thought to ask for. This gift made you feel uniquely special to your best friend. After several years have gone by, that gift is still every bit as awesome as it was the day you received it.

You have never forgotten the best friend that made it possible for you to enjoy such an awesome gift.

Looking at things from this perspective, every born-again believer of our Lord and Savior Jesus Christ was given an awesome gift. This gift was heaven-sent and given to you. This gift contains many attributes designed specifically for you by God. The purpose of gifts and talents is to glorify God and bless others.

The Bible tells us to think about things that are lovely. So, ask yourself, "How will I worship God with my gift? How can I uniquely touch and bless the lives of my fellowman?"

**Dr. Leticia Hardy**

# DAY 126

## GRACE AND FAVOR

> *As every man hath received the gift, even so minister the same one to another, as good stewards of the manifold grace of God.*
> *1 Peter 4:10-12*

At the time, it was 1994 and Pastor Watts was just beginning in the ministry when she met the little boy and his mother at a church in Lake City, Florida. The little boy had grown up and his mother was attending a funeral of Pastor Watts' relative. A conversation at the Home Going service revealed the newly elected Elder of the congregation in Lake City will be led by the young man who attended services there several years earlier. Watts stated to the congregation, "We are here because of His grace, and we are the apple of His eye."

**Grace:** Courteous, good-will. It is given freely. Mercy: Compassion and kindness.

**Jessica Lucas**

## DAY 127

# BELIEVE WHAT YOU HEAR

> *I will praise thee; for I am fearfully and wonderfully made: marvelous are thy works; and that my soul knoweth right well.*
> *Psalms 139:14*

Have you ever been in the middle of a conversation, sharing an idea that you have, and everyone tells you that it's a great idea? "You should go for it." For whatever reason, you decide not to pursue it because you really aren't convinced that it would work. Later on, you see or hear of a similar product that is proving to be VERY successful.

Or a friend of yours tells you of a problem they are having and how they really don't know what to do or where to turn next. As soon as you hear it, you are able to give them specific instructions as to what they should do or point them in the right direction. This is not the first time that you have been at the right place at the right time with the right resources for your friends…somehow it just seems to work out that way.

I call these "small whispers" from a loving God who is trying to show you the important things about yourself that you just don't believe. There are gifts and talents that God has given us that we sometimes have a tendency to downplay and devalue what we may have to offer to others. Sometimes it's just difficult to see or acknowledge the GREATNESS in ourselves that others see in us. I would like to say to you as a child of the creator of ALL things… believe what God has said about YOU!

You are fearfully and wonderfully made. There is no other person on the face of the planet like you. No one has your smile, your quirky sense of humor or that brilliant spark that captures the attention of so many. Believe Him when he says that you are an heir of the promise, you are the righteousness of God, the apple of his eye. I challenge you to say to yourself I will believe it when someone tells me that I am beautiful. Believe it when someone tells you that you're smart. Just say thank you the next time you receive a compliment. Give yourself permission to smile when you see the work of your hands and you just have to say…God, you showed out!

WE DID THAT!

**Lesley Thomas**

## DAY 128

# HIGHER LEARNING

> *A wise man will hear and increase learning. Give instruction to a wise man, and he will be still wiser. Proverbs 1:5a, 9:9a*

While praying on the housetop of a friend, Apostle Peter became wiser and ready for higher learning as he watched a vision from God. He listened and obeyed the instructions. In the vision, Apostle Peter saw heaven open and an object like a great sheet bound at the four corners, descending to him, and let down to the earth. In it were all kinds of four-footed animals of the earth, wild beasts, creeping things, and birds of the air.

A voice spoke, "Rise, Peter, kill and eat." Peter refused, calling the animals common or unclean. But a voice spoke saying, "What God has cleansed you must not call common." Peter saw this vision three times. I believe Peter remembered the three times Jesus directed him before. (John 21: 15-17) While thinking on this higher learning he had received from God, Peter had visitors asking him to go with them. Peter obeyed the Holy Spirit and went with the three men. As he entered the house of Cornelius, a centurion, he explained how unlawful it was for a Jewish man to keep company with one of another nation. But he had heard from God and was obeying His instruction.

Peter preached and the Holy Spirit descended on all that believed. (Acts 10: 1-48) The Holy Spirit is calling us to higher learning. As people of other cultures move into our communities and come into our churches to worship with us, let us obey as the Apostle Peter did. Let's become wiser and minister to them that they receive the Holy Spirit and glorify God in heaven.

**Prayer:** Thank you today for higher learning to draw others into our community so that they may glorify you. In Jesus' name, we pray. Amen

**Mary Smith**

# DAY 129

# PACE = PATIENCE

> *Rejoice in hope, be patient in tribulation, be constant in prayer.*
> *Romans 12:12*

It is often difficult to move in pace and in time with God's rhythm. First, you have to find His rhythm. Then you have to decide to be content and even happy with it. It's hard because when God shows us what He has planned for our lives it is typical to want to see the manifestation of it right away.

We're excited when God tells us He'll use us mightily. We're ecstatic when He calls us to do great works for Him and when He tells us He'll make our name great. We see the vision and we're ready to reap the benefits immediately.

But what we soon find is that every promise of God comes with the process of God. We can't have the promise if we're not willing to endure the process. The process is often painful. Not only because it takes time, but often because it empties us of our selfish, vain ambitions and motivations.

By the time we're ready for promotion and see the promises of God made manifest in our lives, we've been emptied out and offered up. Our will is His and our goal is only that He is satisfied and happy with our total obedience, pure heart, and motive.

We're not obedient because we want to be seen. We're not compliant because we want to be famous. We're not willing because we're seeking to be rich. We're finally ready because we know nothing else on the earth matters other than fulfilling His will.

It's the process and pace of God. It births patience in us. It births peace in us. It births contentment in us. But most importantly, it births purity in us. Purity of heart, focus, and motive. When we've endured the process, we're ready for the promotion of God.

**Cheryl L. Thomas**

# DAY 130

# BREAKING THE SILENCE

> *And they called them and commanded them not to speak at all or teach in the name of Jesus. But Peter and John answered and said unto them, whether it be right in the sight of God to hearken unto you more than unto God, judge ye. For we cannot but speak the things which we have seen and heard. Acts 4:18-20*

When I was a boy growing up, I often listened to adult conversations in my community. Sometimes they would discuss the neighborhood gossip. I remember hearing the terms like "blabbermouth", she has "the can't help-its, she tells everything she hears, her business and everybody's business." Gossip is an activity in which you do not receive awards for your performance. Most people tend to frown on those who engage in this practice.

The Bible says that there is time for everything under the heavens, a time to speak and a time to be silent. Peter and John had seen and heard too many amazing exploits as followers of Jesus, not to blab it. They were threatened with jail time if they kept teaching about Jesus, but they had "the can't help it." There are many occasions when many of us sense the leading of the Lord to share our faith and testimony about what the Lord has done in our lives, but we seem to get a case of self-imposed lockjaw. Our mouths will not move enough to speak of His exploits.

**James Thomas**

# DAY 131

# RUNAWAY RAMPS

> *Where there is no revelation, people cast off restraint; but blessed is the one who heeds wisdom's instruction.*
> Proverbs 29:18

While traveling through northern Alabama and Tennessee, drivers must obey the travel advisories, especially while driving up and down the southwestern part of the Appalachian Mountains. If those warnings are ignored, tragic accidents could occur. Cars and trucks could be pulled down the mountain at accelerated speeds causing some vehicles to become "runaways." When a vehicle loses its brakes, the driver looks for the nearest "runaway ramp" in order to stop the forward movement. Runaway ramps have saved many lives.

Behavioral advisories are being ignored by people in churches around the world. As a result, many believers are becoming "runaways". They are out of control! Some have passed by "runaway ramps" time and time again. Now, many are heading for a tragic awakening because they refuse to take the "runaway ramp" to stop their out-of-control behaviors. Yes, even among believers! Only the grace of God can deter that tragic awakening! Many tragic things are happening in our world today because too many of God's people have not heeded the warning signs that God has sent forth. His word plainly states that when we see the signs of the time, we are to "stand in a holy place." That place is not necessarily inside a church. It is having a posture of holiness; being mindful of God's righteousness at all times. When the righteousness of God is suppressed, runaway behaviors increase. Obedience to God's word brings runaway behaviors under control and averts a tragic awakening. May God continue to work in the hearts of His people as we witness this world spiraling out of control. Are you in need of a "runaway ramp" from God's word?

**Heavenly Father, continue to reveal your truth to me so that my attitude and behavior will always be controlled by the fruit of the Spirit. In Jesus name. Amen.**

**Geraldine Russell**

# DAY 132

# THE WAYS WE GROW

> *And we know that all things work together for good to them that love God, to them who are the called according to his purpose.*
> Romans 8:28

One day, I came across a picture of a tumor that had grown completely out of control and as a result, had taken over the face of a little girl. My heart went out to her, but then the Lord began to speak. Now, a tumor is defined as "an abnormal growth of tissue resulting from uncontrolled, progressive multiplication of cells and serving no physiological function."

Speaking very generally, a tumor grows without caring who sees it, where it is, or knowing what its end result will be. The word *"tumor"* in itself tends to have a negative connotation, but I want to introduce you to a different perspective.

Yes, it gets rough and uncomfortable at times. God steps in and carries us through so that we continue to *grow* in Him. He wants to use our lives as witnesses, and we have to *live* our testimony before we can *tell* it! We don't know how we're going to look at the end of that season, but we do know that it will work for our good! Whether the tumor is benign (harmless) or malignant (harmful), the fruit of the Holy Spirit will be evident.

**Think About It:** What situations has God used to "grow" you lately?

Domonique Brunson

# DAY 133

# LORD, HOW LONG?

> *I had fainted unless I had believed to see the goodness of the Lord in the land of the living. Wait on the Lord be of good courage, and he shall strengthen thine heart: wait, I say, on the Lord.*
> Psalm 27:13-14

Every single person on this earth is waiting for something. Whatever it is, you are thinking and dreaming about it every day and hoping it will come soon. You start out feeling strongly about its deliverance, but, as the days, weeks, months, and years scroll by, your hope begins to waiver, sometimes to the breaking point of giving up and letting go. You begin asking yourselves, "Where is God? Does He care about my situation? How much longer must I wait?" Sometimes you even feel like God's presence has left you. These human feelings and questions make complete sense. God does not hold them against you because God knows you are still human.

The courage to wait on God's timing is like fertile ground. You must create a mindset contrary to the way you feel by trusting God, even in the difficult times of waiting for your breakthrough. During your waiting time, your heart and mind must sow seeds of trust, hope, and patience in God and His Word. Like David, you must remember to *be strong in the Lord and in the power of His might*, knowing that your Father is a faithful God. He will not allow your waiting to go unfulfilled. He is faithful to them that believe.

So, whatever it is that you are waiting on, just remember that your heart can trust in God and all His promises. Our God is the God of **time**, **order**, and **purpose**.

**Dr. Leticia Hardy**

## DAY 134

# JESUS AND ME

> *I have named you friends because I've let you in on everything I've heard from the Father. John 15:15*

Jesus and Me. These three words were echoed by my pastor during one of his sermons and it struck something in my inner being that will forever be etched in my heart. Our relationship with Jesus is contingent upon our obedience to Him and His Word. The scripture states that the Lord has called us friends because He wants us to commune and be with Him in all we say and do.

What does your relationship with the Lord look like? Is it on fire, or are there areas that need improvement? Some will have a lot of work to do to get higher in Jesus, others not so much. But, whatever you do, make sure you are diligent, holy, and steadfast in your stance. Recently, my husband and I were appointed as Pastor and First Lady of a local church within our organization. Now we have the task of covering people's lives and watching over their souls.

As I reminisce over my life in ministry, Jesus and I have been rocking this faith thing since day one. I have had many setbacks and trials along the way, but my triumphs outweigh my tribulations. I know what I have been called to do and that is to help young people find their place in the kingdom and to ensure they are equipped to be strong men and women of God.

**Jessica Lucas**

## DAY 135

# BUY THE SHOES

> *Be careful about nothing; but in everything by prayer and supplication with thanksgiving let your requests be made known unto God. Philippians 4:6*

One day I saw the most beautiful pair of shoes in the store and though they were not the reason that I had made the trip to the store. I decided that I would just take a moment to try them on. My feet are not the smallest, so when I see a pair of shoes that are cute AND in my size; I try to take advantage of the opportunity to get them.

As I tried them on, looked at them in the mirror, and pranced around to make sure that they would allow me some level of comfort as well, something inside said to me… "You know you should save this money in case something else comes up." I thought about it for a brief moment, danced around a little more, and of course, quietly put them back.

This was not the first time I took a step back in my daily life to consider what may or may not transpire in my life when I was given the chance to give or receive. I came to the realization that at the root of my disquiet about giving, which is in turn tied to receiving, was that deep in my heart I thought it would leave me in a place of lack or being without what I needed.

I further realized that it meant that there was a lack of trust that my heavenly Father was not able to keep His promise to provide everything that I would ever need. God softly whispered to me to trust Him enough to supply the things that I needed and the things I wanted.

I have learned that if I trust Him with all of my substance, there is an abundant supply to replace or add to anything that I would ever need. I wish I could tell you that I got this lesson right away, but I didn't. I still have to remind myself that there is nothing that I possess that our Father does not have plenty of and more. He's got me!

**Lesley Thomas**

# DAY 136

# UPGRADED RESUME

> ...Lord what do you want me to do? And the Lord said to him, Arise and go into the city and you will be told what you must do. Acts 9:6

Let's first define our subject: Upgraded Resume. A resume qualifies one for a particular job. An upgrade means that a person has been given a higher position using his/her resume. In this devotional scripture, this happens to Saul of Tarsus, a lawyer, and prosecutor in the book of Acts. As a lawyer, Saul has gotten written authority from the high priest in Jerusalem to travel to Damascus and arrest women or men disciples of the Lord Jesus Christ.

But while he was performing this job, the Lord Jesus Christ intervened and upgraded his resume. The Lord used the light from heaven and spoke the following words: "Saul! Saul! Why are you persecuting me? Saul asked. Who are you, Lord? The voice replied, 'I am Jesus, the one you are persecuting'! Now get up and go into the city, and you will be told what you must do."

Though blinded by the light, Saul obeyed the Lord's voice. He was led by his companions into Damascus. Three days later the Lord used Ananias' hands to perform the upgrade to Saul's resume. He became a disciple filled with the Holy Spirit, and God's chosen instrument to take the gospel to the Gentiles, kings, as well as to the people of Israel (Acts 9).

Each of us can receive an upgrade to our resume today. In this world in which we live, Jesus is still in need of disciples to witness.

Prayer: Abba Father, upgrade our resumes today and use us to do your will. In Jesus' name, we pray. Amen.

Mary Smith

# DAY 137

# REDEFINING PERFECT

> *It is God that girdeth me with strength, and maketh my way perfect. Psalm 18:32*

What is perfect? Who defines it? Is perfect a reality or is it a figment of our imagination? Are there perfect people? Is there a perfect relationship or marriage? Is there a perfect job or career? Is there a perfect church or pastor? What is perfect?

If our current definition of perfect means something, someone, or a situation without flaws, without scars, without baggage, or without blemish, I'm afraid our definition is grossly incorrect.

Every living thing has flaws. That's the beauty of creation and the thing that uncovers our need for each other and God. Yes, I said beauty. It's that beauty that makes us acceptable to one another. Because we recognize that we all have flaws, we can cease being judgmental toward one another and begin to help "bear each other's weaknesses."

God created us for a community so that the weakness of one could be fortified by the strength of another. Are you fortifying your brother or sister in Christ or are you tearing them down? Choose today to be a strength and pillar in the Christian community and a beacon of love and light.

Perfect in action? No, we are not. But, if we continue in the footsteps of Christ, we can be perfect and pure in heart.

**Reflection:** *Tear up the report card you may have assembled for your fellow Christian. Instead, extend an arm of love, hope, and reconciliation. You never know when you will also need that olive branch!*

**Cheryl L. Thomas**

## DAY 138

# ENJOYING THE TRIP

> *To everything, there is a purpose under the heavens...*
> *Ecclesiastes 3:1-13*

Living life to the fullest often requires staying in the moment and being grateful for the bird that is in your hand, not the one that is in the bush. Life will bring you different seasons to mold, shape, and develop you into the vessel that God wants you to become.

On a recent fishing trip with my wife to the Gulf Coast, my mental attitude was that I could take it or leave it. However, my wife's attitude was just the opposite of mine. She was driving along anticipating the day of fishing, admiring all the wildflowers along the roadside. "Oh, how beautiful are those trees!" "Oh, they are so pretty!"

I'm thinking to myself; now that is amazing! She is enjoying the trip! I can use an attitude adjustment. She is enjoying the day God has blessed her with, not looking for the tomorrow that may not come. The preacher was right, "There is a time and a season for everything." We do not set the time nor the season; however, we can be happier when we gratefully accept what God is performing through our lives. Whatever season of life you are currently in, make the most of the opportunity to grow, and genuinely enjoy this precious gift of life and abundance.

Right now is the right time to praise the Lord for all his wonderful blessings!

**James Thomas**

## DAY 139

# GREAT IS HIS FAITHFULNESS!

> *Because of the LORD's great love we are not consumed, for his compassions never fail. They are new every morning; great is your faithfulness. Lamentations 3:22-23*

During the days of Israel's rebellion, God raised up the "Weeping Prophet, Jeremiah". God revealed to him the great sins of his beloved daughter, Zion. He delineated each sin and the prophetic rebukes he delivered through other prophets before and after Jeremiah's call. Their call to repentance was short-lived or ignored. Decades later, there was nothing anyone could do to stop God's decree for the consequences of Israel's rebellion against Him. He decreed, and so it came to past.

One "sobering read" through the book of Lamentations and the reader will be overwhelmed by the depth of emotions Jeremiah must have experienced as God revealed the consequential message he had to deliver to his rebellious people, Israel.

As we take a panoramic view of what's happening in our world today, it causes one to wonder if God has sent another sobering message into the world. Death, dying, and defying stretch from the north, south, east, and west. However, nestled in the midst of it all is the reassuring *hope* of God's great faithfulness to His people, the Church. His compassions are "new" every morning. As believers in Jesus, we have a personalized "key card" to the mercies of God. And there are no limitations on how much believers can gather from the storehouse of "God's Mercy".

Lord, like Jeremiah, my heart weeps day and night for what You have revealed during these troubling times. Help me to access the comfort of your mercy as your warnings are being rejected by family, friends, and those we love so dearly. In Jesus name I pray. Amen.

Geraldine Russell

# DAY 140

## THE RESIDENT IN YOUR SPIRIT

> *But the fruit of the Spirit is love, joy, peace, longsuffering, gentleness, goodness, faith, meekness, temperance: against such there is no law. Galatians 5:22-23*

Let's say you own a house, and you allow someone to come and stay. One of two things will happen. You notice the person has taken care of the house, the things in the house, and all is well; or you find that the house is not being kept up, things have been broken or destroyed, and it has become only a shell of the house it used to be. In the latter case, you regret the moment you allowed that person to live in your home.

Often, just like that house, we allow all kinds of things to live in our spirit. We allow bad residents like sadness or depression, lack of self-esteem, confidence, even malice, jealousy, or strife to live inside of us. If these things are living inside of us, they eventually surface and adversely impact our surroundings just as "the bad resident destroyed the house." On the brighter side, there are good residents known as the fruit of the Spirit, determination, and the Holy Spirit that can take root in your heart and forever transform you for the better. These are the kinds of residents that will uplift, encourage, and inspire believers and non-believers.

**Think About It:** What are the residents in YOUR spirit?

**Domonique Brunson.**

# DAY 141

# SAFEGUARD YOUR HEART

*Keep thy heart with all diligence, for out of it are the issues of life.*
*Proverbs 4:23*

Living as a born-again believer for our Lord and Savior Jesus Christ in such a chaotic world is not always easy on one's heart, especially if our heart is not truly anchored in the Word of God, and saturated in His agape love.

Just like our physical heart, our spiritual heart needs to be attended to. Our earthly physicians recommend an annual checkup for our physical heart, but we must never forget that our spiritual heart needs a daily routine checkup also.

We must safeguard our spiritual heart because it is the key to sustaining a true and pure relationship with God. Our spiritual heart helps us love God, our fellow man, and ourselves. We must keep in remembrance the first and greatest commandment is to love the Lord our God with all our heart and with all our soul and with all our mind.

As Christ believers, we will encounter hurt, pain, betrayal, offenses, anger, and grief; but if our heart is anchored in the Word of God, we can conquer all life's scary weapons that will form against us.

When was the last time your heart had a spiritual checkup?

**Dr. Leticia Hardy**

# DAY 142

# TO LOVE AND TO PRAY

> *In all thy ways acknowledge him, and he shall direct thy paths.*
> *Proverbs 3:6*

Purifying Grace. It comes when we are saved, and we ask Him to come into our hearts. Serving Grace: We are to be faithful stewards of God's Grace (Peter 4:10-12). God's grace will sustain us. Each of us is given grace by the Lord Himself, Watts declared. Sometimes though, we hinder our blessings because we won't get into a position to receive them. All we have to do is align ourselves with the Word of God. Dating and courtship can be fun when there is a purpose in mind. I did have a desire to be married and I knew the Lord was directing my path, and as you will learn, marriage was in God's plan for my life. I didn't know that love and marriage were right around the corner after college. Now, I only had one boyfriend whom I dated my senior year. He was tall, dark, handsome, and a star athlete, but his relationship with Jesus was a little rocky and not as solid as it should be.

Fast forward to 2007, the year after I graduated college, I met a lovely young man at a church convention and we instantly hit it off. My younger brother even liked him and told my mother that this young man was going to be his brother-in-law. Yeah right! I was TOTALLY NOT READY FOR MARRIAGE. I had just met him, but of course, God had other plans.

As we were getting to know each other, our prayer life increased dramatically. Go JESUS!!! We began each date with prayer because we wanted the Holy Spirit to fully connect us as we were preparing for marriage. Yep, exactly one year and one week to the date of our meeting, my boyfriend became my fiancée. We became one.

Fifteen years later, what advice can I give to newly married or engaged couples? I would say prayer is the key to a lasting, fulfilling, and meaningful relationship. Two people are coming together as one unit from different backgrounds, so seeking God through prayer is essential. Heed to the Scriptures and bask in God's presence often so he can reveal to you your personal life and relationships. So, to love is to pray.

**Father, we thank you for your love and for the opportunity to come to you in prayer every day. We pray that through your Spirit, we will keep praying and communicating with you so we can see through your eyes in Jesus' name, Amen!**

Jessica Lucas

# DAY 143

# A PURE HEART

> *Blessed are the pure in heart, for they shall see God. Matthews 5:8*

We think of an individual with a pure heart as one who keeps the great commandments in the law. This is to "Love the Lord your God with all your heart, all your soul, and all your mind." This is the first and greatest commandment. A second is "Love your neighbor as yourself." The entire law and all the demands of the prophets are based on these two commandments (Matt.22:37- 40). As we think about these commandments, we remember they were given to mankind that listened to the voice of God.

Moses was educated in the kingdom of Egypt under King Pharaoh, but Moses' mother was his nurse. Moses knew the true God. So, when Moses saw the burning bush that was not consumed, the Lord had his attention and began to minister to him. It took Moses a while to get to the point of being obedient to God and taking the children of Israel through the desert. Over the next 40 years, Moses became a great listener with a pure heart by listening to God.

As we practice the great commandments of God, we too can become great listeners with pure hearts seeing the Lord our God for who He is. God gave His only Son to be crucified for our sins, and the sins of the whole world.

**Prayer: Abba Father, help me to practice the greatest commandments daily so that I may have a clean and pure heart to follow thee. In Jesus' name, we pray. Amen.**

**Mary Smith**

# DAY 144

## GOOD SUCCESS

> *This book of the law shall not depart out of thy mouth; but thou shalt meditate therein day and night, that thou mayest observe to do according to all that is written therein: for then thou shalt make thy way prosperous, and then thou shalt have good success.*
> *Joshua 1:8*

Everyone wants to be successful at something. Whether it is career, marriage, parenting, or finances, we all have an inner drive to excel at something. So we work, we plan, and often lose sleep to be "successful." This drive to obtain "success" is often so demanding for some that they lose their families, their homes and some even lose their lives in the process.

The question then becomes, is it worth it? This drive, or maybe more aptly put, obsession, we have for obtaining society's idea of success is killing us. Our children are raising themselves. Many marriages are on the verge of collapsing as couples have simply become roommates.

Now, don't get it wrong. This is not to discredit anyone's desire for achievement and advancement, but it does make us ask the question, "Who defines success for you?" Is it television or your friends and neighbors? Is it your ability to purchase fancy cars, large homes, and go on exotic vacations? I don't think that's God's idea of "good success."

God's idea of good success is peace, joy, contentment, love, and every fruit of the Spirit that is found at the feet of Jesus. When we delight in Him, He blesses everything we do. While success can be and often is coupled with great wealth, it cannot be realized nor called GOOD if Christ isn't the center of it.

**Cheryl L. Thomas**

## DAY 145

# EXTREME IMAGE MAKEOVER

> *And God said, let us make man in our image, after our likeness: and let them have dominion over the fish of the sea, and over the fowl of the air, and over the cattle and all the earth, and over every creeping thing that creepeth upon the earth. So, God created man in his image, in the image of God created he him; male and female created he them. Genesis 1:26-27*

Man is the crown jewel of God's creation. There was a divine conference among the members of the Godhead before man was created; something that was not seen at any other time in the creation. Some of the angels had already rebelled against God. He certainly knew what man would do, still through love and grace, He molded the first man "in His image;" referring to man's personality, creativity, and spiritual capacity.

The man was given a place of dominion over the earth, the highest position in all of creation. Man lost his dominion through sin. But that dominion has been regained through Jesus Christ, the last Adam. If any man is in Christ, he is a new Creation, made anew in the image of Christ. Old things are passed away, behold all things become new.

**And be not conformed to this world: But be ye transformed by the renewing of your minds, that ye may prove what is good and acceptable, and perfect will of God, Romans 12:2.**

**James Thomas**

# DAY 146

# CONCEALED IDENTITY

> *For now, we see through a glass, darkly; but then face to face; now I know in part; but then shall I know even as also I am known.*
> 1 Corinthians 13:12

While observing a Zoom meeting among family members, I noticed that many of the participants' video cameras were disabled, although their voices were recognizable when they chimed into the discussion. One of the older participants longed to see her granddaughter. She had not seen her face-to-face for several years. Nearing the end of the meeting, the host asked if everyone could turn their cameras on. That ignited a flurry of intimate chatter! When the older participant saw her granddaughter, her eyes lit up and swelled with tears of joy. Although they were more than 3000 miles apart, their hearts reignited. The older participant kept her eyes fixed on her granddaughter until the meeting ended. Oh, how she longed to see her face-to-face and to feel her loving embrace!

From the beginning of creation until Jesus entered the world, only a few people heard the audible voice of God. When Jesus began his work of bringing the kingdom of heaven to earth, he revealed the identity of God the Father. When Jesus ascended, he sent the Comforter into the world to continue the work he started. His identity could no longer be denied or concealed. Therefore, the "express image of God" had finally been revealed to mankind. The camera was turned on so that all could see the identity of God.

Studying the word of God is like joining a Zoom meeting with fellow believers around the world and Jesus as the Host. Let's turn our cameras on so that other believers may connect and ignite an intimate fellowship with one another and the Host. When this meeting ends, all believers will see him face-to-face. His in-person identity will no longer be concealed. All believers will see him as he is, LORD of lords and King of kings! Oh, I want to see HIM!!

**Prayer: Lord, I'm logging into your word today. Thank you for the <u>invite</u>. Thank you for turning your camera on so that more of <u>You</u> can be revealed to me.**

Geraldine Russell

# DAY 147

# PICKING SIDES

> *No man can serve two masters: for either he will hate the one and love the other; or else he will hold to the one and despise the other. Ye cannot serve God and mammon. Matthew 6:24*

There were billboards on both sides of the highway. On one side, the billboard read, "Topless! Topless! Etc." Then, I looked to the other side and that billboard read, "Jesus Christ...the Savior and Light of the World". Then, it came to me. Billboard number one represents the devil that is on our left shoulder and billboard number two represents the angel that is on our right shoulder. We cannot obey them both at the same time.

We are children of the Most High! As our Divine Father, God knows our hearts. If our intentions are good, He will make a way for us to escape (1 Cor. 10:13). There are times when we want to give in to temptation and there are times when we do, but when we *resist* the devil, he will flee from us (James 4:7)...and then we can flee the temptation! Now, sometimes the enemy may try to sneak up on us. If we keep our eyes and ears open, keep our guards up, and *pay attention* to the Master's warnings, we will be fine. We should never be too proud or grown to listen (Proverbs 16:18) because warnings come before destruction!

**Think About It:** Which side do you give in to most often?

**Domonique Brunson**

## DAY 148

# SAFEGUARD YOUR HEART

> *Keep thy heart with all diligence, for out of it are the issues of life. Proverbs 4:23*

Living as a born-again believer for our Lord and Savior Jesus Christ in such a chaotic world is not always easy on one's heart, especially if our heart is not truly anchored in the Word of God, and saturated in His agape love.

Just like our physical heart, our spiritual heart needs to be attended to. Our earthly physicians recommend an annual checkup for our physical heart, but we must never forget that our spiritual heart needs a daily routine checkup also.

We must safeguard our spiritual heart because it is the key to sustaining a true and pure relationship with God. Our spiritual heart helps us love God, our fellow man, and ourselves. We must keep in remembrance the first and greatest commandment is to love the Lord our God with all our heart and with all our soul and with all our mind.

As Christ believers, we will encounter hurt, pain, betrayal, offenses, anger, and grief; but if our heart is anchored in the Word of God, we can conquer all life's scary weapons that will form against us.

When was the last time your heart had a spiritual checkup?

**Dr. Leticia Hardy**

# DAY 149

# A SERVANT'S HEART

> *And the Lord came and called as before, Samuel! Samuel! And Samuel replied, Speak, your servant is listening. I Samuel 3:10*

We define the word servant as one who serves others. Then, a servant's heart in Christ Jesus has the gift of obeying the voice of God with a praying Spirit of obedience to God's word. Today we think of Samuel who was trained by his mother Hannah to have a servant's heart. He was given to serve the man of God in the tabernacle by his mother Hannah when he was weaned as a child. Therefore, Samuel was taught to listen and obey leadership. He served in the tabernacle faithfully with the priest Eli. He learned to listen to Eli's voice and obey, then to God's voice after being told how to answer. Samuel replied to God's voice saying "Speak, your servant is listening." And for the rest of Samuel's life, he listened as God gave him directions. He became a seer, priest, judge, prophet, and military leader for God.

So, think today, as we read God's word and spend time in His presence, let us be still and listen to what He is saying to us. For He is the same God that directed Samuel. We are so fortunate to be experiencing the third person in the trinity- the Holy Spirit in the world we live in today. We are honored to have Him live on the inside of us in our servant's heart each day giving directions for our lives. However, it requires early morning arrival, listening, and obeying what we hear each day of our life. He will continue to work with us with servants' hearts.

Prayer: Abba Father, we thank you today for a servant's heart. Please direct us in your way. Thank you. It is in Jesus' name we pray. Amen

**Mary Smith**

## DAY 150

# GOD WANTS YOU TO WIN

> *Nay, in all these things we are more than conquerors through him that loved us. Romans 8:37*

Sometimes in our Christian journey, things don't go quite the way we planned.

Obstacles, roadblocks, and setbacks seem to pop up without notice. We are running this race, doing the best we know how but sometimes it doesn't seem like enough.

What does it take to win? Stamina? Persistence? Strength? Fortitude? It takes Jesus! No matter the strategy you use, the tools you have, the people you know, or the resources at your disposal, if you don't have Jesus it will never work.

Here's the good news! God wants us to win! He just wants us to know that it is only possible with Him. Victory is sure if Christ is your guide. The Bible says, "I can do all things through Christ who strengthens me. (Philippians 4:13)"

So, today know this. God is on your side. He is your biggest cheerleader. He is standing at the finish line with your reward in His hand. Run-on, you're already a winner!

> **Reflection:** *When is the last time you asked God for a strategy to accomplish your goals? God is for you. He isn't hiding information from you. He's waiting for you to come to Him and ask for direction. Do it today.*

**Cheryl L. Thomas**

# DAY 151

# FENCES!

> *Then Satan answered the Lord, and said, doth Job fear God or naught? Hath not thou made a hedge about him, and about his house, and about all that he hath on every side? Thou hath blessed the works of his hands, and his substance is increased in the land… Job 1:9-11*

A popular Gospel song says, "Jesus be a fence all around me every day. I want you to protect me as I travel along this way…" Fences are built to either keep desirable things in or to keep undesirable things out. In the story of Job, the Lord had a fence around everything that Job possessed. Fences are usually controlled by the builder or gatekeeper. So, Satan needed to ask permission to enter. I believe that God has built a hedge or fence around all that come to Him in saving faith.

Jesus said all that the Father hath given me, I have lost none. The Father has put them in My hands and no man can take them out of My hands. The Bible says that "The Lord will give His angels charge over us to keep us in all our ways; no evil shall befall thee, and no plague shall come near your dwelling." That sounds like a secure fence, where the Lord is the Gatekeeper. Anything undesirable can only enter by permission. If God allows it to enter, He has prepared us to survive it.

**Be strong in the Lord, and be of good cheer, He will strengthen your heart!**

**James Thomas**

## DAY 152

# PAID IN FULL!

> *For God is not unrighteous to forget your work and labor of love, which ye have showed toward his name… Hebrews 6:16a*

Drowning in debt causes many adverse reactions. One such account happened to a young lady that earned a Doctor's Degree. That degree helped her get a well-paying job. However, by the time she was in position to repay her student loans, they had increased exponentially. After more than twenty years of faithful commitment, the debt continued to accrue interest. Her efforts seemed futile! The mounting debt began to chip away at her emotions. She prayed fervently for God to help her meet her financial obligations. As an inexperienced swimmer fighting against rip currents, her strength began to fail. She was drowning in debt! She asked God to give her strength and courage to endure. She served her church faithfully as she faced overwhelming odds.

A few weeks ago, the young lady called her family together to break the news! Her faithfulness to God had paid off! She was one of the *few* selected to have her student debt forgiven! Over one hundred thousand dollars of debt had been erased from her records! That family gathering was filled with "masks" and jubilee! God had worked a miracle and set her free! Her burden-of-debt had been signed, sealed, delivered, and stamped *"paid in full"* (Jan. 2022)!

Over two thousand years ago, our cumulative sin debt was *paid in full*! By faith, those that are born again are transformed from the *crib of sin* onto the plush *"bed of God's grace"*. Oh, how believers rejoice when they receive the credit report saying, *"Your sin debt is forgiven! Paid in full! Signed, sealed and delivered by Jesus!"*

Is your sin debt forgiven? The blood of Jesus paid the price in full!

**Geraldine Russell**

## DAY 153

# THE MYSTERY OF CONTENTMENT

> *Not that I speak in respect of want: for I have learned, in whatsoever state I am, therewith to be content. Philippians 4:11*

As I was reading one day, God stopped me at one particular topic... *contentment*. How do you learn to be "content" in any stage of life? Well, you must first lay down your desire to have everything on your own terms *all the time*. Sometimes, God has to allow things not to go our way for our own good. As believers, we tend to run ahead of God's format and put things together. Then, we stand back to admire our masterpieces...only to watch them fall apart before our very eyes. In reality, though, our mentality should be that "if God isn't in it, neither am I." To stay content, we should not intentionally tempt ourselves with something we know we can't have. We should stay away from relationships that are physically, spiritually, emotionally, or mentally detrimental. Establishing boundaries for ourselves and keeping our emotions in check will also help.

The only way to do any of these is to completely depend on Christ! And we learn through experience, of course. It may be one of the hardest classes we ever take, but we'll be able to apply it for the rest of our life. No, of course, it's not easy...but, in the end, it will all be worth it.

**Think About It:** Are you content where God has you now?

Domonique Brunson

## DAY 154

# AN EPITOME OF LOVE, OBEDIENCE AND HUMILITY

> *Who, being in very nature God, did not consider equality with God something to be used to his own advantage; rather he made himself nothing by taking the very nature of a servant. Philippians 2:6-7*

We are encouraged to take on the very nature of a servant as Christ did in Philippians 2:6-7. Jesus came into this world equipped with the very nature of God, yet he did not try to compare himself equal to his Father. Rather, he took upon himself the spirit and nature of a humble and dedicated servant. Although he appeared in human form, and walked among men, no guile or condemnation could be found in his character, actions, behavior, or personality. He was such an obedient and humble servant that he never strayed from carrying out his Father's will. The love that he felt for humankind was evident in his path to Calvary.

His death on the cross was accomplished to redeem humankind back to God. Where the first Adam failed, Jesus succeeded. This sacrificial act of love, obedience and humility was greatly honored by God, his Father. This very act of sweet submission that Jesus displayed touched millions of hearts around the world. Giving of his life, so that humankind may gain everlasting life, upon accepting Christ's spiritual nature, and choosing the path of righteousness, will go down in history as the greatest love story and testimony ever told.

**Dr. Leticia Hardy**

# DAY 155

# HOPE

> ...those who hope in the Lord will renew their strength. They will soar on wings like eagles: they will run and not grow weary; they will walk and not be faint. Isaiah 40:31

Looking at the definition of the word hope, we find that it means a feeling of expectation and desire for a thing to happen. We find this hope exemplified in the word of God in the prophet Daniel. Daniel was transported from his home in the land of Judah at the age of sixteen as a young man to be trained in the Babylonian culture. But he continuously refused to become a Babylonian or even adopt any of their cultures. For Daniel believed the word of Jeremiah the prophet that after 70 years his people would return to the land of Judah. (Daniel 9:2) Therefore, Daniel stayed true to the Living God.

However, Daniel and his three friends humbled themselves under the leadership and received permission to eat God's way for their bodies. He prayed to God three times a day, practicing what we know today as communication with God. Thus, the three years of training he was given prepared him to be the "inside person" for God to use in the Babylonian kingdom. (Daniel 1:5b) Daniel's great career began in the Babylonian government when he heard that King Nebuchadnezzar's magicians, astrologers, and sorcerers could not reveal to the King his dream and its interpretation. Daniel declared "There is a God in heaven who reveals secrets." (Daniel 2: 28a) Daniel and his three friends prayed. God revealed the answer to Daniel. Then, Daniel was able to reveal the dream and its interpretation to the King. What a day!

Daniel was given gifts and was made a ruler over the whole province of Babylon and chief administrator over all the wise men of Babylon. (Daniel 2:48)

We are here today hoping and looking forward to Christ's return to earth and receiving our gifts and rewards.

**Prayer:** Abba Father, we thank you for your mighty works in this world. Please give us the strength to continue to hope in you as Daniel did. In your name, we pray. Amen

**Mary Smith**

## DAY 156

# HOW TO WIN IN A LOSING SEASON

> *Trust in the LORD with all thine heart; and lean not unto thine own understanding. Proverbs 3:5*

It has been an eventful time in history, a time of stretching and a time of trusting. We're learning to trust God in so many areas and believe Him for so much more. It is a challenge sometimes. We think we trust and believe God and then our faith is put to the test in so many ways. It challenges us to reach, stretch, and most importantly to ACTIVATE our faith.

We believe in our hearts that it is going to work together for good. We trust that the testimony will be powerful and life-changing. Often, like most people who are not too fond of tests during the test, we often only become ecstatic after the testing is over and we come out victorious. However, victory comes in many ways. Sometimes it is instantaneous, sometimes we have to walk, cry, and pray our way through. Sometimes it is God's victory and doesn't end the way we planned or desired. But no matter the way victory comes, as a win or a lesson, let's make sure to make the most of it.

**Reflection:** *What does victory look like to you? Is it having things turn out the way you want, when you want, and how you want? Have you ever stopped to think that maybe, just maybe, we're looking at victory through the wrong lens? Maybe we should start to see victory through God's eyes. How does He want things to turn out? What would best serve His purpose? Prayerfully look at your goals list again. How would achieving these goals serve God's purpose and not just your own? Sometimes "losing" IS winning!*

**Cheryl L. Thomas**

## DAY 157

# FRUITLESS BRANCHES!

> *I am the vine, ye are the branches: He that abideth in me, and I in him, the same bringeth forth much fruit: for without me you can do nothing. John 15:5*

No matter how self-sufficient we are as ministers and evangelists, only God can bring about kingdom growth, maturity, and a harvest of souls. Big churches, extensive programs, and silver tongue sermons are of little effect unless they are fueled by the Holy Ghost. We should never forget that this is God's operation. He is the Chief Executive Officer, and we are the workers. This is God's world that needs saving, His, not ours.

Let God be God, for there is none like Him! We should remember that we are the branches, and He is the vine, the source of all our spiritual sustenance and power. So, if we stay connected to the vine, we can bring forth much fruit. Branches apart from the vine are fruitless. All fruitless branches are pruned and thrown into the fire. We cannot remain connected to God and be fruitless. In the Bible parable of the barren fig tree, Jesus approached the fig tree expecting to find fruit, but discovered that the tree had nothing. Jesus was not happy and cursed the fig tree forever.

"Thunder is good, thunder is impressive, but it is the lightning that does the work" (Mark Twain).

**James Thomas**

# DAY 158

# CHOSEN

> *For, he chose us in him, before the creation of the world, to be holy and blameless in his sight. Ephesians 4:4*

Years ago, during recess, many elementary students participated in a game called *"kickball."* Before the game started, team captains took turns selecting team players. Those with the best athletic skills were selected first. Those that were not athletically inclined were generally chosen last. Sometimes, they felt dejected. However, those feelings dissipated as soon as the game started. Occasionally, the one that was chosen last would kick a homerun. Afterwards, the teammates would gather around that player with joyful affirmations. That player was never again chosen last.

God, in his omniscience, chose all those that He foreknew would respond to the call to join his team of kingdom players. He knew they would say, "Yes, Lord!" Therefore, he assigned each respondent a position on his team *before the foundation of the world.* Throughout history, that team has had many challenging opponents! Some victories were won at the last buzzer! However, with Jesus as the Captain, that team has never lost a game!

God chose all believers after the counsel of His own will. He knew, before the foundation of the world, those that would surrender to His call to be "set apart," Holy. He knew those that would be intrinsically motivated to develop their God-given skills. He chose all those that He knew would make the "Kingdom Team."

Are you one of God's chosen? Have you responded to His call? Has He set you apart as a kingdom player? If not, He's still choosing team members from this generation. Say, *"Yes, Lord!!"*

Lord, thank you for choosing me for your
Kingdom Team! Amen!

Geraldine Russell

## DAY 159

# GOD IS GREATER

> *Ye are of God, little children, and have overcome them: because greater is he that is in you, than he that is in the world. 1 John 4:4*

When we look at our world today, there seems to be constant chaos swirling around us day after day, right? COVID here...Monkeypox there...you name it. Even when we look at our personal lives and the circumstances we find ourselves in, there always seems to be something else to face. In spite of that, I want to encourage your heart by letting you know that God is and will ALWAYS be greater than our circumstances.

If you're facing the loss of your house or vehicle, God is greater. If you're facing the loss of a job or financial hardship, God is greater. If you or a loved one are facing life-altering illness, God is still greater. If you are battling sadness or depression, God has always been greater! And so, it would seem that the answer to us continuing to move forward to what God has in store for our lives is holding on to the reminder that no matter what the problem might be, God is STILL greater! My challenge to you today is to face each situation with the resolve that GOD IS GREATER and watch your entire perspective change for the better.

**Think About It:** What situation do you need to declare God's greatness over today?

**Domonique Brunson**

## DAY 160

# A PRAYER FOR A PURPOSEFUL LIFE

> *And this is the confidence that we have toward him, that if we ask anything according to His will He hears us. And if we know that He hears us in whatever we ask, we know that we have the requests that we have asked of Him. 1 John 5:14-15*

Prayer is powerful and its effects can bring about everlasting changes.

Merciful God, gracious in all that you do, I come before you in the precious name of your son Jesus Christ. Lord, this is the day that you have made, and it is my desire to rejoice and be glad in it.

As I begin my daily routine, make known unto me my purpose for this day. My desire is to live a purpose-filled life that is pleasing in your sight.

Father, direct my path, guide my feet, and govern my mouth to reach a lost soul, a misguided friend, or a grieving neighbor. Lord, let not your breath of life in which you instilled into me be wasted today.

Lord, help me bless someone this day, whether through a song, words of comfort, financial support, or to render a listening ear. As you live through me, help me to be led by your precepts and examples so that your power of deliverance, hope, and salvation may manifest itself through your servant. Lord, I give you honor, glory, and praise unto your name. Father, thank you for hearing my prayer, and attending unto my desire.

Amen.

**Dr. Leticia Hardy**

# DAY 161

# WIRELESS INTERNET POWER

> *But you shall receive power when the Holy Spirit has come upon you. Acts 1:8a*

When computers are turned on in the morning, we see the monitor lights. We know we are connected to the electrical power source. Next, we check the internet source to receive messages from others from anywhere on earth. This is a power source that God has allowed men to create to communicate with others on this great earth.

However, we have a wireless internet that reaches from earth to heaven that needs no electrical power source. This internet was connected on the day of Pentecost in the upper room. There men and women prayed for ten days to receive on earth this wireless internet that was promised by Jesus when He said "But you shall receive power when the Holy Spirit has come upon you" (Acts 1:8a).

Know that we have to check our computers every morning for a connection to our electrical power and internet; but, our wireless internet with Jesus never loses its power. As long as we present our bodies holy and acceptable to God, we have a wireless internet power source on earth to do His will.

Let us go forth today doing the will of God, always knowing that "Greater is HE that is in us than He that is in the world."

**Prayer:** Abba Father, thank you for our wireless internet. Help us today to use it for your glory. Amen.

**Mary Smith**

# DAY 162

# CONFRONTING FEAR

> *For God hath not given us the spirit of fear; but of power, and of love, and of a sound mind. II Timothy 1:7*

Knots in your stomach that will not go away, sweaty palms, knocking knees, chattering teeth, and pounding hearts are the physical signs of fear. They often appear when we're trying something new and stepping out in faith. Sometimes these signs, as well as the enemy's taunting voice in your ear, seem to overwhelm and paralyze you. Is it worth it to move forward or should you shrink back into the safety of your comfort zone?

The roar of fear is so much louder than its reality. We give too much power to negative possibilities and not enough attention to positive probabilities. Let's change our focus. It has been said that the thing you focus on grows and is magnified. If we focus on our success and work diligently toward it, our success is inevitable. It's only a matter of time before what we see in our spirit is what we'll hold in our hand.

Let's stop running in fear of the possibility of failure. Instead, let's stare fear in the eye and dare it to try to stop us. We have God on our side. And with the help of God, we are unstoppable!

**Reflection:** *Make a list of your fears now. Next to that list, write out the ways you could overcome each fear. For example, if you are afraid of failure, list ways you can overcome it. Read Scriptures that remind you that you are an overcomer, more than a conqueror, and already a winner. Read and rehearse those Scriptures until they resonate in your spirit.*

**Cheryl L. Thomas**

## DAY 163

# GOING IN THE WRONG DIRECTION!

> *Now the word of the Lord came unto Jonah the son of Amittai, saying, Arise, go to Nineveh, that great city, and cry against it; for their wickedness is come up before me. But Jonah rose to flee unto Tarshish from the presence of the Lord, and went down to Joppa, and found a ship going to Tarshish; so he paid the fare thereof and went down into it to go with them to Tarshish from the presence of the Lord. Jonah 1:1-3*

You can run but you cannot hide from the Lord! When God's man is out of fellowship with Him, it causes problems not only for himself but for those around him. Though God's human servants may be in disobedience to Him, He sometimes uses nature (nature, ie., wind, fire, water, animals, and even a donkey) to bring about His correction or redirection to His will.

We may not like where God tells us to go, but when we see in scripture what happens to those who choose to disobey, we should be fully warned of the consequences of non- compliance and rebellion.

"And Samuel said, hath the Lord as great delight in burnt offerings and sacrifices, as obeying the voice of the Lord, to obey is better than sacrifice and to hearken, than the fat of rams" ( I Samuel 15:22).

**James Thomas**

# DAY 164

# RENEWAL

> *This is my comfort in my affliction: for thy word hath quickened me. Psalm 119:50*

Glistening white snowflakes as far as the eye can see are covering every inch of ground, roofs, and tops of every tree. Crispy winter days have come. Still underneath piles of falling snow, life lays dormant, waiting for the first rays of spring to shine through. As rays of light trickle through melted openings in the snow, plants and animals began to spring to new life.

As it is in creation, so it is in the hearts of those that allow the word of God to penetrate their lives during difficult times…like rays of sunshine on a snowy day. Reading the living Word of God causes the fruit of the Spirit to spring forth abundantly in hearts that have lain cold and dormant for many years. Love springs forth! Joy, peace, meekness, and gentleness spring forth! Long-suffering, temperance, and faith spring forth when the Word of God penetrates a cold and dormant heart.

Winter comes to all believers' lives. However, winter is always followed by springtime when life seems to spring forth abundantly in nature. No matter how cold life seems, God's Word causes new life to spring forth.

**Heavenly Father, renew our resolve to study your life-giving Word daily.**

**Geraldine Russell**

# DAY 165

# GIVE GOD BACK YOUR LIFE

> *Before I formed thee in the belly I knew thee... Jeremiah 1:5*

Imagine a person who is an amazing artist going to buy a blank canvas for the first time and expecting to produce a masterpiece painting in hours. Sounds a little foolish, right? I know. But, if we are honest, that artist sounds just like you and me sometimes. We are the CREATION, not the CREATORS of our lives, yet we have the tendency to take our lives and matters into our own hands as if we know best. The truth is we know next to nothing about how best to live our lives without the leading of the Holy Spirit.

After all, He is the Master Teacher and always knows what's best for us. Yes, at times, it may feel difficult to release the reins and our sense of control over our lives. However, Psalm 46:10 tells us to be still and know that He is God! It makes much more sense for us to let God have our lives because He knew us before we were even formed in our mother's womb and STILL knows us at this very moment. He knows more about us than we do, and He knows EXACTLY what He created us to become. Personally, and I hope you agree. I want to be ALL that God wants me to be.

**Think About It:** Have you been acting as the CREATION or the CREATOR?

**Domonique Brunson**

## DAY 166

# A CLARION CALL TO WITNESS

> *The harvest is plentiful, but the workers are few. Therefore, beseech the Lord of the harvest to send out workers into his harvest*
> Matthew 9:37-38

<u>What is the harvest?</u> It is the world of sinners and unbelievers. <u>Who are the laborers?</u>

Born Again Believers of our Lord and Savior Jesus Christ.

According to St. Matthew 28:19, Jesus commands believers to journey throughout every nation, teaching and baptizing them in the name of the Father, and the Son, and of the Holy Ghost. Believers have no need to fear when witnessing the gospel, for there is no failure in God. There is no greater joy than to be chosen to proclaim and declare the gospel, which is the good news of our Lord and Savior, Jesus Christ.

God has given believers His heart of love and compassion which motivates and compels them to teach, preach, and pray for the lost, misguided, ungodly, and poverty-stricken people.

He has equipped believers with power and boldness which gives them the courage to preach in season and out of season. Boldness gives them the fortitude to risk ridicule and to endure scorn.

When God saved us, He gave believers His power of authority to heal the sick and cast out demons according to St. Mark 3:14 15.

Be it resolved, "For God has not given us the spirit of fear, but of power, and of love, and of a sound mind. (*2 Timothy 1:2*)

**Now Go!**

**Dr. Leticia Hardy**

# DAY 167

# FLOWING RIVER

> *He who believes in Me, as the scripture has said, out of his heart will flow rivers of living water. John 7:38*

In the United States, the Mississippi River is one of the most popular and helpful rivers. Its system accounts for about 92% of the nation's agricultural exports and 28% of the world's feed grains and soybeans. The river flows from north to south through about 10 other states. These state rivers are helpful to the Mississippi River by serving the United States exports.

Note this, we have a river of life flowing out of our hearts of everlasting life. This is a gift to every man/woman, boy/girl that believes in the Lord Jesus Christ. We can have a 100% export of saving grace to offer every day to everyone we meet, talk to on the phone, text, or email.

The greatest thing about our flow of living water is that it never runs low. I am sure that in the dry season of the year, these rivers have less water flowing. Therefore, there is less traveling of the water.

But, Jesus says for those of us who believe, out of our hearts will flow rivers of living water. Let us plan today to let the living water flow, drawing others to our Lord and Savior Jesus Christ.

**Abba Father, thank you for flowing in my heart. Please touch others as I minister today in Jesus' name. Amen**

**Mary Smith**

## DAY 168

# SEEING IS NOT BELIEVING

*For we walk by faith, not by sight. II Corinthians 5:7*

How do we ignore what we see? How do we not look at our circumstances but stand on what we firmly know God has impressed upon our spirit? That is a difficult thing to do. It seems as if we're being challenged. Challenged how? Challenged to not always trust what we see. That is often difficult for our human nature to grasp, especially when we've grown up on catch phrases like, "Seeing is believing."

Well, if we are Christians and are to believe in the Word of God and not our natural eyesight, seeing is NOT always believing. We must learn to trust the Word of God more than we trust the physical manifestations that are contradictory to it.

Anything we may see with our natural eyesight, or in our current situation that does not affirm the Word of God is not the truth. The truth can only be what God has spoken in His Word over our lives. If He has decreed a thing to be, then it shall be. We must reframe our words, because "Seeing God" is what believing is all about.

**Cheryl L. Thomas**

## DAY 169

# HIS GRACE IS SUFFICIENT!

> *Not that I speak in respect of want for I have learned, in whatsoever state I am, therewith to be content. I know both how to be abased, and I know how to abound: everywhere and in all things, I am instructed both to be full and to be hungry, both to abound and to suffer need. Philippians 4: 11-12*

Grace is God's unmerited favor, given but not earned. Favor comes often because of obedience to God. We have heard the expression that favor is not fair, which may or may not be true. One thing we know, an obedient child will taste the grace. Life with or without abundance can oftentimes be frustrating if we do not have a clear head concerning grace and favor. Life rarely goes exactly according to our plans.

We plan grand and rich lives for ourselves, but often what we get is something in between. I believe that God is in control of favor, and when a man's way pleases God, He will cause even his enemies to be at peace with him. The scriptures teach us that whatever state we are in to be content. However, in this present age, contentment is a lost virtue. Those that have, want more. Greed is the unspoken language of our culture.

Father, we know that Your grace is sufficient for us and that You will supply all our needs according to Your plan for our lives. Help us to live lives of contentment.

James Thomas

# DAY 170

# PSALM 51

> *Create in me a clean heart, O God; and renew a right spirit within me... Psalm 51:10*

During the reign of King David, there was a war between the Israelites and the Ammonites. Instead of leading the charge into battle, David lounged around the king's palace. The lust of his eyes and the desire of his heart caused him to commit several abominations against his Holy God. He devised several plans to try and conceal his sins. However, he could not escape the watchful eyes of God and the evil that tormented his mind.

Consequently, as David's ill-conceived son lay dying in the palace nursery, he laid prostrate before God, weeping bitterly for Him to have mercy and save his beloved son. Reciprocally, his son died. When the servants told David the heartbreaking news, he rose from his bed of sorrow and worshiped God. He knew that his sins had generated the harsh consequences he was enduring. After he cleaned himself outwardly, he asked God to cleanse him inwardly.

That's when Psalm 51 "spilled" out of his heart. His repentance and his love for God caused him to be called, "a man after God's own heart." All of his sins were forgiven! Now, he's one of the most revered men in biblical history, and his throne is now occupied by one of his descendants; the King of all kings, Jesus!

**Lord, help me to humbly confess <u>all</u> of the secret sins that have been tucked away in my heart for years. Create in me a clean heart, O God!**

**Geraldine Russell**

## DAY 171

# GOD CAN DO IT!

> *For with God nothing shall be impossible. Luke 1:37*

I want to briefly encourage you that we serve a God Who is able to do ALL things! Luke

1:37 tells us that *with God, NOTHING shall be impossible.* That means anything that you can conceive in your mind that feels too big of a dream for you is just right for God. Anything that you can desire in your heart that your circumstances tell you will never happen CAN happen with God. Anything you want to speak out loud but are afraid to because others will think you are crazy to even think that big...is POSSIBLE in God!

We, as humans, are fairly limited in what we can do on our own. Scientists even testify that we only use about ten percent of our brain power on average. However, the things that God can do in and through us are limitless. The possibilities are endless...FOR YOU! Therefore, I challenge you not to worry about what your circumstances look like, but to tell your circumstances that with God, all things are possible. Then, believe it!

**Think About It:** What do you need to believe God to do in your life?

Domonique Brunson

# DAY 172

## STAY IN GOD'S PRESENCE

> *I have set the Lord always before me; Surely, He is at my right hand, I shall not be moved. Therefore, my heart is glad, and my glory rejoiced; my flesh dwelleth in safety. Psalm 16:8-9*

Only in the presence of God can we find true joy and happiness. Only in the presence of God can we find release from pain, escape from danger, and recovery from loss. Life is so much sweeter when we experience the presence of the Lord.

There is a deep sense of contentment and security in knowing that God is always near and he extends an everlasting invitation for us to come into His presence day and night. This invitation comes in the form of prayer, meditation and reading of God's word.

When we continuously dwell in the presence of the Lord, he promised to be our protector, our deliverer, and a very present help in our times of trouble. We can trust in his promises with assurance that he will never leave us nor forsake us in the good times and the bad times.

The constant awareness of God's presence within us and around us is like a shield of protection against the fiery darts of enemies. The presence of God will be our light down any dark path.

May God's presence always remain with you and in you.

**Dr. Leticia Hardy**

# DAY 173

## A DAILY RENEWAL

> *Though outward we are wasting away, inwardly we are being renewed day by day. II Corinthians 4:16 NIV*

As a young child, I often followed my mother around the house as she worked doing her jobs. With a song coming from her lips, she moved quickly from one job to the next. As she grew older, the same jobs took longer to finish because her movements were slower; however, the song sounded the same coming out of her mouth.

It seems very clear what was happening to my mother – her outward body was decaying. However, I know that "if our early house of this tabernacle is dissolved, we have a building of God, a house not made with hands, eternal in the heavens." (II Cor. 5:1) We must remember that our inward man is renewed day by day. For we walk by faith not focusing on the things which are seen.

Our goal is to share the gospel of Jesus Christ each day in whatever we do or say. So, we must seek each day to be renewed in the spirit and strong in the power of God. For we are led by the spirit, knowing that we are weak, but we have an entire dependence on Jesus Christ. We know this because we have a life of abiding fellowship with Him.

Now that I am older, I can see clearly as I heard the songs coming from within my mother, that she had an abiding fellowship with God that carried her throughout the day.

**Heavenly Father, daily renew my spirit within so that I may reverence you the more. In Jesus' name, I pray. Amen.**

**Mary Smith**

## DAY 174

# TUNNEL VISION

> *Forget the former things; do not dwell on the past. Behold, I will do a new thing; now it shall spring forth; shall ye not know it? I will even make a way in the wilderness, and rivers in the desert. Isaiah 43:18-19*

When horse trainers are training, they put blinders on horses so all the horses can focus on is what is in front of them. Even if the horses pass something of interest or even something that made them afraid, it only lasts for a moment because just as soon as they physically pass it, it's no longer in view and therefore no longer relevant.

Christians would do well to adopt this practice. Once God has brought us through a trial, we must dust ourselves off, seek healing and help, then get up and continue on our path to purpose. Yes, it was hurtful. It may even have been painful. But it's over. It's in the past and there is no life in looking back. We must move on.

Whatever is in your past is over. It's no longer relevant. You must resist the urge to revisit dead things. You are alive and made it through that difficult and trying season. You escaped. Hallelujah!

**Cheryl L. Thomas**

## DAY 175

# IRON SHARPENS IRON!

> *Iron sharpeneth Iron; so, a man sharpeneth the countenance of his friend. Proverbs 27:17*

The Bible says that he that has friends must first show himself friendly. Proverbs talks about the countenance of a friend. We can often tell when our friends and close associates are in a low place in life struggles. It is shown in their facial expressions and can be easily detected by a friend. A close friend has the unique ability to convince his friend that all is well, that the burden is shareable, and together they can make it. The power to uplift one in times of depression and disappointment is how iron sharpens iron. We can lift the face of our friends with words and actions.

The story of David and Jonathan is a good illustration of how friends sharpen one another. When David was distraught about Saul's plans to kill him, it was Jonathan who protected and encouraged him. The Bible says that the soul of David and Jonathan was knit together. Also, the Bible shares for us the relationship of Job's friends, who were not so helpful in lifting his countenance when he needed them the most. They came, they saw, and they criticized their friend.

Iron is sharpened when it is stroked by a stronger type of metal. To be an iron sharpener you must be sensitive, caring, and empathetic. One must have the ability to put himself in another man's shoes and feel his pain, only then, can you lift the countenance of your friends.

**James Thomas**

# DAY 176

## WHEN TOMORROW BECOMES YESTERDAY

> *If it had not been the LORD who was on our side… Psalm 124:1a*

Medical challenges can become depressing when they seem to come one after another. On one occasion, an aging lady was informed by her specialist that she would have to undergo surgery to remove a cancerous tumor. When the pathology report came back, she was informed that a second surgery was needed to remove additional tissue from that same area. Three months later the surgeon reopened that four-inch incision and removed another mass of cancerous tissue.

Two months following the second surgery, she was informed that thirty-four days of radiation therapy were needed to prevent the cells from multiplying. After trudging her way through all of those intense medical and emotional processes, she made her way to the other side of her dreaded "tomorrows."

Today, she looks at those "yesterdays" with a joyful heart and continual praise on her lips. She knew that if it had not been for the Lord who was on **her** side, the enemy of "death" would have consumed her during those ten months of overwhelming, mental duress. He has been her Savior and Healer for more than fifty-four years, and will be forever! He's a mighty God! What's your testimony?

**Lord, thank You for all of my weary "tomorrows" that you decreed to become my "yesterdays." Thank You, Jehovah Rapha! Amen!**

### Geraldine Russell

# DAY 177

# OUR STORY ENDS IN VICTORY

> *...for the LORD your God is He who goes with you, to fight for you against your enemies, to save you. Deuteronomy 20:4*

As we continue to walk this journey called life, it is a guarantee that we will face some trouble. Jesus promised us that we would in His Word, and He never lies. We have seen our fair share of sickness, heartache, sadness, pain, and complete chaos, especially over the past couple of years. But I want to let you know that reading the Word of God will enlighten you to the fact that our stories do NOT end with our trouble nor our storms. In many biblical instances, trouble arose, but the Lord delivered.

See, I've personally read the last page of the book of Revelation, and I can tell you with certainty that in the end, WE WIN! Everything ends up all right! Isn't it such an encouragement to know that we serve a God who not only walks through this life with us, but Who also will not leave us hanging? For me, it definitely is. I challenge you to hold on to your faith that tells you that if things are not going your way and don't seem to be working out, it is not the end of your story because your story ends in victory!

**Think About It:** In what area of your life do you need to declare victory again?

**Domonique Brunson**

## DAY 178

## SEEKING GOD

> *O God, thou are my God, early will I seek you: my soul thirsts for you, my body longs for you in a dry and weary land, where there is no water. Psalm 63:1*

It is not difficult to find God. Unfortunately, many people are seeking God in the wrong places. It has always been God's initiative for you to draw closer to him and to seek him for guidance, protection, deliverance, healing, and daily needs.

Seeking God is a lifestyle. It means that you are willing to establish an eternal relationship with him. In the book of James 4:8, it reads, come near to God and he will come near to you. Only through studying and meditating on God's word and fervently praying unto God can we gain a closer walk and establish a lasting relationship with him.

There is a phrase that says, **"To know me is to love me."** In any relationship, there are conditions attached. Are you willing to submit your life to God? Are you willing to deny the ungodly lifestyle of this world? Are you willing to allow Christ Jesus to be the Lord and Savior of your life? Are you willing to say, "Yes," to God and his designed way of living?

If you desire anything from God, you simply must ask. The Lord said to ask, and it shall be given unto you., "Seek and ye shall find me. Knock and my door will be open unto you. He is a rewarder of those that diligently seek him."

Seeking God is a conscious choice. How close to him do **YOU** want to get?

**Dr. Leticia Hardy**

# DAY 179

## A GUIDING FORCE

> *When He, the spirit of truth is come, He will guide you into all truth. John 16:13a*

In the early years of revival in churches, the pastor and members spent days and sometimes weeks in prayer preparing their hearts and minds to receive from the Lord; what the revivalist would speak from the Lord. This was a time of repenting of sins known and unknown.

The revivalist entered a church building of worshippers with power ready to receive from the Lord with hearts desiring for souls to be added to the kingdom of God. Those were all the "Good Old Days."

Guess what, we are still living in the world free to prepare our hearts each day for a revival. We do not have to wait for someone to call a meeting or contact us. We can start each day from within the guiding force of the Holy Spirit.

Let us be early risers spending time with our Father yearning for a revival in our hearts as the congregations did in the early years. Our Father is still in the business of saving souls for His kingdom.

**Abba Father, we thank you for the "Spirit of Truth" in our hearts. Please renew your spirit in us and guide us today in praying for souls to be added to your kingdom. In Jesus' name, we pray. Amen.**

Mary Smith

## DAY 180

# FREE YOUR MIND

> *Thou wilt keep him in perfect peace, whose mind is stayed on thee: because he trusteth in thee. Isaiah 26:3*

With so much going on in our world today, it's easy to see how anyone can become overwhelmed with life. We live in such a seemingly complex world. A world that is spinning out of control with issues.

We claim the victory over the enemy even though our arteries are clogged. We're plagued with migraine headaches, kidney disease, heart disease, strokes, high blood pressure, chronic depression, obesity, and mental and physical exhaustion. Our bodies are collapsing under the extreme pressure in our minds.

Studies reveal that 90% of all hospital visits are stress related. It's the outward sign of inward duress. Our bodies are telling on us, crying out for help. Help cannot be found until we address the maladies in our minds.

Let's pray for healing. Real healing. Total and complete healing. Our first healing has to be healing for our minds and our souls. Only as we have freedom and peace of mind, can we really be free.

Lord, heal our minds, heal our bodies, and heal our souls. Though the cares of the world try to distract and disturb our peace, we will rest in YOU, the author and finisher of our faith and the captain of our souls.

**Cheryl L. Thomas**

## DAY 181

# MY BROTHER'S KEEPER

> *And the Lord said unto Cain, where is thy brother? And he said, I know not, am I my brother's keeper? And he said, what hath thou done? The voice of thy brother's blood crieth unto me from the ground. Genesis 4:9-10*

"Am I my brother's keeper" is one of the more recognizable phrases in the Bible. This was spoken by a man who had only one little brother to deal with, and yet he failed to cope with jealous rage, and murdered his sibling. We must have a tender heart, especially for those who are our brothers in the Lord, and also to our brothers and sisters everywhere. The Bible says, "let brotherly love continue."

Love covers all members of the local assembly, regardless of financial status, heritage, race, color, or creed. We must not count ourselves better than our brothers. We must be concerned about their well-being and safety as well. We are encouraged in the scriptures to do good unto all men, especially those who are of the household of faith. We fall but we get up, such is the state of brotherly fellowships. We pick up the wounded soldiers, put healing salve on their wounds and help them in the recovery room. Love covers a multitude of sins.

**Lord, help us to carry our brother when he needs carrying with an attitude that says he is not heavy because he is my brother.**

**James Thomas**

# DAY 182

# LOST TREASURE

> *But if our gospel be hid, it is hid to them that are lost:*
> *II Corinthians 4:4*

A true story was told about a poor, uneducated farmer who found a nice heavy rock that he could use to keep his door ajar. He enjoyed the breeze that kept the house cool, especially during the hot summer months in the south. One day a wealthy farmer came by for a chat and noticed that the rock was valuable. Sensing that the poor farmer had no idea of its value, he offered him a few dollars in exchange. The poor farmer wanted to give him the rock. However, the wealthier farmer insisted on an "exchange." He gave the poor farmer a few dollars, took the rock, and headed home rejoicing. He knew that he had gained a great treasure. He had it appraised and discovered that it was worth far more than his entire estate. The poor farmer forfeited an opportunity to rise above poverty when he exchanged his valuable treasure for a few dollars.

"Salvation" is a treasure that many people think has no immediate or lasting value. They regard it as a prop to keep the doorway open to the comforting, cool breeze of the world. When they finally realize the value of salvation, sometimes it's too late. That treasure is lost; sometimes forever!

Let's not be like the wealthy farmer that hoarded earthly wealth. If he had revealed the truth about the valuable rock, both he and the poor farmer could have shared the wealth. Instead, the poor farmer remained poor and the wealthy farmer increased in riches.

Fellow believers, are we hoarding the valuable riches of salvation? Have we noticed the needs of those that are "poor in spirit?" Have we uncovered the lost treasure of salvation to those whose eyes have not been opened to "truth?" If not, let's share the "wealth!"

**Lord, open our eyes to see the hidden treasures of salvation in the hearts of those who need to understand that what they have is worth far more than earthly comfort and riches. Help us to show them that they have a golden treasure that is far more valuable than the riches of this world. Lord, help them to understand that salvation has a value that can never be lost. It is eternal. In Jesus' name. Amen.**

**Geraldine Russell**

## DAY 183

# WE NEED GOD

> *And those who know your name put their trust in you, for you, O Lord, have not forsaken those who seek you. Psalm 9:10*

Many times, we find ourselves walking through life's sunny days focused on how good things are going and how much we have going for ourselves. We congratulate ourselves on how well we've done with our gifts and talents, and we do our best to enjoy the good times. You know, the calm times. The one thing that we don't think about as often during these amazing times, though, is how much we STILL need God! We love to call on Him when times are rough and the storms of life are raging, but do we realize that we need God just as much in the calm times as we do during the stormy times?

Yes, we may have to try a little harder to keep that fact in perspective when things are going well, but the fact remains that we need God at ALL times and in ALL ways. There is nothing we have that we have acquired on our own and there is no achievement that we've reached on our own either. We must always remember that no matter how far we go, there will never be a time when we don't need the love and protection of the Master Himself.

**Think About It:** In what areas of your life have you been trying to do things on your own?

**Domonique Brunson**

## DAY 184

# MY FRIEND JESUS

> *Ye are my friends, if ye do whatsoever I command you.*
> *John 15:14*

"Jesus is our friend because he loves without limits. He makes it possible for us to live a life of friendship with him. Through friendship, we come to know God. Through friendship we enact the love of God."

Father, God, I thank you for giving me such a wonderful true dear friend. You knew how dearly I needed one, and you knew just who to send. A devoted friend who will always be there to lend me helping hands. A shoulder I can always cry on with a heart that understands. You did not send just anyone, or any mediocre thing. You sent a precious jewel, your son a Savior and King.

**Dr. Leticia Hardy**

# DAY 185

# A LIFE OF PRAYER

> *I urge you, first, to pray for all people. Ask God to help them, intercede on their behalf, and give thanks to them. Pray this way for kings and all who are in authority so that we can live peaceful and quiet lives marked by godliness and dignity. I Timothy 2:1-2*

When we think of a "Life of Prayer," we think of a life daily connected with God. Jesus taught His disciples that they should always pray and never give up. (Luke 18:1b) So, a life of prayer continues throughout one's lifetime.

Then, as we search scripture, we find Daniel was such a man. Daniel was a captive and taken to Babylon around the age of sixteen. He was trained for three years in the language and literature of Babylon. However, Daniel decided to give his heart wholly to God.

Nevertheless, he was always gracious toward those in authority.

God gave Daniel an unusual aptitude for understanding every aspect of literature, wisdom, and a special ability to interpret the meanings of visions and dreams. Daniel prayed three times a day. (Dan. 6:10) God closed the lions' mouths for him in the lions' den. He was one of the administrators under King Darius.

God used his "Life of Prayer" to transform the kingdom under King Darius' reign. (Daniel 6: 1-28) What a life! We too can have a life of prayer today as we spend time with the Lord, praying for all people, interceding on their behalf, giving thanks for them, and praying for kings and all who are in authority!

Abba Father, Thank you for the life of Daniel. Help us today as we present our bodies to do your will. It is in Jesus' name we pray. Amen

Mary Smith

# DAY 186

# BUSINESS OR BUSY-NESS

> *Come unto me, all ye that labour and are heavy laden, and I will give you rest. Take my yoke upon you, and learn of me; for I am meek and lowly in heart: and ye shall find rest unto your souls.*
> Matthew 11:28-29

Everyone is busy these days with iPads, iPhones, Facebook, Instagram, TikTok, whirlwind tours, and demanding careers. We need iPhones and Androids to hold all of our "essential" appointments, two or three personal assistants to keep us on track, a marketing team to promote our agenda, a public relations team to keep us together... Oh, can we simply catch our breath and live?

Now, I am not opposed to any of these great inventions. In fact, I use many of them myself. But when our career, iPhone, Twitter, and Facebook friends get more of our attention than God and our family, that is a problem.

What is this obsession with being busy? If our schedule doesn't have an appointment each and every day, does that make us less important? No. Busy does not equal important. Most of the time, it only equals tired. We are too tired to spend time in prayer, devotion, and celebration with our Savior. We are too tired to spend quality time with our family and friends. We are too tired to be refreshed, reenergized, and revitalized. We are too tired to be of any real help to anyone. So, we must remember to take time to turn off those devices and spend quality time with our Savior and family. Those are moments we'll treasure for a lifetime and cannot be replaced.

**Cheryl L. Thomas**

# DAY 187

## NO MORE EXCUSES

> *Whither shall I go from thy spirit? Or whither shall I flee from thy presence? If I ascend into heaven, thou art there; If I make my bed in hell, behold, thou art there... Psalm 139:7-10*

God calls men and women to perform the special task for His purpose and glory. Sometimes we feel inadequate to accomplish. Oftentimes, excuses are made as to why we are not the person that the Lord needs for this task. We say, "Please let someone else do it." God knows who is right for the job. He will always apply the necessary pressure to get His man, even if he has to take him through the belly of hell. Jesus tells the parable ... "And they all with one consent began to make excuses."

The following excuses were offered. (1) No one should buy land without having previously examined it. (2) I just married a wife... and (3) I just bought ten oxen and I need to go prove them. Excuses can be reasonable when viewed through human lenses, but the call of God is greater than the call of Uncle Sam. When Uncle Sam calls, you will report for duty one way or the other, and you will make no excuse.

**Verse to remember:** Whither shall I go from thy spirit? Whither shall I flee from thy presence? Psalm 139:7

**James Thomas**

# DAY 188

## BLOOD WORK

> *In whom we have redemption through his blood, the forgiveness of sins, according to the riches of his grace. Ephesians 1:7*

The battle against sicknesses and diseases will never be won until Jesus returns and removes the curse of sin. When a person is feeling ill, he/she may schedule an appointment to see a doctor. Upon arrival, one of the first things ordered is a blood test. After the blood is drawn, it is taken to a laboratory to be assessed. Technicians examine the sample to see if there are any viruses, germs, or other contaminants that may be causing the illness. Once the assessment is complete and the cause of the illness is determined, the doctor can proceed with a diagnosis and treatment. Hospitalization, surgery, or prescriptions may be required for that person to recover. If the doctor's instructions are followed, healing or improvement will occur.

When an individual realizes that he/she is sin-sick and lost, scheduling appointments with the Word of God ensures the individual that healing will occur. Through faith, the blood of Jesus will be infused into that person's life. Once the infusion is complete, that person is healed from the sickness of sin forever. If he/she continues to obey the instructions of the Word, there will never be a cause to doubt the lab report – "**You are healed by the blood of Jesus forever.**" All those that the Son sets free from sin-sickness are truly free from the viruses and germs that contaminate the blood.

Has Jesus done blood work on you? Is there anyone you know who needs to make an appointment to hear the Word of God? If so, lead them to a "doctor-of-the-Word" that has truly been sent to preach the gospel. Through faith, the healing blood of Jesus is available to all that will acknowledge, accept, and apply the Word of God to their sin-sickness. His blood cleanses believers from all unrighteousness that causes contaminants to appear in an individual's blood work.

**Heavenly Father, help me to surrender to the blood work of Jesus and to lead others to the cleansing power of His Holy Word. In Jesus' name Amen.**

**Geraldine Russell**

## DAY 189

# JUST SAY THANKS

> *O give thanks unto the LORD; for he is good; for his mercy endureth forever. 1 Chronicles 16:34*

For the most part, we make the choice to do what we want, when we want, during our days. We go where we want to go and plan our days accordingly. Have you ever sat down and thought about just how much time we have been allotted each and every day and how much of that time we simply use giving God praise? I mean, God has blessed us with 86,400 seconds in EVERY day of the week…yet, how many of those seconds do we set aside to appreciate Him? Our God deserves all of our praise for EVERYTHING He has done and undoubtedly, just for Who He is. In fact, He's the only one who rightly deserves the glory.

We did not acquire anything we have on our own because this earth is the Lord's and the fullness thereof. It **all belongs to Him**! My challenge for you today is to take at least one of the MANY seconds of your day and simply give God thanks. I must warn you, though, you might not be able to stop once you start, but that's completely OK because all of the glory, honor, and praise belongs to Him anyway!

**Think About It:** When was the last time you paused just to give God praise?

**Domonique Brunson**

# DAY 190

# PITFALLS TO AVOID ON THIS CHRISTIAN JOURNEY

> *He that handles a matter wisely shall find good; and whoso trusted in the Lord, happy is he. Proverbs 16:20*

On this Christian journey, we must constantly pray asking God to help us to walk with him and listen to him when he speaks for our enemy is as a roaring lion seeking whom he may abound. Believers must avoid the pitfall of "Neglecting Our Personal Family Relationships" by overly committing themselves to church activities, events, meetings, conferences, and duties. Pressures from these entities can greatly affect us personally, physically, emotionally, and spiritually. Believers must take necessary precautions in balancing church and home life.

Avoid the pitfall called "Seeking Self-Gratification and Glory." Believers must always remember that we are only servants and vessels of the almighty God, and it is God who should be glorified for the things He is doing through us. Keep in mind that although God has granted us the privilege to be used by Him, it is the Lord Almighty Who is doing the work. We must always give God all the glory, honor, and praise for the great things that He is doing in our ministry.

Another pitfall to avoid is called "Self-Centered Ambition." We are not saying that ambition is a bad thing, but it must be utilized as a righteous motive. The Bible informs us that if a person seeks an office or position, he must strive lawfully and righteously.

When desiring positions, spiritual gifts, and prosperity, it is vital that we examine our motives for seeking them.

Dr. Leticia Hardy

# DAY 191

# A STUDENT'S PRAYER

> *Show me the right path, O Lord, point out the road for me to follow. Lead me by your truth and teach me, for you are the God who saves me. All day long I put my hope in you. Psalm 25:4-5 NLT*

We think of a student as someone who is studying in a school to enter a particular profession in life. Some years before a student is ready to graduate from high school, he/she is taught to start thinking of what he/she wants to do in life/work, etc.

A counselor may advise according to what he/she sees as strengths in subject matters. But it is always up to the individual student to choose his/her path in life. A Christian student will begin to pray "Show me the right path, O Lord, point out the road for me to follow. Lead me by your truth and teach me for you are the God who saves me. All day long I put my hope in you." Nevertheless, a student is to listen to parents, counselors, pastors, and those in authority. But, the final decision must be settled between the student and God. (I Peter 5:5) Then, continue each day praying for directions, "not my will but thy will be done" in my life today.

What a great thought: we are students in Christ Jesus, each day being guided in his ways as we follow the right path.

**Abba Father, thank you for showing us the right path to follow today. It is in Jesus' name we pray. Amen**

**Mary Smith**

# DAY 192

# NOW IS THE TIME

> *I must work the works of him that sent me, while it is day: the night cometh, when no man can work. John 9:4*

There is a popular saying in Christendom, "I'm waiting for my change to come." I personally think we say it so often and sometimes without even knowing what is meant by that statement. It has become one of our favorite church colloquialisms and Christian jargon. It sounds good. We like the response it elicits from others when we say it. What change are we looking for, a new house, car, or job? Or, maybe we desire a deeper relationship with Christ, a better relationship with family members, or more recognition in the community?

Now don't get me wrong, change does come. However, it often has its genesis with you. There is a famous quote that says, "You must be the change you want to see in the world." So instead of sitting in church **"waiting"** on your change, come from behind those pews, go out into the world and **Be** the change. The world awaits your coming.

**Food for Thought:** *What are you waiting on? What is holding you back? Why are you not doing what God called you to do? Decide today that you'll put down those perfectly laid out plans and stop waiting for the "perfect" moment and instead choose to begin walking into your destiny! The purpose lived out one day and one step at a time. Begin that step now.*

**Cheryl L. Thomas**

# DAY 193

# PRAYER: A POWERFUL PRINCIPLE!

> *And I set my face unto the Lord God, to seek by prayer and supplication, and with fasting and sackcloth, and ashes. Daniel 9:3*

A principle is the foundation of one's Christian belief system. With that as a fundamental starting point for this discussion, the Bible says that men ought to always pray and not faint. Giving up should not be an option for the believer, "for the just shall live by faith." Jesus urged his disciples to "watch and pray" so that they might not enter temptation.

If they are not prayerfully watching, they would not be prepared for the tragedy that is about to happen. He counseled them that the spirit is willing, but the flesh is weak. Our regenerated selves may have good intentions. We must control our bodies to gain spiritual victories. When prayer is the foundation of our spiritual life, victories will come.

Prayer and fasting were Daniel's basic daily routine. He prayed three times a day. He set his face to know God. Because of the principles of prayer, Daniel found grace in the sight of God. He was delivered from the den of lions, and the furnace of fire. He was promoted to the second-highest position in the Babylonian Kingdom. I think that is a good return on his daily prayer investment.

**Father, help us to prioritize and have a daily encounter with you, so that we may know your heart for our lives.**

**James Thomas**

# DAY 194

# WHEN TRUTH IS REJECTED

> *Then you will know the truth, and the truth will set you free.*
> *John 8:32*

Living on the opposite side of "Truth" has deadly consequences. During the past two years (2020-2021), deception has caused many people to ignore the truth. That ignorance (refusing to acknowledge truth) has caused hundreds of thousands of people to "die before their time." (Ecclesiastes 7:17) Scientists discovered a deadly virus that blanketed the earth before measures could be taken to mitigate the spread. Within a few months, a global pandemic had been declared. Death swept across every major continent on earth like a tsunami. Scientists worked around the clock to develop a vaccine that would slow the rapid spread and curve the tide of death. However, in a demonstration of political correctness and solidarity, many people refused to adhere to expert, scientific advice. They rejected truth because it was declared by someone they disliked. Consequently, many lives have been "snuffed out." Two years and millions of deaths later, some people are just now realizing that the "truth" had been proclaimed from the beginning.

Just as it was during the unbelieving world of Noah's day, truth is still being ignored today. Noah preached for 120 years that destruction was on the horizon. The people refused to believe it because they had never heard of a flood caused by rain. Therefore, they laughed, jeered, and taunted Noah until it was too late. When God commanded the fountains of the air and the deep to operate in full glory, no one outside Noah's ark was spared. Death swept over the entire earth in a matter of days. Wailing surrounded the ark, but it was too late! Today, millennia later, another cry for repentance is going out into the world.

However, the world is full of rebellion. "Truth" is being laughed at, jeered, and mocked. As a result, the masses are being swept away by death! Therefore, believers, "Cry aloud! Spare Not! Lift your voice like a trumpet! Show the people their transgressions! Tell them to repent!" Maybe, God will relent!

**Heavenly Father, help us to proclaim your truth in our world today. Amen.**

**Geraldine Russell**

# DAY 195

# JUST KEEP PRAYING

> *Jesus said unto him, if thou canst believe, all things are possible to him that believeth. Mark 9:23*

Every time I think about the fact that God is omnipotent, it floors me. I mean, we serve a God who holds all power in His hands and Who is able to do ANYTHING but fail. Even when we fail daily, Jesus NEVER fails! That also means that He can turn around any situation He wants to at ANY time He wants! He is so much in control that our sense of time does not affect Him in the least. He operates outside of our circumstances so that He can step in or out of them whenever He gets ready.

No matter whether you are struggling emotionally, mentally, financially, physically, with family or friends, or even spiritually, God can turn it around for you if you want Him to. He can switch the direction of events in your life with just a word. The only thing the turnaround requires from us is that we KEEP PRAYING and KEEP BELIEVING that God is well able to perform it! The older saints used to sing the song, "Only believe...all things are possible if you only believe." I just want you to remember today that it's possible for you, too, if you only BELIEVE!

**Think About It:** What situation do you need to PRAY and BELIEVE God for?

Domonique Brunson

## DAY 196

# LOVE IS WHAT LOVE DOES

> *A new commandment I give unto you, that ye love one another, as I have loved you, that ye also love one another. By this shall all men know that ye are my Disciples, if ye have love one to another.*
> *John 13:34-35*

Love is a subject that has stirred the interest of mankind from the beginning of time up until the present and will forever more.

There have been thousands of songs, novels, poetries, and movies written or produced about love. The general perception of the world is that love is an emotion to be felt rather than a lifestyle to be lived.

People love what they value the most. The evidence can be seen by what they devote themselves to and it is reflected in their actions and motivations.

God's love towards mankind is amazing, incredible, incomprehensible, and immeasurable. God loves us so that he gave His only begotten son, Jesus Christ, as a ransom to remove the Barrier of Sin that once separated us from him. God's love canceled the debt of our sins and removed our sins far from ever existing again.

God's love is the only love that heals us physically, emotionally, mentally, and spiritually. God knew we were once sinners, yet his love forgave us of our sins. God knows our shortcomings, yet he chose to love us despite of. God sees our many diseases, yet his love keeps healing us. God sees our ungratefulness and slackness, yet he keeps giving us good gifts with benefits. God sees when we deserve justice for our wages, yet he grants us mercy. Even when we fall into a pit, God hears our cries, and His love pulls us out. God even calls us friends! What greater love than a friend would lay down his life for a friend?

**Dr. Leticia Hardy**

# DAY 197

## COMMISSIONED AROMA

> *For we are to God the pleasing aroma of Christ among those who are being saved and those who are perishing. II Corinthians 2:15*

Planning a vacation to get away from everything and everyone we are around all the time can be very exciting. But, as we travel meeting others that we have not met before, we are commissioned to spread the aroma of the knowledge of Jesus Christ. It is the most important relaxing aroma that makes the highlight of a vacation worthwhile. We get to spread God's aroma to new believers in Christ and share with the unbelievers. Then, the vacation becomes not just about relaxing and getting away from everyone and everything we know, but it becomes a process of reaching others for Christ.

Oh, thanks be to God, who always leads us in Christ's procession and uses us to spread the aroma of the knowledge of Him everywhere. "For we are to God the pleasing aroma of Christ among those who are being saved and those who are perishing." (2 Cor. 2:15) So, we can never leave our commissioned aroma behind us no matter where we go. It is who we are and the highlight of each day no matter where we are on this earth.

**Abba Father, thank you for your aroma, and please commission me again to spread it to everyone I meet. In Jesus' name. Amen.**

*Mary Smith*

# DAY 198

# LET'S MEDITATE

> *This book of the law shall not depart out of thy mouth; but thou shalt meditate therein day and night, that thou mayest observe to do according to all that is written therein: for then thou shalt make thy way prosperous, and then thou shalt have good success. Joshua 1:8*

As Christians, have we allowed the world or the secular arena to benefit more from meditation than us? I must admit that I myself let it take on a somewhat "spooky" sinister meaning or connotation. But meditation began with God's admonition to the Israelites. The Bible admonished them to meditate, think on, and ponder the true meaning of His Word. I also believe it is important and powerful for us to meditate on the Word and how it affects our existence.

I believe one of the advantages of meditation is focus! With the hectic lives we all seem to live, it is often hard to find the time to think. We run to and fro without direction because we haven't stopped long enough for God to show us where to focus. He longs to give us direction, but often we're too busy to stop and listen.

God wants to fine-tune our focus so we will know His will clearly and be able to create the steps and strategy necessary to procure it. Let's begin to meditate on His Word and what it means to us specifically. As we seek His direction, He will begin to whisper His plans for our life.

**Food for Thought:** *Are you having trouble with your focus? Seek God. Pick out one day this week and make it your business to seek God and meditate on His plan for you so you can fine-tune your focus and clearly hear His direction for your future.*

**Cheryl L. Thomas**

# DAY 199

# RAINY DAYS AND RAINY NIGHTS

> *We are troubled on every side, yet not distressed; we are perplexed, but not in despair; persecuted, but not forsaken; cast down, but not destroyed. II Corinthians 4:8-9*

Troubles! Troubles! Why so many troubles are sometimes the sigh of the believer. Why me, Lord? That fate is the common fate of all – into each life some rain must fall. Some days are dark and dreary. Behind the clouds the sun is still shining (Longfellow).

The Apostle Paul describes the challenges that Christians will likely face at some point in time. They will have mountain top experiences. There will be days of gloom and days when it seems like the enemy has the upper hand. We know that no matter how dreary the day or dark the night, God sits on the circle of the earth.

He looks high and He looks low. He promises that He will never leave us nor forsake us. I believe His word, that He watches over His Word to perform it, and none of it will fall to the ground unfulfilled. I will sing as David sang. I will dance as David danced. I will say of the Lord, He is the joy and strength of my life. He will perform that which concerns me and my household.

*Life is filled with swift transition, none on earth unmoved can change, you ought to build your hopes on things eternal, and hold to God's unchanging hand.*

**James Thomas**

# DAY 200

## THE LEAST AND THE GREATEST

> *For it is the one who is least among you all who is the greatest. Luke 9:48c*

The political state of the nation has become a battleground between the greedy and the needy. Those that have risen to the top of wealth are trying to keep others from rising to the top with them. In many cases, those that are in need are the ones that are being suppressed and hindered from becoming successful.

In the kingdom of heaven, those who are on the top are the ones at the bottom. In the kingdom of heaven, those who are "looked down on" will be those who are "looked upon." In the kingdom of heaven, the lesser are the greater. In the kingdom of heaven, the poor are the rich. In the kingdom of heaven, the despised are the ones that are celebrated. In the kingdom of heaven, the ones that are hated are the ones that are loved. In the kingdom of heaven, the losers are the winners. In the kingdom of heaven, the weak are powerful. And, in the kingdom of heaven, there are NO self-righteous people. All that enter the kingdom of heaven must humble themselves before God. Only then will they become great.

Believer, do you feel unappreciated, looked down on, or like a loser? Surrender those thoughts to Jesus. He will lift you above the cares and concerns of this life and give you a glimpse of glory. He will lift your head. He will supply your every need. When your circumstances cause you to hang your head down, just remember that in the kingdom of heaven, "down is up". When Jesus returns, there will be many surprised people. Therefore, be encouraged to press on toward the mark of a higher call in God's kingdom.

**Lord, lift my head to Your embrace. Help me to see me as You see me…through the eyes of Your loving grace.
In Jesus' name. Amen.**

**Geraldine Russell**

# DAY 201

# THE BEAUTY OF HIS PROMISE

> *There failed not ought of any good thing which the LORD had spoken unto the house of Israel; all came to pass. Joshua 21:45*

As I was riding along the other day, the weather was in perfect condition to produce a rainbow. I looked around for one. When I spotted it, I was in awe because real life rainbows are so beautiful and always remind me of God's promises still covering my life. Now, when someone makes a promise to you, you expect them to keep it, right? After all, the Bible does tell us that it is better to not even make a promise than to make one and not keep it. The thing is that all of us are guilty of making a promise and for whatever reason, we have to break it.

However, there is Someone whose promises are unbreakable and unfailing no matter the situation and that Someone is Jesus Christ. Every promise He has ever made to us has, is, or will come to pass. EVERY SINGLE ONE! He is the absolute only one that we can always depend and rely on to come through for us. That's why we ought to stay in our Word so that these promises can come to light and shine on our problems and issues. There is NO problem that can outshine or outlast the promises of our God.

**Think About It:** What promise has God shown you?

**Domonique Brunson**

# DAY 202

# HOW DEEP IS OUR LOVE FOR GOD AND ONE ANOTHER?

> *Hereby perceive we the love of God, because he laid down his life for us; and we ought to lay down our lives for the brethren. 1 John 3:16*

Love is doing what is best for others no matter the cost. God gave his only son to save the world from his wrath-what a great price. In Genesis 19:8, Lot was willing to give up his daughters to save Sodom and Gomorrah. In 1 King 3:16-28, Solomon revealed how the rightful mother was willing to save her baby's life by giving him over to the lying woman who claimed to be the baby's mother. Abraham was willing to sacrifice his promised son to please God. Job was willing to be slain by God to prove his love, loyalty, devotion, and trust to him (Job 13:15). Esther was willing to perish to save the people of the most high God.

Love is more than just a feeling. Love is action, doing, and behaving. Love is the way we treat God and His people.

There is a song entitled, "**I've Got the Love of Jesus, Deep Down in My Heart.**"

We can be good at our job, our position, or skilled in planning events, completing multiple tasks, organizing projects, or playing an instrument, but poor at allowing God's AGAPE love to flow out of us like a true disciple of God bearing the name of Christianity.

Loving one another means always being ready to believe the best about each other. This does not mean you are gullible. Love is clear-sighted, even when it can recognize the wrong in an individual. However, love will always give the benefit of the doubt.

As Christ loves us, we must love one another. When God's love is in us, His love helps us to endure one another, trust one another, have faith in one another, and have hope for the improvement of spiritual growth within our fellow brothers and sisters. God has never commanded anyone to do anything that He has not already empowered them to do.

**Dr. Leticia Hardy**

# DAY 203

# ASK FOR WISDOM

> *If any of you lacks wisdom, let him ask of God, who gives to all liberally and without reproach, and it will be given to him. James 1:5*

We are living in a world today where man's knowledge is growing daily with the utilization of technology. It is one thing in which a child can say "I know more than my parents." And yes, as parents we must acknowledge this, but continue to love them and teach them about the Savior who died for their sins. As we incline our ear to wisdom and apply our heart to understanding…For the Lord gives wisdom; from His mouth comes knowledge and understanding. So, when wisdom enters our hearts, knowledge becomes pleasant to our souls so we can grow together. (Proverbs 2:2,10)

We praise God for wisdom to live in this world that is growing with knowledge and technology at such a fast pace. We can continue to smile and know that God is still in charge of everything that He has made. He is still allowing things to be made far above our understanding to ask or think. Wisdom!

**Abba Father, thank you for wisdom this day to serve you in this world. In Jesus' name, we pray. Amen.**

Mary Smith

# DAY 204

# TURN ON THE LIGHTS

> *Thy word is a lamp unto my feet, and a light unto my path.*
> Psalms 119:105

Have you ever had so many things you needed to get done that it clouded your thinking? All the items on your checklist seem to mock you, each of them vying for your immediate attention. They all fit into the scheme of your plan. They are all pieces to the master puzzle. Oh, but where do you begin?

Perhaps it's time to lay down our puzzle pieces and ask, "God, what is my next step? I moved when You said to. I'm in the place I believe You called me, preparing to do what I believe You called me to do. What next? Do I forge ahead, or do I keep this holding pattern? Is the timing right? Is my focus correct? Are the necessary people in place? I have all of these puzzle pieces, but have no idea how to correctly place them."

It is sometimes so easy to know the destination but another thing entirely to find the correct path. Our daily prayer should always be, "Lord, be a lamp unto my feet and a light to my pathway; so that I end up in the exact place you ordained for me!"

**Food for Thought:** *Feeling confused about the path to take? Relax and do not stress. Lay your puzzle pieces down at the Master's feet and rest. In time, He will illuminate the path, the people, and the strategy. If it is His purpose you're seeking to fulfill, He will provide every resource you need to complete it.*

**Cheryl L. Thomas**

# DAY 205

# RELIGIOUS STORM WARNING!

> *Now unto him that is able to keep you from falling, and to present you faultless, before the presence of his glory with exceeding joy.*
> *Jude 1:24*

There is a gospel song that I listen to that says, "There is a storm out on the ocean, and it's moving this away. If your soul is not anchored in Jesus, you will surely drift away..."

Apostle Paul warned the saints of his day about the great falling away before the coming of the Lord. It is believed that the opposition Paul writes about would come from within the church. This takes on added significance in the light of recent developments in the church world. Men who once stood tall as mighty men of God, and proponents of moral purity, have been deceived by misinformation, conspiracies, falsehoods, and are now teaching a lifestyle that is contrary to the Gospel of Jesus Christ. Paul was right to warn us of these times.

What are some of the things we should watch out for? In the last days, perilous times shall come; having a form of godliness but denying the power thereof; false teachers; heady; and calling evil good and good evil, etc. How can we avoid becoming caught up in a world gone mad with greed and pleasure-seeking at the expense of truth and the Word of God?

**Wherefore let him that thinketh he standeth take heed lest he falls (I Cor. 10:12).**

**James Thomas**

## DAY 206

# A STOLEN BLESSING

> *Let us therefore come boldly unto the throne of grace that we may obtain mercy, and find grace to help in time of need. Hebrews 4:16*

Jesus performed many miracles to fulfill his prophetic identity as the Son of God. On one occasion while in Galilee, a ruler named Jarius came to him and asked if he would come and heal his dying daughter. While enroute to Jarius' house, a woman that had been sick for twelve years sneaked behind him and "stole" a healing. She said within herself that if she could touch the hem of Jesus' cloak, she believed her body would be made whole. Sure enough, immediately after her hand and faith touched his garment, she was healed. She tried to sneak her way back through the crowd, but was caught before she could escape. She bowed before him and confessed her behavior. Jesus told her not to be afraid because her bold faith had made her whole. She left rejoicing! The woman had not experienced that kind of joy in twelve years. On her way home, she boldly proclaimed the healing power of Jesus!

Jesus is still seeking those that will come to him for healing and deliverance. It doesn't matter what the issue is, he's still healing the sick, saving the lost, and setting the captives free. His throne of grace is still available to all that will come to him boldly and in faith. They will find help in their time of need.

**Geraldine Russell**

## DAY 207

# PEACE, PURPOSE AND HOPE

> *For I know the thoughts that I think toward you, saith theLord, thoughts of peace, and not of evil, to give you an expected end.*
> *Jeremiah 29:11*

Quick flashback: in our school days, we learned in ELA that there is a difference between the past, present, and future tenses. That fact also holds true in real life. If something happened in our past, that means it did already happen and what is happening in our present could be very different, just as what is happening in our here and now is no match for what God has planned for our future.

Many of us have pretty "colorful" pasts, which we may not want to re-live. However, the amazing thing about God is that He is willing to bring peace to all that turmoil so that we can move forward in the present because He has purpose for us to walk in. There is someone who will need to hear the story of our past so THEY can get through. And for all of us currently walking in our purpose, just knowing that there is a reason for all our experiences ought to give us hope that God has great things in store for our futures. Little does the enemy know that our strength lies in our hope!

Think About It: What in your past do you need to allow God to bring peace to?

**Domonique Brunson**

## DAY 208

# WHERE ARE THE LABORERS?

> *Then he said to his disciples, The harvest is plenteous, but the laborers are few. Ask the Lord of the harvest, to send out laborers into his harvest field. Matthew 9:37-38*

Working is an everyday way of life. We invest our time, energy, effort, focus, and finances into various areas of our lives with high expectations of a return. Ecclesiastes 3:13 states, "That every one of us should eat, drink, and enjoy the good of our labor, this is a gift of God". Although we thank God for his daily benefits, our workday is not quite over. St. John 6:27a states, "Labor not for the meat which perishes, but for that meat which endures unto everlasting life." John is encouraging us to invest or sow our time, energy, effort, focus, and finances into that which is eternal, SOULS!

There is a harvest of valuable souls waiting on you to make an investment. When Jesus looked on the multitude of souls, He was moved with compassion to take action on what he saw. Teaching and ministering to their needs became His primary focus.

Where are the laborers? Look in a mirror; you'll find the answer!

**Helen V. Tate**

# DAY 209

# EVANGELISM EXHORTATION/GOD'S POWER

> *But he said to me, "My grace is sufficient for you, for my power is made perfect in weakness." Therefore, I will boast more gladly about my weaknesses, so that Christ's power may rest on me.*
> II Corinthians 12:9

Once a little girl found a cocoon hanging from a limb in the forest. She took it to her room and placed it in a jar, expecting one day to see a butterfly emerge. One day, she saw the butterfly within the cocoon trying to get out. It was struggling and trying to push its way out of the tight opening. To help the poor insect, she very carefully slit open the cocoon. After that, the butterfly was able to easily exit the cocoon. But a strange thing happened. Instead of spreading two beautiful wings, the butterfly had two withered, shriveled, useless, ugly wings hanging by its side.

No, we are not butterflies, but we need the pressures and trials of life, if we are to develop into all that God has saved us to be. Just like that butterfly, we will find that the trials and the sufferings of life will refine and prepare us to take flight for the glory of God. We need to understand that the things we may be called upon to endure may not be over in an hour or a few days. God is doing something special in your life and in His time; He will make that perfectly clear!

**Missionary Sheila F. Jones**

# DAY 210

## INSTANT REPLAY

> *Fear not, little flock; for it is your Father's good pleasure to give you the kingdom. Luke 12:32*

Why do we waste time replaying the past? What is it in our yesterdays that makes us yearn so to return? Is it because it was that good or wonderful? Hardly or not always. I believe sometimes our fixation on our past stems from our fear of the future. It is not always that the events of the past were so glorious, it is often the fear of our future that frightens us.

A lot of fear may be rooted in a belief that there is nothing better for us. But there has to be. With God, being the loving Father that He is, He would never take us from good to bad. It is always from good to better and from better to best. So, know that BEST is coming. The waiting process is often difficult, but it is always worth the wait.

What are you anxious about? Do you fear the best years of your life are over? Confront that fear today. God always takes us from faith to faith and glory to glory, so we never have to worry that He's run out of good things for us.

Lord, please help us to patiently wait on You. We trust that You know what is best for us. Help us to not seek our own path in frustration but help us to know that waiting on Your best is worth the wait. Amen.

**Cheryl L. Thomas**

## DAY 211

# GOD IS A HEALER

> *And Jesus went about all Galilee, teaching in their synagogues, and preaching the gospel of the kingdom, and healing all manner of sickness and all manner of disease among the people. Matthew 4:23*

Six weeks after open-heart surgery, I found that a cyst burst in the back of my head and was cancerous. My doctor sent me to a surgeon who was and is a Christian and allows the Lord to perform successful cancer procedures while praying for his patients to be healed.

Afterward the doctor was reluctant to tell me what the x-rays revealed for fear that I would start crying. But I assured him that I knew someone bigger than cancer. The doctor asked me who I knew that was bigger than cancer and I responded by telling him that I knew God. Within a few seconds, the doctor had crossed the room and grabbed me to let me know that he was going to pray, and I would be healed, delivered, and set free. At that point, I told him that I would touch and agree with him and I would be healed.

Every time I am scheduled to go for a checkup, my oncologist tells me that he was dumbfounded because they drew four vials of blood and ran every test in the book. He recalls the fact that no radiation was given, neither did they have to treat me with radiation therapy. After the doctor told me all the data that was found, I simply responded, "But God!" God is the same yesterday, today, and forevermore.

**Evelyn Beachem**

## DAY 212

# LORD, HELP ME TO TRUST YOU IN EVERY ASPECT OF MY LIFE

> *Then Jesus said to his disciples: Therefore I tell you, do not worry about your life, what you will eat; or about your body, what you will wear. Luke 12:22*

God already knows what we will encounter each day. He says that he knows the hairs on our heads and even a sparrow, though sold for two pennies, does not fall from the sky without his knowledge. He says that we are more valuable than many sparrows (Matthew 10:29-31). If even the sparrow is not forgotten, how much more will he take care of us. It is so easy to see God's hand in something AFTER we have gotten through the trial and are looking back to see what he brought us through. While this is nice to thank God in the AFTER, how much better to thank him in the NOW. Oh, how he desires for us to trust him in the NOW.

He wants us to know that we may not see how it is going to work out, but by trusting in his word, we KNOW that it is. Yes, it is easier to say it, than to do it. However, it works out our faith muscles when we do. This furthers our testimony and ability to reach the masses. When we can share how we are currently walking through something and trusting God in the NOW, not just the AFTER, it helps other people going through their trials to know that God is also with them in the NOW.

**Prayer:** God, you know my heart, my needs, my desires, and my struggles. You know what I am going through, and you know what this day will bring. Thank you for going before me and putting people and plans in motion to see me through this. Thank you for your provision. Thank you for being with me in the NOW. Help me to trust you when I cannot see how it will work out. Help me to trust you when I feel weak. A mustard seed of faith is all that is required. Lord here is my seed. Amen!

**Lynette Whitfield**

# DAY 213

## LIFE BLUEPRINT

> *For I know the plans I have for you… Jeremiah 29:11a*

A blueprint is a designed plan or a detailed plan of something to be done. In the context of building a home, engineers test the soil before pouring a foundation per the blueprint. The foundation is the support upon which something rests. A foundation can develop cracks. If not formulated correctly it can also disintegrate. How can our foundation develop cracks and or disintegrate? There is one word that defines it: "sin."

How can one have a firm foundation in Jesus Christ? Seek God and study the word of God because our foundation is predicated on the word of God. God is not slack concerning His promises for our heavenly Father has a plan for our life that will give us an expected end. If you worry about situations in your life read Matthews 6:34. If uncertainty overtakes you, read Jeremiah 29:11.

You may design your blueprint for your life but seek God to see if you are in His will for your life. Our heavenly Father knows our thoughts, actions, and the paths that we will take in life. If one deviates from the blueprint that God has ordained for you, know that all things work together for our good, and remember that God chastens those who He loves.

**Prayer: Heavenly Father, thank you for my life blueprint. Help me to seek you daily so that I may align my heart, mind, and spirit endeavoring to do your will and not my own. Amen.**

**Sharon Smith**

## DAY 214

# TIME OF REST

> *There remains, then, a Sabbath-rest for the people of God; for anyone who enters God's rest also rests from their works, just as God did from his. Hebrews 4:9-10*

Do you ever take the time to relax by reading, writing, or simply to reflect with no interruptions? Most individuals that relax by these means are taking the time to restore themselves. Restoration is essential in order to be able to continue on a journey. If an individual continues to work without a break, the result could be a physical and mental crash.

When Jesus Christ was on earth, He always found time to rest, so that He could be prepared mentally and physically for the journey He was on. During Jesus' time of relaxation, He spent time with God, in order to build a closer relationship with Him, and to be strengthened for the journey ahead. Jesus understood that His purpose called for moments of restoration, especially after consistently ministering to people, feeding individuals spiritually and naturally, and supporting the disciples through spiritual development. Jesus was intentional about praying and spending time alone with God for restoration.

Are you intentional about your natural as well as spiritual restoration? Do you spend time alone with God through prayer and meditation? It is indeed necessary to recharge for the spiritual journey ahead.

**Brittany Rudolph-Montgomery**

# DAY 215

## SALT OF THE EARTH

> *Ye are the salt of the earth: but if the salt has lost his savor, wherewith shall it be salted? It is thenceforth good for nothing, but to be cast out, and to be trodden under foot of men. Matthew 5:13*

In nature, salt is ineffective unless it is exposed to elements or substances that it can influence or change. Salt usually changes everything that it comes into contact with. If it contacts metal, the metal will corrode. If it is exposed to meat or vegetables, the flavor changes. If it is dissolved in water, the water ceases to be H2O. Neutrality is not the characteristic of salt. It is a change agent. Salt can lose its savor if it is significantly diluted or polluted.

Salt is best kept in a container. We are the container, salt shaker, or box. However, salt in the shaker has greater utility. Shake a little here, a little there, and a little everywhere. Salt in the box has no chance of exposure, and no opportunity to be an influencer. The Lord wants Christians to become change agents in this manner. We are expected to be a positive influence on those that we encounter.

If I can help somebody know that he is going wrong, then my living shall not be in vain. If I can help somebody as I travel along this way, then my living will not be in vain (Mahalia Jackson).

James Thomas

# DAY 216

# A REST THAT REMAINS

> *There remaineth therefore a rest to the people of God. Hebrews 4:9*

Many of our fore parents lived during the difficult time of "sharecropping." Landowners would "hire" poor people to labor on their farms from sunup to sun-down, Monday through Saturday. On Sundays, they were given a day to "rest." Early on Monday morning, laborers were taken back to the fields to harvest more crops. Day after day, they worked for a small percentage of what they deserved. This process continued until the end of the harvest season. Workers were paid only a few dollars and given a bushel of peas or beans as their wages. In addition, they were given the "unwanted" portions of the livestock that had been butchered during the year. Many of those weary laborers died before they experienced a real vacation; a time to rest, relax and rejuvenate before the next harvest.

Sometimes, working for Jesus may feel like "share cropping." However, at the end of our harvest season in the Lord's vineyard, there awaits a reward that lasts forever! All believers will truly rest from their labor. The grandest vacation resorts on earth with all their amenities cannot compare to the splendor of the rest that awaits believers. There is a "rest" that remains in heaven's Eternal Resort. Kingdom harvesters will truly rest from all their labor! Press on, believers! There's still another rest.

**Geraldine Russell**

# DAY 217

## BE A WARRIOR

> *Finally, my brethren, be strong in the Lord, and in the power of his might. Ephesians 6:10*

In our BC days (Before Christ), many of us may have the testimony that we were professional worriers. Maybe you worried about how you would pay the light bill or whether the car would start the next morning or whether you would have enough food to last through the week, etc. The list could go on and on.

However, after Jesus walks on the scene, there is no longer any need to worry because the control of the circumstances and situations in our lives now lies in His more than capable hands. Now that we are on the Lord's side, we can give up our title as WORRIER in exchange for the title of WARRIOR! Doesn't that feel better? We have the weapon of prayer on our side and prayer changes everything! We do not need to worry because we are not helpless anymore, but we have the greatest help we could ever have in our corner. We can, with great certainty, declare that Jesus is our help, and He gives us the strength to walk in victory over every trial and every test. We can rest in that fact daily.

**Think About It:** Will you be a worrier or a warrior today?

**Domonique Brunson**

## DAY 218

# THE BUDDY SYSTEM

> *And five of you shall chase a hundred, and an hundred of you shall put ten thousand to flight, and your enemies shall fall before you by the sword. Leviticus 26:8*

Webster defines the Buddy System as a cooperative arrangement whereby individuals are paired or teamed up assuming responsibility for one another's instruction, productivity, welfare, or safety.

The U.S. Army has what they call a "battle buddy" system. It works by having every soldier accompanied by another soldier of the same or opposite gender wherever they are. This rule is there for the protection of individual soldiers. Soldiers are extensively trained, uniformed, and fully armed. They are physically and mentally ready for battle. Their military creed states "no soldier left behind." Indeed, we are our brothers' keeper.

Jesus also has a buddy system in place for his soldiers in the army of the Lord. "And He called the twelve to Himself, and began to send them out **two by two**, and gave them power over unclean spirits." Mark 6:7

It's a two-by-two strategy. We are stronger together. There is an added impact when two or more soldiers are winning souls for the kingdom of God. So, the next time you're on the battlefield, grab a Buddy and remember Leviticus 26:8.

**Helen V. Tate**

## DAY 219

# ALONG THE WAY

> *Now the God of peace... Make you perfect in every good work to do his will, working in you that which is well pleasing in his sight, through Jesus Christ; to whom be glory for ever and ever. Amen.*
> *Hebrews 13:20-21*

I always hear people speak of pursuing destiny and purpose. I seldom hear people talk about the dark and often lonely road you must travel on your way there.

We fantasize about the result, but do not spend enough time counting the cost of preparing ourselves (mentally, socially, spiritually) for the rigors of the journey. Most people do not even have a clear picture or idea of what the journey will involve until well on their way.

I believe it is the things we learn along the way that make the difference in life. It is the things that we learn about ourselves and others, the things we learn about God, the things we learn about life and even about our place on earth that matter.

Something wonderful happens along the way. We learn, we grow, and we evolve into the individuals God has designed. Now that is powerful!

Lord, please help us to remain steadfast as You work through us. Help us to remain focused, unmovable, and resolute in Your purpose for our lives no matter the obstacles we may face. Remind us that You are always with us through every storm and trial and hold our hands and our hearts as we journey with You. Amen.

**Cheryl L. Thomas**

## DAY 220

# GOD USES WHOMEVER HE WILL

> *Behold, I have given him for a witness to the people, a leader and commander to the people. Isaiah 55:4*

Being diagnosed with what doctors described as "stubborn hypertension, I was hospitalized twice within 5½ weeks. The first hospital stay lasted seven days, in which I was given different medications to help stabilize my blood pressure and to bring my potassium up to a normal level.

After having returned home, I found that I contracted the flu and had an allergic reaction to one of the medications. The reaction caused me to break out in fine intensely itchy bumps over the majority of my body. In addition to the reaction I was experiencing, I had an accumulation of fluid in my body. Once again, I was ordered by my doctor to report to the emergency room. This visit resulted in a 5-day stay.

Three young ladies would come into my room every day when they had a break just to talk to me. Being a child of God, I would talk to them about the Lord. One of these young ladies was a young mother trying to get her life straight with the Lord. The morning before my discharge she told me how much she enjoyed talking to me. She further explained that when I talked about the Lord, chill bumps came all over her. I could only smile because God was using me to witness to this young lady, thus allowing the Lord to use me for His purpose.

**Evelyn Beachem**

## DAY 221

# TODAY IS A NEW DAY TO BEGIN AGAIN

> *Forget about what's happened; don't keep going over old history. Be alert, be present. I am about to do something brand-new. It is bursting out! Don't you see it? There it is! I'm making a road through the desert, rivers in the badlands. Isaiah 43:18-19*

How often do we go over our previous day and think about what we could have done or said differently? How often do we replay the story in our minds over and over with different variations and outcomes? Here is the fact, we cannot change it. No matter how long we linger over what we did "right" or "wrong", yesterday is done. What we can do is make better choices today. We can show more love, more patience, more gratitude, more understanding, more grace, more mercy, and more forgiveness today.

Thankfully, when we open our eyes to a new day, we have another opportunity to let the light of Jesus shine more brightly through us. The Bible says "God's loyal love couldn't have run out; his merciful love couldn't have dried up. They are created new every morning. How great your faithfulness!" (Lamentations 3:22-24) I am so grateful for his merciful love that renews daily.

**Prayer:** Lord, thank you for renewing mercy. Thank you for seeing my flaws, faults, and shortcomings and still seeing purpose and greatness in me. Thank you for not going over old history. Help me to forgive myself as quickly and completely as you do. Keep me growing in your word. May each day of renewal bring me closer to you and show the light of your love to all those I encounter. Amen!

**Lynette Whitfield**

## DAY 222

# BE WATCHFUL!

> *Be watchful, stand firm in your faith, be courageous, be strong.*
> *I Corinthians 16:13*

Spiritual watchfulness consists in watching over one's soul in a careful and circumspect manner so that no evil may befall thee. Spiritual life is a precious and desirable treasure to the believer, far excelling the entire world and all that is in it. Luke 21:36 communicates that one is to "Watch, therefore, and pray always that you may be counted worthy to escape all these things that will come to pass, and to stand before the Son of Man."

Revelation 3:1-3 "To the angel of the church of Sardis – I know your works that you have a name that you are alive, but you are dead. Be watchful, strengthen the things which remain, that are ready to die, for I have not found your works perfect before God. Remember therefore how you have received and heard; hold fast and repent. Therefore, if you will not watch, I will come upon you as a thief, and you will not know that hour I will come upon you. Be watchful so that you may live.

"Live" is defined in the context of physical and spiritual.

Your life can be taken away in a blink of an eye. Tragedies are occurring each and every day. We must be mindful for our adversary is seeking whom he may devour. One needs to stand firm in the faith, be courageous and be strong. Watch, pray, and be cognizant of the Holy Spirit operating within you.

I decree and declare that my life is in God's hand, and I stand on the word of God by watching and praying in and out of season.

Sharon Smith

# DAY 223

## SEEK OUT GODLY COUNSELORS!

> *Blessed is the man that walketh not in the counsel of the ungodly, nor standeth in the way of sinners, nor sitteth in the seat of the scornful. But his delight is in the law of the Lord. And in his law doth he meditate day and night. Psalm 1:1-2*

Happy and empowered to prosper will be the person who seeks the wisdom of a Godly mentor. Knowledge is important and it is equally as important from whence that infusion of information comes. The person who takes pleasure sitting at the feet of a wise and Godly mentor will receive, in my opinion, the best of both worlds - the carnal and the spiritual, the temporal and the eternal.

Advice, everybody has some advice these days, but the Bible teaches us that if we acknowledge God in our affairs, He will direct our pathway. Biblical history reveals through the ages that when God's people sought out His guidance and counsel, they were prosperous. When they sought the advice and guidance of other gods and those who stood in the way of sinners, they suffered His displeasure. God wants His people to seek Him for direction in navigating this life.

**They soon forgot his works; they waited not for his counsel.
Psalm 106:13**

**James Thomas**

# DAY 224

## A "BUT GOD" MOMENT

> *This is the Lord's doing! It is marvelous in our eyes!*
> Psalm 118:23

Four young people were on their way to Bethune Cookman College when they had an accident while traveling north on Interstate 95. Each had their own conflicting account of the incident. The passengers in the back seat were asleep and could not recall all the details. The driver said the car flipped 7 times.

The front seat passenger said it flipped 5 times before it landed "wheels down" onto the southbound lanes of I-95. Miraculously, they were able to scramble out of the car and push it into the median just before an eighteen wheeler whizzed by in that lane. If it had not been for the grace of God, they could have been killed. Their testimonies were not the same as the four young people that were in the SUV parked near their vehicle in the salvage yard. The yard manager stated that "No one in the SUV survived that rollover," one week earlier.

At 10:15 that same night, God moved upon the mother's heart to pray fervently for her sons. Shortly afterward, she received a call informing her that there had been an accident. All had survived with only a few cuts, bruises, and aches. God had saved her sons and their friends! When she saw what was left of her son's car, she worshiped God and rejoiced. She knew that had been a "But God" moment! Her sons are still serving God!

**Geraldine Russell**

## DAY 225

# COVERING THE FAMILY

> *The LORD bless thee, and keep thee: The LORD make his face shine upon thee, and be gracious unto thee: The LORD lift up his countenance upon thee, and give thee peace. Numbers 6:24-26*

This world that we live in has taken the concept of love and twisted it into so many different shapes and forms that it is almost unrecognizable from God's original intent. The best reflection of real love can be found, though, in the Word of God. 1 John 4:8 tells us that God is love, so Who better to tell us what love is than the One Who embodies it?

There is No One Greater! And one area of our lives that requires our utmost love and prayer is with our families. We all have some family members we are close to and some with whom we are a bit distant. We have those whom we talk to all the time and those whom we share a few words with every now and then. No matter what the relationship looks like, the fact remains that as believers, we are still called to love and pray for them.

Many of our family members are going through situations we can personally do nothing about except place them in God's hands. When we cover our families in prayer, we show them how much we truly desire their well-being and God's best for them.

**Think About It:** How can you cover your family in prayer today?

**Domonique Brunson**

# DAY 226

# SOUL WINNER'S DECLARATION

**Hear Ye, Hear Ye! I hereby make the following declarations:**

**I decree and I declare!**
That I am a witness for the Lord according to Isaiah 43:10

**I decree and I declare!**
That Holy Spirit has endowed me with the wisdom needed to win a soul According to Proverbs 11:30

**I decree and I declare!**
That I am the salt of the earth, and a light unto the world according to St. Matthew 5:13 & 16

**I decree and I declare!**
That I will lead many to righteousness. With wisdom I will shine with the brightness of heaven
According to Daniel 12:3

**I decree and I declare!**
That I will allow the Fruit of the Spirit to be evident in me at all times
According to Galatians 5:22-23

**I decree and I declare!**
That I will minister from the command of "Go and Compel" according to St. Luke 14:23

**I decree and I declare!**
That I will convert a sinner from the error of his ways, thus saving his soul from death According to James 5:20

**I am fully aware that**
Winning souls is the process of evangelizing or witnessing, communicating the message f salvation to unbelievers.

**Therefore, I decree, and I declare that I am a soul winner!**

Helen V. Tate

## DAY 227

# FIGHT ON!

> *Fight the good fight of the faith. Take hold of the eternal life to which you were called and about which you made the good confession in the presence of many witnesses. 1 Timothy 6:12*

What do you do when you are tired? You have fought a good battle, but you know you are not done. It seems as if the fight is gone out of you, and you do not feel you have any strength left. It is often so easy to tell others to fight on, but what do you do when it is you who is seemingly left without any energy?

As much as we sometimes hate to admit it, sometimes we are left depleted and burned out. We have run so hard toward our goal that when we can finally see the ribbon clinging to the finish line our strength wanes.

How can we get so close that we "see" the finish line and still faint? How could we have endured so much, run so far, and worked so hard only to give up before obtaining the prize? I know you are tired. I know it seems like you have been running forever. I know you are weak and just ready to see the light of day. But I want to encourage you today to never give up until you receive your reward.

You see, it does not make sense to go through everything you have had to go through, to fight and win all the battles you've encountered along the way to just throw in the towel in the 11th hour. You have gone through too much to give up. You have endured too many struggles to walk away.

If you are on this road and "see" your finish line seemingly mocking you in the distance, somewhere deep inside of yourself you must find the strength and courage to fight on.

Victory is within your grasp. Reach again.

**Cheryl L. Thomas**

# DAY 228

# UNITY

> *Behold, how good and pleasant it is when brethren dwell together in unity. Psalm 133:1*

The word *unity* is defined as being able to work with, live with, and worship the Lord together in peace, love, and joy. It is being of one mind and spirit and being on one accord. We are told in God's Word that there is strength when we can worship God in peace and love. When we fail to dwell together in unity, we allow Satan to come in and bring about confusion. Therefore, we miss out on being in true fellowship with the Lord because God tells us in His Word that He is not the author of confusion.

Having unity among the household of faith does not require that we agree on everything, and on matters that are based on religious issues. However, on fundamental concepts, we should reserve subordinate matters in order to make room for different viewpoints. In all these things, there should and must be a spirit of love.

As individuals, we are all different, but that should not prevent us from working together. We may disagree as long as we continue to be agreeable and motivated by love. Always remember that we are not enemies. The real enemies of unity are jealousy, grudges, backbiting, and lovelessness. We should always strive for unity and not division.

**Abba Father, please help us to dwell with one another in unity. In Jesus' name, we pray. Amen.**

**Evelyn Beachem**

# DAY 229

# IT STARTS WITH A THOUGHT

> *Summing it all up, friends, I'd say you'll do best by filling your minds and meditating on things true, noble, reputable, authentic, compelling, gracious—the best, not the worst; the beautiful, not the ugly; things to praise, not things to curse. Put into practice what you learned from me, what you heard and saw and realized. Do that, and God, who makes everything work together, will work you into his most excellent harmonies. Philippians 4:8-9*

Life and death are in the tongue, but before it reaches your lips it starts in your mind. Our habits, behaviors, and attitudes are born in the mind, which stems from the thoughts that we entertain. Isn't it amazing that we can literally change our life by changing our thoughts? What we focus on (thoughts), we give life. I do not know about you, but I want to breathe life into great things. Health, financial prosperity, spiritual growth, close knit family, the works. Refer to Proverbs 23:7 where it says, "For as he thinks within himself, so he is."

It does not get much clearer than that! What we think about strongly influences what we will become. But what about all those negative thoughts that bombard me daily? Well, we cannot change our thoughts without God's help. Afterall, the mind is a battlefield. To combat the negative, we must fill our minds with the good. It is the only way to flush out the bad. We must guard our eyes and ears by filtering what we watch, hear, and with whom we keep company. God will honor our desire to please him and will give us the strength to keep our minds focused and filled with right thinking.

Prayer: Thank you Lord for giving us the ability to change our life with our thoughts. Help us to fill our minds with good and pleasing things to you. Remind us to redirect our thoughts to you when they begin to drift. Remind us that a negative situation and circumstance can begin to shift in a positive direction when we focus on you. Help me to surrender my thoughts to you. Amen!

Lynette Whitfield

# DAY 230

# WASTED TIME

> *So, then, be careful how you live. Do not be unwise but wise, making the best use of your time because the times are evil.*
> *Ephesians 5: 15 – 16*

Time management is the process of planning and exercising conscious control of the time spent on specific activities especially to increase effectiveness, efficiency, and productivity. Organize your time intelligently so that you use it more effectively. There are only 24 hours in a day. Can you account for every second, minute, or hour of your day? If you were to keep a journal of your daily activities, would you find that you have spent time doing useless or unnecessary things that could be considered a waste of time? Wasteful is defined as consuming, spending, or employing useless or without adequate return, using to no avail or profit, or squandering. God was not wasteful.

Ephesians 5:15 -16, states that we are to be wise, making the best use of our time. Perform a self-examination on giving God what is due to Him. God does not like waste because time is precious, and life is precious. Time is a blessing from God, and you must engage your time profitably to maximize your life. Minimize waste in any area of your life and you will surely begin to experience a spiritual turnaround in your life.

We spend time building relationships horizontally but what about our vertical relationship with our Lord and Savior Jesus Christ. How much time do you spend reverencing God daily? We are to pray without ceasing. Time is precious, and life is precious. Give God what is due unto Him.

Heavenly Father, forgive me for wasting time in my life on my endeavors. Help me to see areas of wasted time; thereby enabling me to maximize my destiny as ordained. Amen

Sharon Smith

## DAY 231

# STANDING ON HIS PROMISE!

> *And being not weak in faith, he considered not his own body now dead, when he was about a hundred years old, neither yet the deadness of Sarah's womb: he staggered not at the promise of God through unbelief, but was strong in faith, giving glory to God; and being fully persuaded that, what he had promised, he was able to perform. Romans 4: 19-21*

*Standing on the Promises* is a gospel song that always seems to refresh my spiritual resolve. Part of the lyrics start like this: "Standing on the promises of Christ my King, listening every moment to the Spirit's call; resting in my Savior as my all and all, standing on the promises of God…" The story of Abraham as described here should add muscle to every believer's faith. Faith grows bigger when it is exercised, just as our body muscles grow bigger when exercised.

Consider Abraham's faith dilemma. God made the promise to him when he was 75 years old. After 25 years of waiting on the promised child, the Bible says that he staggered not at the promise of God with unbelief. It is amazing, he considered not his own body, now being dead. He continued to believe that someday, someway, and somehow, that what God had spoken, He was able to make it good. We too must learn to see beyond the physical and the natural systems and trust God's power to perform the supernatural.

**James Thomas**

## DAY 232

# RELEVANT FOREVER

> For ever, O LORD, thy word is settled in heaven. Psalm 119:89

The "great falling away" from God's Word is evident across the world. People who once believed God's Word was the ultimate authority in all human affairs are now bowing under pressures. Many are beginning to compromise the Word to appease people that are not fully surrendered to God. Some surmise that because God is loving, kind, longsuffering and compassionate, He will allow them to become self-indulgent without fear of consequences. They make excuses for behaviors they know are unacceptable. Many continue to move the "stakes of righteousness" in a futile attempt to validate their wayward behaviors. However, when God penned the commandments, there was never a need for "century-updates". His Holy Word is settled forever!

Times, seasons, ages and people will change. However, God's holy principles will never change! It may be challenging to maintain a "holy" life in the midst of this increasingly ungodly world, but it **is** possible. When Jesus ascended on high, He sent the Holy Spirit back into the world to empower all believers to live and do as Jesus commanded. If it were not so, He would have emailed believers by now. Therefore, it is time to gird up the loins of our minds and recommit to God's commands, because His Word is settled in Heaven both now and forever!

**Geraldine Russell**

# DAY 233

# BORN IS THE KING

*And she shall bring forth a son, and thou shalt call his name JESUS: for he shall save his people from their sins. Matthew 1:21*

Each day, my heart is just humbled more and more that a God so high above us would come down so low just to save us...to save me. The fact that he would even consider taking on this flesh that we walk and suffer with every day just so He could understand this life is just beyond me. And because of that, I want to share a favorite Christmas lyric from the hymn, "O Come All Ye Faithful." The song says "...Come and behold Him, born the King of Angels."

Why? Well, every time I sing it, I picture the swaddled Baby Jesus and all those who gathered around Him in worship. I put myself right in the middle of the crowd, gazing at someone Who was BORN A KING! Nobody else can say that. Sure, they may have become king at young ages, but Jesus is the only one who was born as a king and STILL sits on the Throne to this day. And even more special is the fact that He did not grow up to wear a crown of gold, but a crown of thorns, making Him the reigning King. That makes Him royalty and so am I!

**Think About It:** When was the last time you reverenced the King?

Domonique Brunson

## DAY 234

## LOST AND FOUND

> *I say unto you, that likewise, joy shall be in heaven over one sinner that repenteth, more than over ninety and nine just persons, which need no repentance. Luke 15:7*

Have you ever lost something that you deemed valuable, leaving you with feelings of despair, bewilderment, or panic? Whatever you deem valuable, will determine the intensity of your search and recovery efforts. In St. Luke Chapter 15, we read of three losses that were of the utmost importance to their owners. The parables of the lost sheep, the lost coin, and the lost son.

What exactly led up to these losses? Regardless of the circumstances that led to these losses, the heart of the Father is such that he is "not willing that any should perish, but that all should come to repentance." (2 Peter 3:9b) It is important that we recognize the value of lost souls.

In the eyes of the owners, each was unique in purpose, part of a whole, irreplaceable, and deemed priceless. The owner's search was relentless. Their recovery efforts, victorious. Let us be diligent and relentless in our search and recovery efforts for those that are lost. Souls are priceless!

**Helen V. Tate**

# DAY 235

# LOVE WINS

> *Unto the angel of the church of Ephesus write; These things saith he that holdeth the seven stars in his right hand, who walketh in the midst of the seven golden candlesticks; I know thy works, and thy labour...Nevertheless I have somewhat against thee, because thou hast left thy first love. Revelation 2:1-5*

**Frozen. Immobilized. Stuck.**
These words depict the state of the American church. We are stuck. We have not had much forward progress in a long time. Now do not get me wrong, we are having service. As a matter of fact, we are having more services than we have ever had.

Often, we are so busy in our efforts to save and disciple a lost generation that we forget the LOVE that brought us in. We only need to retrace our steps to that moment when God's love overshadowed our lives and changed our hearts. That is the same love God requires us to walk in everyday as we seek to serve Him.

We will not draw the world with our power or our eloquent words. God draws them by the overwhelming might of His love! Let us share the LOVE that won us!

*Lord, help us not forget the reason we serve You. Help us to always be mindful that it was Your incredible love for us that drew us out of a sinful life to a glorious life where we are accepted as Your sons and daughters. As we go about our daily lives, help us to model and exemplify that same love to others. Amen.*

Cheryl L. Thomas

# DAY 236

# IMITATING GOD

> *Be imitators of God, as beloved children. And walk in love as Christ loved and gave himself up for us, as a fragrant offering and sacrifice to God. Ephesians 5: 1-2*

When our daughter was about 3 years old, we noticed that she picked up many things and habits from us. We thought it was cute until one day she decided to imitate her father and shave her soft, clear face.

We were unaware that she had slipped into the hall bathroom, lathered her face with soap, and began to shave. For the first few seconds, our daughter was okay. Suddenly, we heard a shrill cry of pain. She had cut her face and blood began to form on her face. My husband and I both ran to the bathroom and were sorely distressed. Thanks be to God, there was only a small scratch, just enough to sting and cause a little blood to form on her face. Nevertheless, the scar remains on her face even to this day. We never had to worry about that imitation, again.

Children are great at absorbing and copying others, but that incident reminds me that we too are called to be imitators, as well. As we observe the characteristics of our Lord and Savior, Jesus Christ, through our study of the scriptures, and the way that Jesus responded to those around Him, we begin to pick up God's habits and mannerisms. He has formed a new spirit in me, one of love, sacrifice, and forgiveness.

**I declare and decree that I am an imitator of God, as one of His beloved children. I declare and decree that I also walk in love as Christ loved and gave Himself up for us, as a fragrant offering and sacrifice to God. Amen.**

**Evelyn Beachem**

# DAY 237

# STAGNATION

> *It will come about at that time That I will search Jerusalem with lamps, And I will punish the men Who are stagnant in spirit, who say in their hearts, The Lord will not do good or evil!*
> *Zephaniah 1:12 (NASB)*

Zephaniah stated that spiritually stagnant people are those who don't care because they think God doesn't care. People become stagnant when they isolate themselves from God and stop responding to the needs of others. That is when spiritual decay sets in. Spiritual decay also smells because sin stinks in the nostrils of God. We sometimes think that managing the status quo is good enough. Some take the merry-go round approach to church.

It's as if everyone keeps moving with the flashing lights shining bright as they listen to happy music without complaints. Some even try the "don't rock the boat" approach. They think that if we all remain very still in the boat, it won't turn over; but it also won't go anywhere. We must move beyond entertainment into engaging Christ's mission.

What we need to move us from ruts to routine is a transformational mindset and clarity of focus that comes from finding the grace of God more enthralling and exciting than anything else.

Heavenly Father, please search my heart and wash my spirit in your word so that I will not become complacent nor stagnant in my spirit. In Jesus' name, I pray. Amen

**Sharon Smith**

## DAY 238

# THE PRICE OF INTEGRITY!

> *So went Satan from the presence of the Lord, and smote Job with sore boils from the sole of his foot unto his crown... Then said his wife unto him, Dost thy still retain thine integrity? curse God, and die. Job 2: 7-10*

Integrity is defined as the quality of being honest and having a strong moral principle. Not so many years ago, I recalled that in our culture, a man's word was his bond, his yea was yea, and his nay was nay, a handshake, and the deal was sealed. Oh, what a change! Since 1990, it has become popular to have an accountability partner. This is another person who coaches and follows up to make sure you keep your commitments.

The Bible says that Job was a perfect and upright man. He did not need a coach to keep his commitment to his God, even though Satan had stripped him of all his health and wealth. The final kick in the gut was when Job's wife said to him, "Dost thou still retain thine integrity? Curse God and die." Many are the temptations and afflictions of the righteous, but God will deliver us out of them all. Integrity is described as what a person will do when he thinks no one is looking. Job was not a sellout.

What is the price of your integrity? Will it be financial gain, power, and fame? What would you give in exchange for your soul?

**James Thomas**

# DAY 239

# JESUS WEPT!

> *For we have not an high priest which cannot be touched with the feeling of our infirmities; but was in all points tempted like as we are, yet without sin. Hebrews 4:15*

As Lazarus lay dying, his grieving sisters wondered if Jesus would arrive in time to heal him of his sickness. However, he did not get there until Lazarus had been buried and began to mortify. As Jesus approached the tomb of Lazarus, He allowed Himself to feel the depth of human sorrow. He wept with Mary, Martha and the mourners gathered at the tomb. After His moment of grief, He demonstrated His power over death by raising Lazarus from the dead. Can you imagine the joy that filled all those that witnessed His miraculous power? That was further proof that Jesus was the Son of God.

Death and dying are all around. Sorrow is flooding every community. Many are wondering if Jesus will "stay" the spread of the virus that has taken the lives of millions. Some people may be wondering if Jesus cares. The response is, *"Yes, Jesus cares about everything that is happening in our world and in our lives."* Because He was fully human, Jesus experienced all of the emotions known to humankind. He gives us permission to sorrow, but not as those who have no hope. He feels the sorrow that so many are experiencing. He hears, sees and feels every tear that falls from a believer's eyes. He sends divine comfort to all who will call upon His name. Jesus promised that sorrows would be turned into joy. He promised that one day He will wipe all tears from our eyes. Jesus promised that He will never leave or forsake His people! He knows what it means to weep over the loss of a loved one.

He knows what it means to be separated from His Father. He knows what believers are enduring! Jesus knows it all! He feels it all! He sees it all! And He's listening for your heart's call! Yes, He cares!

**Heavenly Father, I place my grief at your feet. Thank you for being my High Priest that feels what I feel. Send your comfort to my family, friends and loved ones as we walk through the valley of sorrow. Take my hand, Precious Lord! Amen.**

Geraldine Russell

# DAY 240

# THE PERFECT SEASONING

> *Let your speech be always with grace, seasoned with salt, that ye may know how ye ought to answer every man. Colossians 4:6*

The thermostat of *respect* for people has been modified to fit a person's own values. Some people believe that only a select few should be respected. This attitude has caused many to categorize people into various groups. When some groups are engaged, disrespect and harsh treatment seem to flow easily. With others, it takes a lot to cause those same people to become agitated.

Consequently, many innocent people have endured unjust treatment. God, in His infinite wisdom, foreknew that times like this would come and inspired Colossians 4:6 to be recorded. He did not categorize people into *"respect"* and *"non-respect"* groups. He commands all speech to be seasoned with the salt of *"grace."* When we approach issues with *grace*, the unmerited favor of God will be demonstrated.

Throughout Paul's missionary journeys, he endured intense persecution. However, he controlled his emotions in such a way that even his enemies knew that he was a follower of Jesus. He took the *seasoning of grace* into and out of his troubles. As a result, he is classified as the world's greatest missionary. His commitment to God commanded respect from the paupers to the king's palace.

How hard is it for you to gauge your temperament when you are treated unjustly or disrespectfully? Pray now for self-control because emotional temperatures are rising.

**Lord, help me to be seasoned with the salt of** grace.

**Geraldine Russell**

# DAY 241

# THE SAFE SIDE OF FAITH

> *Lord, I believe, help thou mine unbelief. Mark 9:42*

The majority of my life I've been living on the "safe side of faith." Just what is that you ask? It's where you "try" to live by faith but hold something back "just in case."

Just in case of what you ask? Just in case things do not work out quite like you planned. You see, after living through several disappointments, I just found it easier to "brace" myself.

I braced myself so I would not get hurt - again. But it never worked. Why? Because life happens to everyone and hurt, and pain are inevitable. We can either deal with the pain of things not working out according to our plan or we can deal with the pain of living isolated and imprisoned by fear.

I thought I could be my own shield. But now I know God is our only shield. And when He chooses to not shield us from the pain of life, He is the best safe place and shelter ever. I now know that true faith does not have a "safe side." It is all or nothing. We either believe or we do not.

When life throws a painful curveball, we know that our heavenly Father is there to catch us and love us back to health.

**Lord, help us to release our worries, anxieties, and cares daily to You. We know you know what is best for us. In the times we want to believe, but the "past" threatens our faith, help us hold on to Your faithfulness and love for us. Amen.**

**Cheryl L. Thomas**

# DAY 242

## CLEANING THE CLUTTER OF YOUR MIND

> *Wherefore gird up the loins of our mind, be sober, and hope to the end, for the grace that is to be brought unto you, at the coming of Jesus Christ. I Peter 1:13*

Every year, around this time, I begin to see the need to take down, put up, and pack different items in boxes to take to Goodwill, hoping that there will be something in these boxes that will prove to be beneficial to someone in the upcoming year. As I get rid of multiple items, I pack other items in neat piles so that the closets and other locations throughout the house will not appear to be cluttered.

My mind began to reflect on the Christian walk with God and how from time to time, we need to check our hearts, minds, souls, and spirits to pray to the Lord to help us remove all the negative aspects of our hearts that will only cause confusion, tensions, and negative thoughts among the household of faith, thus creating a comfortable place for Satan to set up camp. These attitudes will only hinder the works of Christ and hinder souls from being saved.

As saints go out into a hostile world, Christians can sometimes become rattled and confused in times of persecution. Always remember that a girded mind is strong, composed, and ready for action. A girded mind will keep you prepared for action.

Dear Heavenly Father, help me to gird up the loins of my mind, and to be sober so that I may be prepared to go about my daily activities. Amen

**Evelyn Beachem**

# DAY 243

## DO YOU UNDERSTAND?

> *Trust in the LORD with all your heart; do not depend on your own understanding. Proverbs 3:5*

Sometimes in life, we feel that we can conquer anything that crosses our path. Sometimes we live a life based on our intellect and if the outcome appears to be positive, we feel justified in how we felt and how we responded to the outcome.

Have you ever asked yourself, that even if the outcome was positive, was it pleasing to the Lord? Automatically, if the result or results were negative, we would reply that it was not pleasing to the Lord. However, I often wonder how many blessings have been delayed or denied because I leaned upon my own understanding. Note that a positive outcome does not necessarily mean that the Lord is pleased with the result. Isaiah 55:8-9 states, "For My thoughts are not your thoughts, neither are your ways. My ways, *declares the LORD*. For as the heavens are higher than the earth, so My ways are higher than your ways and My thoughts than your thoughts".

Do you take the time to pray and ask the Lord to lead and guide you in the right direction? Or, are you too busy thinking about what you know about the situation? Do you take the time to consult God's Holy Word for guidance? "Trust in the Lord with all your heart; do not depend on your own understanding."

**Prayer: Dear Heavenly Father, forgive me for relying upon my intellect. Please lead and guide me according to the Word. In Jesus' name. Amen**

**Sharon Smith**

# DAY 244

# THIEF ON THE LOOSE!

> *The thief cometh, not but for to steal, and to kill and to destroy. I am come that you might have life and that they might have it more abundantly. I am the good shepherd, the good shepherd giveth his life for the sheep. John 10:10-11*

Jesus declared I am the door or entrance to the sheepfold. It is by him and him alone. This door is the entrance to all the blessings of the Kingdom, salvation, peace of mind, family relationships, health, wealth, rich and long productive lives, job security, and prosperity. Everything that pertains to abundant living in this world is found through this door!

The enemy of our faith, the thief, the robber, that Jesus warned the believers about is making his presence felt. He comes to steal every ounce of faith that you have been given, that God will keep his promise to you. God said that he wants us to prosper. So, get up, go prosper, and make it happen. The Bible says that he wants you to be in good health, get up and do the things to be healthy. He wants you to have an abundant life; well, resolve to settle for nothing less. Put feet and muscle to your faith and watch things happen for you and your family. The just shall live by their faith. Stop the steal by believing and achieving!

**And I say unto you, ask and it shall be given unto you; seek and ye shall find, knock, and it shall be opened unto you. Luke 11:9**

**James Thomas**

# DAY 245

# ONE SIZE FITS ALL

> *By grace are ye saved through faith; and that not of yourselves: it is the gift of God. Ephesians 2:8*

Many department stores carry a line of clothing with a label that says, "One size fits all." The company wants as many shoppers as possible to purchase the item without the fear of it being too small or too large. Even so, many shoppers would prefer an item that fits their individual physique. Many buy items that are made especially for them. Some hire their own designer and seamstress. They want outfits that are one-of-a-kind and uniquely designed. Some would never purchase a one size fits all outfit!

Ephesians 2:8 says, *"By grace are ye saved through faith; and that not of yourselves: it is the gift of God."* It doesn't matter who a person is or his/her economic status, the "grace" of God fits that individual's case. Large or small, rich or poor, famous or not famous, believer or non-believer, God's grace is tailor-made to fit each person's physique (each case) when faith is activated.

Is there anyone you know that the enemy has ravished and it seems like there is no hope of deliverance? If so, that person is tailor-made for the grace of God. Grace is designed to fit every situation known to man. The grace of God covers every sin, every rebellion, every unbelief, through faith in the finished work of Jesus Christ. When Jesus died for the sins of man, He reconciled mankind back to the Father. That dispensation of "grace" has been designed and extended to all men. It fits all - large and small!

Heavenly Father, thank You for Your grace. When I sin against You, Your grace covers me and draws me into Your loving arms of forgiveness. Your grace is so amazing!
Thank You, Lord! Amen.

Geraldine Russell

# DAY 246

# GOD'S PROMISE

> *I will never leave thee, nor forsake thee. Hebrews 13:5*

We truly live in the type of world where it seems that there is always something else happening, even if there is nothing new under the sun. The news and the internet do their best to shock us with the latest updates and catastrophes, right? However, we should not be surprised by any of these things because we live in a fallen world where the enemy is running rampant and trying all he knows how to distract the people of God. That is his job, after all. But I am so glad that God left a promise with us that He may allow bad things to happen, but He will always be with us through it all, no matter what.

He is definitely a promise keeper! Bad things may still happen because we are born into a sinful nature and people will do what they want to do (we all know that!). However, our God will be there in the good times and the bad. We never have to worry about Him keeping His promises because He has never failed! So, I challenge you to remember that God is with you when you experience any situation that seems a little rough. We expect that life may not always be "peaches and cream", but we also expect that our God will be with us always!

**Think About It:** What promise from God do you need to be reminded of?

Domonique Brunson

## DAY 247

# STRUGGLED STARTS

> *Fear not, for I am with you; be not dismayed, for I am your God; I will strengthen you, I will help you, I will uphold you with my righteous right hand. Isaiah 41:10*

Starting is never easy. Typically, you do not have everything you need. You are scared that you will not succeed, and it seems as if all eyes are on you... Waiting, watching, counting the days to see if you can really pull it off.

What if it does not work out like you planned? What if you were wrong? What if, what if, what if?

The real question we should be asking ourselves is, what if we are right! What if it does work? What if it goes better than anything we could have ever imagined? Instead of looking for the bad things that could happen, why not look for the great things that God has promised instead?

We must change the way we think if we are ever going to change the way we live. So, you are starting out with only a vision and a prayer. That is all God needs to multiply it into a full-fledged multi-billion-dollar enterprise.

He is not asking you to have everything in place. He does not even expect you to. That is why He is there. He has everything you need. If you need provision for the vision... He's got it. If you need people to walk the vision out... He has got them too. If you need faith to conquer your doubts, He's got you covered. Remember the mustard seed?

No matter how small your mustard seed of faith is, that is all God needs to move the mountain of fear, doubt, and anxiety from you. You are His child. And God always takes care of His own.

**Cheryl L. Thomas**

# DAY 248

# I SURRENDER ALL

> *Love the Lord your God with all your heart, with all your soul, and with all your mind. Matthews 22:37*

Surrendering all to God means to yield up, transmit and entrust. A believer completely gives up his own will and subjects his thoughts, ideas, and deeds to the will and teaching of our Lord and Savior Jesus Christ.

How strong of a hold do your possessions have on you? If faced with the loss of something valuable to you, how resistant would you be to living without it? When everything inside you is saying you cannot do this or get through it – remember that Jesus Christ surrendered all. He surrendered Himself to the Father's will and purpose.

Surrendering all is about one's relationship with Christ. Communicate to Jesus Christ your desire to be free from worry and the cares of this life. There is no one-stop way to surrender to God, it is a daily moment-by-moment choice to give it to God. It is a continual work in progress. If you love Jesus and truly desire to be an ambassador for Him, then surrender and trust the one who is Alpha and Omega (beginning and the end)?

Let go of preconceived ideas about how things should be and rest in the wisdom of greater Divine power. Let go of what, how, when, and who. Let go of how we think things must be and allow Jesus to oversee our life. We are not meant to keep certain parts back but surrender our whole life to Him in an act of obedience and complete trust.

Prayer: Heavenly Father, help me to surrender my will to thy will. Help me to not yield or surrender to the cares of this life to others but unto my Heavenly Father. Amen

Sharon Smith

## DAY 249

# WHAT DOES GOD REQUIRE OF ME?

> *He hath showed thee, O man, what is good; and what does the Lord require of thee, but to do justly, and to love mercy, and to walk humbly with thy God? Micah 6:8*

In a world with so many choices and so many voices, information, and misinformation, where do you turn for a less complicated way? As a young Christian, trying to navigate what all the dos and don'ts, the cans and the can'ts were, I became spiritually traumatized and made the false choice to just climb into my spiritual bubble. That bubble consisted of going to work, going home, going to church, reading my Bible, and going to sleep.

That was my daily routine. I was intent on not making any mistakes that would keep me out of heaven. There is a saying for this way of thinking, "I became so heaven bound that I was no earthly good." When I read and understood Micah 6:8, it was liberating, eye-opening, and burden lifting. "These things have I written unto you that believe on the name of the Son of God; that ye may know that ye have eternal life…" (I John 5: 13-14). These two scriptures were immensely helpful in freeing me from my self-imposed religious bubble. Perhaps they will help you find your way home also!

**May your Word alone be our guiding light as we weigh the value of all the voices and choices that engulf our world daily.**

**James Thomas**

# DAY 250

# THE "GO-TELL-IT" SYNDROME

> *Then said Jesus unto them, "Be not afraid: go tell my brethren that they go into Galilee, and there shall they see me.*
> *Matthew 28:10*

While observing a six-year-old boy and his four-and-a-half-year-old sister interact, it was clear that she liked to tattle. Every few minutes she would come running to her aunt trying to explain what her brother had done. She wanted him to get in trouble each time she brought a report. On one occasion, before she could finish her report, the aunt asked her to give an account of her own behavior which caused her brother's response.

She stopped in the middle of her exclamation and said, "But, I didn't do nothing!" She got teary-eyed and continued to explain why her brother was the one in trouble. Her aunt talked to her about becoming a "tattletale." Afterward, she returned to the room and had a pointed discussion with her brother about his behavior, not hers. The exchange was hilarious. She acted so innocent, and she litigated her case well. A few moments later, they were laughing, running, playing, and squabbling again.

Can you imagine the squabbling and finger-pointing Jesus' disciples may have experienced after they abandoned him to be crucified? Fear had gripped each one because they had not understood the real Plan of Redemption. When Jesus met the women while they ran to tell the news of the empty tomb, He told them to go and tell His disciples that He would meet them face-to-face in Galilee. Bubbling over with joy, they ran to tell His disciples the good news of seeing Jesus alive and well!

As this world continues to spiral out of control, we must develop a "Go-Tell-It" syndrome. Let's go tell the world that "He has risen, just as He said He would!" He will meet believers in their own "Galilee." He will speak peace to their fears and empower them with the Holy Spirit which will lead and guide them until they see Him face-to-face in all His glory!

**Geraldine Russell**

# DAY 251

## LOVE'S PURE LIGHT

> *And she brought forth her firstborn son, and wrapped him in swaddling clothes, and laid him in a manger. Luke 2:7*

I love this season of the year because it inspires a time of reflection and it is also a time when some of the most beautiful songs ever created are sung, songs that specifically celebrate the birth of our Lord and Savior Jesus Christ. One lyric that particularly blesses me from "Silent Night" is "Son of God, love's pure light…" We honor Jesus as the Son of God, but at Christmas, we remember that He came to earth as an actual human baby and that seems to really drive home for me that He came to me…to be like me…so He could save me…from me!

That intent to save me from myself is love's purest light because real love comes to make you better and shine a light on what needs to be done to get you there. I am so grateful that Jesus was truly Lord from birth and the grace He brought with Him redeemed all of mankind. That silent night so long ago was silent, not because there was no sound, but because the sound of the Blessed Baby crying was the most awe-inspiring and humbling sound ever heard. Allow your heart to stand in awe when you remember Jesus.

**Think About It:** Where in your life do you need God's pure light to shine?

**Domonique Brunson**

## DAY 252

# HERE'S TO THE FUTURE

> *Trust in the Lord with all your heart, and do not lean on your own understanding. In all your ways acknowledge him, and he will make straight your paths. Proverbs 3:5-6*

Many years ago, there was a song with a refrain that said, "My future is so bright, I've got to wear shades." I absolutely loved that song. It kept in the forefront of my thinking the wonderful things God had prepared for me.

I loved reflecting on what He'd promised. I would daydream for hours thinking of what it would feel like to walk in my purpose, my promise, and my destiny. It fed my spirit and soothed my soul.

So, when days are dark and my promise seems so far away, I reflect on that song and the promise it bears. When disappointment knocks, I think of a faithful God who has never failed in producing. I think of all the times He has come through in my life and look happily forward to the fulfillment of every dream and every promise.

My future is still bright. As long as God is on the throne, it forever will be. Even in dark times, our future shines brightly. Even when we can't see the way, we only need to remember that Jesus is the way. He'll make good on every promise.

I'm excited about my future. I do believe it's time to pull out the shades!

**Cheryl L. Thomas**

# DAY 253

# CHECK YOUR MOTIVES

> *All the ways of a man are clean in his own sight. But the Lord weighs the motives. Proverbs 16:2*

Motives may be defined as a reason for doing something, especially one that is hidden or not obvious. There are various examples given throughout the bible where God lets us know that we must examine our motives.

For example, prayer, giving to the poor and fasting are activities encouraged throughout the Bible, but Jesus underscores that God will not reward those who do them for selfish reasons (Matt 6:1 – 18). Another example is baptism by water. It can be undermined by one who submits to it but is not inwardly changed. (Romans 2: 5-29, Matt. 3: 7 – 8) One must be extremely cautious in deducing others' motives merely by observing their actions. For instance, Jesus rebukes the disciples for jumping to inappropriate conclusions about people and their deeds after observing only their actions (Matt. 26: 6 -13).

You may think what you are doing is good but if your motives are not right the deed is dead. Selfish motives can hinder one's prayers. We can operate from a variety of motivations. For example, pride, anger, revenge, a sense of entitlement, or the desire for approval can all be catalysts for our actions. God sees what no one else sees. He knows why we do what we do and desires to reward those whose hearts are right toward him (I Cor 4:5) We can keep our motives pure by continually surrendering every part of our hearts to the control of the Holy Spirit.

**Prayer:** Heavenly Father, help me to constantly evaluate my motives and help me to be honest with myself about why I am choosing to carry out a certain action. Amen

**Sharon Smith**

# DAY 254

## SECURITY BLANKET!

> *He that dwelleth in the secret place of the Most High shall abide under the shadow of the Almighty. Psalm 91:1*

When my oldest brother was drafted into the Army during the Korean war, I was a little boy. I remember my mother giving him the only advice that she had, and that was her faith in God's ability to keep him alive. She gave him instructions to read Psalm 91 every day so that the Lord would protect him in battle. In later life, he told me that every night he would read Psalm 91 and placed the Bible on his chest before going to sleep. For him, this became his security blanket. There is a place in God that the believer can go and experience God's daily covering as a shelter from the uncertainties of life.

When I read and meditate on the words of Psalm 91, I can visualize the hand of God hovering over and going before me, just as the Word says no evil shall befall me. He will give His angels charge over me to keep me in all my ways. If you will make this a daily confession, imagine the thought of daily dwelling under the shadow of the Almighty. Finally, can you only imagine a long and satisfying life of promise? Believe His Word and this can become your security blanket also.

Only God can issue a security policy that covers you from the cradle to the grave!

**James Thomas**

# DAY 255

# A "SHO NUFF" BLESSING

> *This is the Lord's doing! It is marvelous... Psalm 118:23a*

While traveling to Dothan, Alabama for a funeral, God shielded eight members of my family and me from certain death. Heading north on Interstate 95, I was completely flanked in by an eighteen-wheeler to my right and an out of control, careening pickup truck heading across the grassy median toward my driver's door. Just before impact, I braced myself, gripped the steering wheel and yelled, "JESUS!" Seconds before impact, the front bumper of the pickup scooped up about ten pounds of grass, rock and soil that jettisoned onto my windshield and driver's window. That reduced my visibility to zero.

Therefore, when I looked in the right, side view mirror, I saw the miracle God had so graciously performed. Although there was a fatality, God had saved us from what could have been a horrific tragedy, if the pickup had continued its path. Instead, it hit the embankment, became airborne, flipped 90 degrees, and hit the rear axle of the refer trailer that was being pulled by the eighteen-wheeler. The impact caused the eighteen-wheeler to stop its forward movement.

When I saw that it had stopped along with the traffic in the other lanes, I was able to pull over and stop on the right shoulder. I got out and scraped the debris off the windshield and driver's door while worshiping God! When I realized what God had done for me and my family, I shifted from worship to panic. In that state of panic and confused thinking, I looked back at the accident and thought everyone was okay. I got back into the van and drove on to my destiny. It was only when I returned that I found out how tragic the accident had been. If God had not heard my "one-word" prayer, my family and I could have been added to the list of fatalities. Though tragic, it was a "Sho Nuff" blessing! I am so glad I knew Jesus!

**Lord Jesus, I just want to say, "Thank You!!" Amen!**

Geraldine Russell

# DAY 256

# LOVE GOD AND OTHERS

> *By this shall all men know that ye are my disciples, if ye have love one to another. John 13:35*

The greatest commandment that God gave us was for us to love Him with all our heart, mind, and soul. And although we know this intuitively, we still tend to offer Him SOME of our heart, SOME of our soul, and SOME of our mind. We should, however, desire to be fully obedient to Him because partial obedience is still disobedience. We should desire to LOVE GOD with our total being.

After all, He loved us first and out of everyone, still loves us most. And the thing is, if we genuinely love God, then we will have no choice but to also love people. 1 John 4:20 tells us that we cannot say we love God and hate others at the same time. It just doesn't work like that. I know there are times when we may not necessarily like someone else, but we are still called to love them because that is the only way they will know we are Christians--BY OUR LOVE! Will it be easy? Not always. Is it possible?

Absolutely, but only through the power of the Holy Spirit. And this is not a process that we only go through on Sundays, but one that we must repeat daily. Love God...Love People...All Day...Every day. So many are looking for love in all the wrong places these days, but if we show them the love of Christ, they will not have to look any further.

**Think About It:** How can you show the love of Christ today?

**Domonique Brunson**

## DAY 257

# WALKING THROUGH DARKNESS

> *God is our refuge and strength, a very present help in trouble. Therefore, will not we fear, though the earth be removed, and though the mountains be carried into the midst of the sea; Though the waters thereof roar and be troubled, though the mountains shake with the swelling thereof. Selah. Psalm 46:1-3*

It is sometimes difficult to walk through dark seasons. Every step you take seems like a struggle. You wonder and pray for the next flicker of light. All you must go on is a Word from God. At times you even begin to second guess that Word. You ask yourself, "Did I really hear Him correctly?"

Everyone has a dark season. A season of trusting God when His presence seems so distant and His voice so faint or seemingly nonexistent. It is how you walk through this season that makes all the difference. You may feel like you are wandering without leadership or direction. You may sometimes feel like you have been abandoned or left to fend for yourself.

It is in this season that you must dig deeper, pray harder and study longer. It is in this season that you must lean on the support, advice and wisdom of others who have been where you are now trying to go.

What you will learn from your prayer time, study and fellowship is how to rest in God's promise, how to wait on God without losing your faith and that life is a process.

Your dark season is not punishment, but training for reigning. It is designed to build the necessary strength and fortitude you will need on your next level of dominion. Do not seek to rush or escape your season of test and trial. You are going to need the strength of that fire to operate in the next dimension!

**Cheryl L. Thomas**

# DAY 258

# TAKING THINGS FOR GRANTED

> *Everything in the world is about to be wrapped up, so take nothing for granted... I Peter 4:7a MSG*

The word granted is defined as a feeling or sense of security and permanence about something that is not, in reality, secure, or permanent. We should not take waking up from a state of sleep for granted. We should not take our loved ones for granted. We should not take our livelihood for granted. More importantly, we should not take our Lord and Savior Jesus Christ for granted. One cannot go around casually assuming that he or she can complete an activity tomorrow.

In a blink of an eye, your life can change. An accident can happen, illnesses can happen, banks can foreclose, and the stock market can crash. The economy can take a turn for the worse. One can meditate on things that one should not be dwelling on that will bring about feelings of insecurity and anxiety.

Life is not promised for we live, move, and have our being in our Lord and Savior Jesus Christ. We need to acknowledge our Lord and Savior every day by walking in the Spirit and not in the flesh. For we know that we are to crucify our flesh daily. Meditate on the goodness of Jesus and what He has done knowing that Jesus is the same yesterday, today, and forever more.

Great is God's faithfulness toward us. According to God's word, He has no respect of persons and He reigns on the just and the unjust.

Trust in the Lord and lean not to your own understanding. Seek the Lord, knowing that He is a sustainer and the giver of life.

**Prayer: Dear Heavenly Father, forgive me for taking You and life for granted. Help me to seek You daily and help me to lean and depend only upon You. Amen.**

**Sharon Smith**

# DAY 259

# CANDLELIGHT!

> *No man, when he has lighted a candle, covereth it with a vessel, or putteth it under a bed, but setteth it on a candlestick, that they which enter in may see the light. Luke 8:16*

I am persuaded to think that one of the hardest things for Christians to do is one of the simplest commands which is to "let your light so shine before men…" What makes this so hard and causes your light to flicker in the darkness? Disrespect, disbelief, disobedience, disappointment, dishonesty, and disregard will cause your light to flicker. I call these attributes the <u>diseases</u> of life. Submission to God is the eternal flame in our Christian candle that will mitigate most of these <u>diseases</u>.

The lyrics in the song written by Chris Rice entitled, "Go Light your World" captures the emphasis that the Lord intends us to understand. "There is a candle in every soul…so carry your candle, run to the darkness, seek out the lonely, the tired, and worn, and hold out your candle for all to see. Take your candle, go light your world." Jesus is the light of the world. He is asking you to be the earthen vessel through which he wishes to shine. He simply wants us to let our light shine.

**Lord, help me to be the brightest candle on my street, the candle that never stops flickering, the candle that runs to the darkness serving as a lighthouse for some wayfaring stranger, trying to find their way home.**

**James Thomas**

## DAY 260

# PRICED OUT OF PARADISE

> *This know also, that in the last days perilous times shall come. Men shall be lovers of themselves... II Timothy 3:1-2a*

In a continuing quest for power and control, many wealthy property owners continue to expand the gap between the needy and the greedy. They desire to invest in areas that will generate the largest profit margin and excite the Stock Market. Consequently, millions of people are being priced out of communities. Many have become homeless. Some have young children that will suffer irreparable emotional damage for years. Without a change of heart among those in authority, there will be no end to manmade sufferings in this wealthy nation! Tragic!

Although God's Word declares that times like these would come, there is still hope for the homeless and suffering. The answer is to *surrender*. Jesus said, "*Come to me, all ye that labor and are heavy laden, and I will give you rest.*" That rest may not be owning a beautiful home, or landing a well-paying job; it means having confidence that all things will work out for one's good. When a person surrenders to Jesus, He supplies all that is needed to live in peace in the midst of this cruel world. Being priced out of communities on earth paves the way for all to own a heavenly mansion. Rich or poor, heaven is accessible to all that will humble themselves and surrender to Jesus. If you have been *priced out*, just remember that it's only temporary. You can't be *priced out* of God's kingdom. All that come to Him will never be turned away because **He** paid the first, the last, and the eternal premium for all. Many rich people will be *priced out* of Heaven because the price of *humility* is far too great! May God renew our sense of humility!

**Geraldine Russell**

# DAY 261

# LET THEM SEE YOU IN ME

> *I will be glad and rejoice in thee: I will sing praise to thy name, O thou most High. Psalms 9:2*

I often sit down and just ask myself what people think of God when they see me. Why would that question even matter? Well, as a believer in Jesus Christ, we are called to be living reflections of Him on the earth. When people look at us, they ought to be able to see His light shining through us and when they see how we go through, they ought to be able to tell simply by the WAY we go through, that the God we serve is good.

Yes, this life will present us with opportunities to throw tantrums and look a mess because of our circumstances and sometimes we might want to but take my advice and DON'T DO IT! Instead, take the other route and show others that it is possible to go through with joy and praise. We are supposed to give those around us a reason to ask how we can still smile amid chaos. And when they ask, we should be ready to tell them that we are able because God is able!

We should be able to share with them as CeCe Winans sings, "All my life You have been faithful, all my life You have been so so good, with every breath that I am able, I will sing of the goodness of God!" And I can definitely say that His goodness has been evident in my life over the years, which MAKES me give Him praise.

**Think About It:** Who do people see when they look at you?

**Domonique Brunson**

# DAY 262

## SAYS WHO?

> *Looking unto Jesus the author and finisher of our faith; who for the joy that was set before him endured the cross, despising the shame, and is set down at the right hand of the throne of God. Hebrews 12:2*

Everyone else is the expert. Everyone else is smarter. Everyone knows better than you. Says who?

Now don't get me wrong. I certainly believe in coaches, elders, and others that God will call to walk alongside you to counsel and guide you during your journey. That's not what I'm talking about here. What I'm warning you against is surrendering the trajectory of your life to other people who do not wish you well or who constantly attempt to thwart your success.

What makes them the expert in your life? Why do you think they are smarter? What has given them insight to know better than God and you which path to take? If your critics can mock you and then you adjust your plans then you have given them the right to control your destiny.

Why? Do you fear what they say is true? Do you see them as the authority? Absolutely not. God has the final say in your life. If He has declared that you are a winner, you are. If He says you're more than an overcomer, you are. If He says you are a leader, you are. If He says you are a millionaire, you are!

Close your ears and open your heart to the only One who can take what He says and make it a reality in your life. Your life is not at the mercy of your critics, it is at the blessing of your Savior!

**Cheryl L. Thomas**

# DAY 263

# GOD IS ALL-KNOWING

> *God is greater than our heart, and knoweth all things. I John 3:20*

Nothing takes God by surprise. For God is aware of the past, presence, and future. God is the source of all knowledge because He knows all that there is to know and all that can be known. For God to be sovereign over His creation of all things, whether visible or invisible He has to be all-knowing.

God knows not only the details of our lives but also our very thoughts, even before we speak forth. (Psalms 139:4) There is nothing too hard for an omniscient God, know that He promises never to fail us as long as we continue to live in Him and for Him. Omniscient is defined as all-knowing, all-seeing, or wise.

The omniscience of God assures our salvation. (Heb. 4:13) The omniscience of God assures us of present provision. (Matt. 6: 25-32) The omniscience of God assures our future. (Matt. 10:29-30) The omniscience of God assures us that justice will prevail. (I Cor. 4:5) The omniscience of God assures us that all questions have answers. (Psalms 147:5)

Trusting in God's omniscience assures us that while we may never understand some things in this life, we can trust that God knows what He is doing, and His perfect purposes will be for our good and God's glory.

**This is my prayer to the all-knowing and wise God our Savior. Order my steps in your word dear heavenly Father for I realize that in you I live, move, and have my being. Amen.**

**Sharon Smith**

## DAY 264

# DO YOU HAVE A SERVANT'S HEART?

> *Lay not up for yourselves treasures upon earth, where moth and rust doth corrupt, and where thieves break through and steal. But lay up for yourselves treasures in heaven, for where your treasure is, there will your heart be also... Matthew 6:19...25*

The question was asked if I have a servant's heart. The answer is yes, I do have a servant's heart. When our priority is spiritual, God will take care of the material. Where God guides, He provides.

The attention of the believer is directed toward treasures in heaven. The two kinds of treasures are conditioned by their place, either on earth or in heaven. The concept of laying up treasures in heaven is not pictured as one of the benefits, but rather as one of the rewards for faithful service.

**No man can serve two masters: for either he will hate the one and love the other; or else he will hold to the one and despise the other. Ye cannot serve God and mammon. 25- Therefore I say unto you, take no thought for your life...** (Matthews 6:24, KJV)

Total loyalty to God cannot be divided between Him and loyalty to one's material possessions. A master is a lord or an owner. God claims total lordship.

Jesus now deals with the equally dangerous tendency of those who have few possessions: worry! Taking no thought means not being anxious. To set one's heart on material possessions is to live and deprive oneself of the spiritual blessings of God.

Walter L. Booth, Sr

# DAY 265

# NO GREATER LOVE

> *Greater love hath no man than this, that a man lay down his life for his friends. John 15:13*

What Jesus did at Calvary demonstrated the ultimate kind of agape love possible for us all. It was unselfish and unconditional. He did not consider race, gender, color, or creed, just mankind! Now for me, the question becomes what shall I render? How much do I owe him? How can I demonstrate a similar kind of agape love among my fellow man for this gift of unmerited favor?

Various passages in the gospels reveal how the Lord might answer my question: "Do good unto all men, especially those that are of the household of faith. Love one another as I have loved you. As ye would that man do unto you, do also unto them. By the love you show one to another all men will know that ye are my disciples. Love your neighbor as yourself." These are the building blocks of agape-type love and faith. Unconditional and unselfish love will be greatly magnified when undergirded by prayer and fasting.

**Father, I thank you for this wonderful gift of salvation that you paid in full at Calvary, not only for me alone but for "whosoever believeth should have everlasting life." Help me to be a vessel through which others may receive this gracious gift. Amen!**

**James Thomas**

## DAY 266

# THE FIRST RIDE HOME

> *Blessed and holy is he that hath part in the first resurrection...*
> *Revelation 20:6a*

During the early days of integration, children jostled to be the first ones to board an overcrowded school bus. There were times when drivers were required to take one group home, then return to pick up those that remained. Sometimes, younger siblings were separated from their older siblings. Most, if not all children wanted to take the first ride home. These first and second rides home continued until funds were made available to purchase additional buses.

Today, people are jostling to get aboard an imaginary train that takes them to the portals of riches, fame, prestige, and influence. Much to their surprise, the conductor (money) permits only a few to climb aboard. Sadly, that train is heading off the cliff called "death". When that happens, what then? Will passengers be prepared for the first ride from earth to heaven, or will they have to wait for the second ride that leads to eternal damnation? Whatever the case, that home will last forever. There will be no return trips! God's Word reminds us in Revelation 20:6, "*Blessed and holy is he that hath part in the first resurrection: on such the second death hath no power...*" Perilous times are pointing believers towards the "first ride home". The second ride is for those that did not heed the signs.

**Lord, grant me courage and strength to hold on to my position to take** the first ride home. **In Jesus' name. Amen.**

**Geraldine Russell**

# DAY 267

# SPIRITUAL AND NATURAL

> *O come, let us worship and bow down: let us kneel before the LORD our maker. Psalms 95:6*

Many times, we try to separate this natural life from our spiritual life, and it never seems to work. Why? Because the two are intricately and inseparably connected since we are both natural and spiritual all in one. It is no coincidence that the state of our spiritual lives can often be reflected in the state of our natural lives. For example, are you disciplined in your Bible reading and devotional time with God? No?

You may very well struggle with being disciplined in your everyday life as well. Is your relationship with God on the "struggle bus" and kind of here and there? Well, your natural friendships and relationships may also be struggling. Ultimately, we worship God most deeply when we realize that we are called to worship Him through EVERY moment of our lives, not just in church or amongst other believers because that is where our truest dependence on Him is displayed. We are supposed to praise Him despite the pain we periodically experience, be thankful even during trials and tribulations, and trust Him even when we are tempted to sin as Jesus was when He walked this same earth.

We are called to surrender our entire beings to Him when we are suffering and love Him with our whole hearts even when He seems distant. Our deepest worship is poured out during those moments and if you think about it, those moments can be reflected in our natural mirrors every day.

**Think About It:** How is your spiritual life influencing your natural life?

**Domonique Brunson**

## DAY 268

# SPEAK LIFE

> *Death and life are in the power of the tongue: and they that love it shall eat the fruit thereof. Proverbs 18:21*

Often, we come across a fellow Christian who has been battered and bruised by the cares of life. Like shipwrecked vessels, their spirits are broken, their peace is threatened, and their hopes are dwindling. They are doing everything in their power to stay strong and keep the faith but are dying for the lack of power that can be found in a comforting word.

Something wonderful happens when you speak encouraging, reassuring words to others. Spirits lift, peace is resuscitated and hopes rise. As children of God, we have been given the unique power, with just the simple utterance of our words, to lift the weary souls of our sisters and brothers in the faith.

One word from a caring person can ease pain, lighten loads, and build community. Often in the harried paces of our lives, we don't stop long enough to see that there are many of our fellow soldiers who are dying for the lack of a comforting word.

We rush through life attempting to fight our own battles so we don't often take the time to look around to see how we might help someone else. Is there someone aching for a comforting word housed in your spirit?

Slow down. Look around. Someone needs your spirit-laced words today.

**Cheryl L. Thomas**

# DAY 269

# FULLY ALIVE IN CHRIST JESUS

> *I came that you might have life and have it more abundantly. John 10:10*

God has given us an example of a fully alive person in Jesus Christ. Jesus is our example and model for who we are to be. As a human being, Jesus lived fully into the design of what it meant for him to be human.

Jesus had to do the work of hearing God's calling, as a human being, just like we do. For instance, in the baptism experience, God speaks and Jesus' calling as the Messiah is fully imparted. As disciples of Christ, we follow his example. Jesus heard the Father's plan for His life and He followed it. We are to do the same, not our will but let God's will be done in our life. Jesus came to give us a full life. A full life is a missional life (missionary lifestyle). John 15 expresses the full life that Jesus came to give us. John 10:10 states that Jesus came so that we may have life and have it more abundantly. We cannot live this abundant life unless, like a branch, we are connected to Jesus, the vine. We bear fruit when we are connected to Jesus. We become like Jesus, fully human and fully alive.

In John 14:12, Jesus says that those who follow Him and become like Him will do "greater works than these". That is the full life that Jesus offers us because being fully alive in Christ Jesus means our foundation is so strong that even when storms come, we can live through them.

Dear Heavenly Father, help me to live a full life and walk in the abundant life that Jesus Christ has ordained for me. Amen.

Sharon Smith

# DAY 270

# SOME ME TIME!

> *Let the words of my mouth, and the meditation of my heart, be acceptable in thy sight, O LORD, my strength, and my redeemer.*
> Psalm 19:14

I am reminiscing on a spiritual song that says, "There are days I would like to be all alone with Christ the Lord. I can tell Him all about my troubles all alone." Do you ever feel like life has gotten to be too stressful, too complicated, and you long for a return to a simple place and time? **Some Me Time** is a time to declutter my own life. To some, the thought of asking for **Some Me Time** is an act of selfishness.

However, this may be the best self-enhancing time that one can aspire for. In the pursuit of happiness, we often work non-stop to achieve the American dream. And in doing so, sometimes we sacrifice quality time with God, family, and friends. There are times I just need a getaway to talk to God about ordering my steps and prioritizing the mess I have made trying to do it alone. I need time with Him to restore my failing health and relationships, and to revive my spirit again. Ecclesiastes 4:6 says, "Better is a handful with quietness than both hands full with travail and vexation of spirit."

**Lord, help me to order my steps in your Word so that I may live a long and prosperous life according to your Word.**

**James Thomas**

## DAY 271

# FROM...TO

> *Therefore, if any man be in Christ, he is a new creature: old things are passed away; behold, all things are become new.*
> II Corinthians 5:17

Cooking a delicious, old fashioned pound cake takes time to master. The ingredients must be exact and must be blended into the batter sequentially. When all of the steps are followed precisely, the results will be beautiful and delectable. If the steps are not followed, the cook will never be able to "un-blend or un-cook" the ingredients, so that each could return to its original state of matter. The cook will have to settle for the one that was cooked or start the process again. Either way, the ingredients will have to change *from* blended batter *to* cooked batter before it becomes a beautiful, delicious pound cake.

Modern religion teaches that all a person has to do to be saved is go to church, give the preacher your hand, and be baptized. Too many people do not understand that being *saved* will start a lifetime of transformational processes. A true believer in Christ Jesus will become a brand-new creature. He will change *from* being a "sinner" *to* a "saint". He's no longer the same. He is being blended into a new person, a holy person. Once that transformation begins, it's sealed forever! Many will be tempted to return to old habits, but the desires will never be the same. Once a believer is truly born of God, he will never be the same again. He changes *from* being an acquaintance of God *to* a child of God!

**Geraldine Russell**

# DAY 272

## WATCH WHAT YOU SAY

*Whoever would love life and see good days must keep their tongue from evil and their lips from deceitful speech. 1 Peter 3:10*

It's easy to speak too quickly when in the heat of an angry, disappointing discourse. It seems as if the words rush into our minds and out of our mouths in a matter of milliseconds. But it is often not a good thing to speak in these intense situations.

Words uttered out of disappointment and anger are typically sharp and biting. Instead of being laced with love and compassion, they are often stained with hurt and anger. No matter what the famous nursery rhyme told us, words can hurt. Deeply.

They are powerful, effective, and lasting and cannot be erased with a simple apology. This is why it is so important to be careful and mindful to pray before speaking. The words we say in any given moment have the power to give life, help, and healing or they can cause great wounds that can be difficult to erase.

Our words should always bring life and love. Even if the words that we must speak are given for correction and rebuke, we should always speak to them in love so that our brothers and sisters and Christ can receive them, grow from them, and use them to help others as well.

**Cheryl L. Thomas**

# DAY 273

# THE ALTAR OF OUR HEART

> *I the Lord search the heart and test the mind, to give every man according to his ways, according to the fruit of his deed." Jeremiah 17:10*

For God to show himself mighty through His people, they must first place their hearts **back on the altar** to be transformed by the renewing of their minds. By doing so, believers can clearly understand and carry out the perfect Will of God.

We believe that God has called every believer to be Spirit-empowered (Acts 1:8), Spirit- filled (Ephesians 5:18), and Spirit-led for such a time as this. We must not allow alternative altars of materialism, voyeurism, relativism, narcissism, consumerism, immoralism, and atheism to replace God's authentic corporate, ecclesiastical altar and the domestic home- based altar that keeps us connected to our Risen Lord.

God is calling for every believer to construct a spiritual altar and mark out sacred spaces, both at home and at church. This requires self-denial. It involves a deliberate choice to ignore critics and embrace God's life-changing power.

The altar is the quintessential place where believers receive God's grace to live victoriously in a fallen world. The altar is a spiritual necessity.

More than ever, we need to return to the altar of our faith. We must be reminded that the altar is not just a place to go when we have a problem, but it is a lifestyle and place where we can experience the presence and power of our sovereign God.

May this generation's prayer and praise, poured out in corporate and private moments of deep intercession, rise to the very throne room of God.

**Dr. Leticia Hardy**

# DAY 274

# WHAT A WONDERFUL WORLD

> *Truly God is good to Israel, even to such as are of a clean heart. But as for me, my feet were almost gone; my steps had well-nigh slipped. For I was envious at the foolish, when I saw the prosperity of the wicked. Psalm 73: 1-3*

When we read the thoughts of the psalmist as he expresses his wavering emotions, life can become unsettling indeed. Life is often viewed through the window of what we possess and that we do not have what others possess. The psalmist's frustrations were only comforted when he went into the sanctuary of the Lord, then he saw what was in store for the unrighteous.

In contrast, jazz songwriter Louis Armstrong offers these lyrics in his song, *What a Wonderful World*: "I see trees of green, I see red roses too. I see skies of blue and clouds of white, the bright blessed day, the dark sacred nights, and I say to myself what a wonderful world."

Abundant life is enhanced when one praises God for the half-full glass, rather than complaining about the glass being half-empty. The choice is ours to make. We can begin to see things as God sees them and aspire for the better. Or we can choose to see through a hopeless lens, "while sitting on the dock of the bay, watching the tides roll away."

**Lord, help me to see your glory with all its splendor and say to myself, what a wonderful world! Oh, yes!**

**James Thomas**

# DAY 275

# BRANDED!

> *And grieve not the Holy Spirit of God, whereby ye are sealed unto the day of redemption. Ephesians 4:30*

Chuck Conners starred in an old western series called "Branded". He was charged with abandoning his army regiment where all of his fellow soldiers were killed in battle. Because he was the only one left to give an account of the incident and casualties, no one believed his report. Consequently, he was branded as a traitor. He was stripped of his dignity, duties, and his uniform. Then, he was banished from the security and camaraderie of being stationed in the fort. He spent the rest of his life trying to prove his innocence while solving crimes.

When believers surrender their lives to Jesus, they become *branded*. Many times, they are banished from the prestige and comforts of society, not for dereliction of duty, but for their stand *against* ungodly, societal norms. Instead, they take a stand *for* holiness. As a result, many are *branded* as traitors to the progressive world. Some spend the rest of their lives trying to prove their innocence. In the interim, they help unbelievers understand that the solution to society's problems is to be washed in the blood of Jesus and *branded or* sealed for life.

**Lord, it's uncomfortable to be branded, but I am so thankful for your seal of protection. Lord, grant me the courage to persevere. Amen.**

Geraldine Russell

# DAY 276

## KEEP IT MOVING!

> *Be strong and courageous. Do not be afraid or terrified because of them, for the LORD your God goes with you; He will never leave you nor forsake you." The Good News: Keep going, no matter what other people say. Your one true companion throughout life is God and He will never abandon you. Deuteronomy 31:6*

People may criticize God's decision to use you. They are baffled that you've been so successful in your endeavors. They simply cannot understand your methodology. However, what you have to realize is that often people criticize what they do not understand. That doesn't mean you have to answer or even acknowledge their musings.

They're not impressed with your gift. So what? They don't have to be. You're not in a popularity contest nor are you out to win their approval. You are God's choice, and His approval is all you need.

They may never understand why God selected you. They may never understand the way you flow in your gift. But the good thing is they don't have to. God's selection of you is not a corporate decision. He chooses whom He will to best accomplish His purpose.

He doesn't take a vote. He does things out of the counsel of His own will. The enemy sends the chatter of your critics simply to divert your attention and focus from your ultimate purpose and goal. If you're not careful, you'll find yourself paying more attention to the rumblings of your critics and not enough attention to the whisper of your Savior.

You have too much work to do to be distracted. There are too many people awaiting your gift to waste time with those who do not see God's glory in you. Don't leave the field of your dreams to participate in their cleverly crafted nightmare. You're on a mission. Keep it moving!

**Cheryl L. Thomas**

# DAY 277

# SHAKE, SHAKE, SHAKE!

> *Be sober, be vigilant; because your adversary the devil, as a roaring lion, walketh about, seeking whom he may devour... I Peter 5:8-11*

"This world is *filled with swift transition. So, build your hopes on things eternal,*" is basically all that we have come to know as normal. We are having to deal with shifting moral values, political ethics, and religious integrity. What once was considered right, is often met with doubt; a lie is considered truth; and the truth is called a lie. However, we know that God's Word has not changed. God's Word says to the believer that your enemy is the devil.

The gospel song, "Shake the Devil Loose," seems to indicate that you can shake, shake, shake, and he will simply leave. This is not so. He has the speed, agility, tenacity, and cunningness to attack, trap, and swallow up his prey. He is a fierce predator. To win this fight, trust the Holy Spirit to give you the wisdom to escape (1 Corinthians 10:13). If one does not resist him, he will ride, then the shake will be powerless. This is spiritual warfare. *Shake* is not a battlefield weapon. The Word says, "Resist the devil and *he* will flee from you" (James 4:7).

**JESUS has defeated the devil and therefore, we now have the POWER to defeat him. JESUS knows how to win. Let us trust His strategy.**

**James Thomas**

# DAY 278

# PEACE

> *Peace I leave with you, my peace, I give unto you... John 14:27a*

Two little ones get to visit their great-aunts often. From the breaking of day until well into the night, they have continuous bursts of energy. They run, squeal, wrestle, squabble, snack, and eat, again and again. The *g-aunts* dare not fall asleep while the two are awake! Only when they are sound asleep will they get a few moments of peace and relaxation. After two full weeks of regenerating energy, the *g-aunts* have to readjust to having a peaceful surrounding. It takes two to four nights of uninterrupted sleep to settle the nervous system after the little ones return home. They always look forward to their next visit with their *g- aunts*!

Unlike the little ones that will eventually settle down and fall asleep, the unnerving crises in our communities seem to continue from sunup to sundown every day of the year. Some situations cause many believers to shake their heads and wonder if there will ever be a break in hearing about one crisis after another. In the midst of it all, God's word reminds believers that there will come a day when crises end. Then, there will be *peace* once again. Until that day comes, believers are commanded to live in the *peace of God that passes all understanding*. He's the Sovereign Lord over all the earth. In His timing, troubles will cease, and *Peace* will return!

**Lord, help us to accept the peace that Jesus offers. In His name, I pray. Amen.**

**Geraldine Russell**

# DAY 279

## GOD'S CHOICE

> *According as he hath chosen us in him before the foundation of the world, that we should be holy and without blame before him in love: Ephesians 1:4*

We live in such a critical and competitive generation. Everyone is trying to outdo everyone else. It almost seems as if we're living to prove ourselves to others. But why? Why do we even put ourselves through the trauma of trying to please people who most likely aren't even paying attention to our shenanigans?

We seem to crave their approval or affirmation. We want them to celebrate the call of God on our lives. We want them to accept us, believe in us and support us. However, everyone will not affirm your call. Some will, some won't.

No matter what you do, there will just be those who refuse to celebrate with you. The wonderful thing about God is that He doesn't need their celebration. He called you. He confirmed you. The evidence of your calling is not in the masses of people who celebrate you, but in the anointing and fruit in your life.

There will always be people who disagree with your call. But they can never argue with fruit. They can say someone else is better, but they can never disprove the results that follow an anointed soul.

So, forget about winning the approval of everyone. It may not ever come. We are God's workmanship and His choice. As long as He is satisfied with our work for Him, that's all that matters.

**Cheryl L. Thomas**

# DAY 280

## APPLES OF GOLD

> *A word fitly spoken is like apples of gold in pictures of silver. As an earring of gold, and an ornament of fine gold, so is a wise reprover upon an obedient ear. Proverbs 25: 11-12*

I am reminded of a wisdom key that my sixth-grade teacher shared with the class. He quoted this saying, "Hearts are like doors that open with ease, with very few keys, and don't forget that two of these are, 'thank you sir' and 'if you please' (*Author Unknown* ).

This basic concept has served me well as I have navigated my personal life. Many doors of opportunity will swing open if we are measured in the manner of *word* choices and conversations because *words* matter. Stubborn hearts can often be changed by kind words and pleasant mannerisms. The Bible says that harsh *words* stir up wrath.

The spoken word is powerful; it can be used to build up and tear down the human spirit. The saying, "sticks and stones may break my bones, but words will never hurt me," is false. Our choice of words can often be mean, malicious, and intentionally destructive. The Bible encourages us to "be ye kind one to another, tenderhearted, forgiving one another, even as God for Christ's sake hath forgiven you" (Ephesians 4:32).

"Be careful little tongue what you say, for the Father up above is looking down on you, so be careful little tongue what you say."

**James Thomas**

# DAY 281

# HOV LANE

> *Preach the word; be instant in season, out of season… II Timothy 4:2a*

Tony Evans reminds believers that our travel from earth to heaven is comparable to taking the High Occupancy Vehicle (HOV) lane on the freeway or interstate highways. Jesus commanded his disciples to *go into all the world and preach the gospel and teach them to observe all things.* By doing so, believers invite new believers to climb aboard the HOV so that all will make it to their destiny, heaven. If a driver is caught traveling the HOV lane with no other passengers, they are ticketed for violating the law.

How many times have believers passed by would-be passengers stranded along the *roadside of life*? How often do we speed by those in need of the gospel, or look in the opposite direction of their gaze? How many times have believers forfeited an opportunity to welcome a homeless passenger into the cool breeze of an HOV? How many times have believers trusted God to dispatch guardian angels to protect them from potential danger when they stopped to help a family in need that was stranded along the *roadside of life*?

**Lord, help us to see the needs of your people and welcome them aboard the spiritual HOV You have leased to believers as they travel along** Highway Earth. **Grant us hearts of compassion that will see, feel, and supply their needs, as you provide the resources. In Jesus' name. Amen.**

**Geraldine Russell**

## DAY 282

# TAKE NO THOUGHT

> *Therefore, take no thought, saying, What shall we eat? or, What shall we drink? or, Wherewithal shall we be clothed? (For after all these things do the Gentiles seek:) for your heavenly Father knoweth that ye have need of all these things. But seek ye first the kingdom of God, and his righteousness; and all these things shall be added unto you. Matthew 6:31-33*

Take no thought. It's a simple phrase but often misunderstood... just like the word ignore. Often when people advise us to ignore something we look at them as if they're asking the impossible. "How are we supposed to ignore something that is real?" we ask.

We wonder how they can expect us to do it. They expect it because they know it can be done. They are simply asking us not to give the adverse situation attention. To not respond to its invitation. To place our thoughts, attention, and focus elsewhere... on the God that has the final say in everything.

We have the power to ignore any setback or difficulty and take no thought of it because our faith rests in Him alone. We ignore those who say we can't accomplish a task because God has already told us we can.

We ignore the taunting of the enemy because God has already told us that we're more than conquerors through Jesus Christ. We take no thought of failure, because we know in the end, when all is said and done, we'll always come out on top.

We cease to worry about things in which God has the ultimate say. We learn to leave it in His capable hands and instead place our thoughts on the victory we are promised. We ignore what is not our concern.

Our only job is to be obedient to God, so we ignore everything that is contrary to bringing about that outcome. Why? Because that's God's job. If we're faithful to be obedient and do our job, God is always faithful to do His.

**Cheryl L. Thomas**

# DAY 283

# LANGUAGE OF THE BEE

> *Go to the ant, thou sluggard; consider her ways and be wise…*
> *Proverbs 6:6-8.*

If the ant could talk, I wonder what it would say to us that King Solomon did not say! The ant is a member of the family of social insects, such as bees and wasps, that are highly organized.

Solomon suggested that we visit the lowly ant. What are we to look for in their behavior? They work while it is day. There is a division of labor assignments. They stay in their lane, guard the house, gather food for the queen, and brood as they prepare for the hard times of winter.

As a student in college, I took an apiculture class titled: *The Language of the Bee*. This was a study of the physical behavior of the insect. The buzzing, dancing, twirling, and flapping of the wings are methods of communicating the need of the insect colony. There are specific assignments for male and female workers, queens, and drones, with no overlapping. The queen's job is to eat royal honey and lay eggs only. **Do your job!!!**

There is a group of workers who are assigned the job of locating food sources such as nectar and pollen. Upon returning to the hive, they communicate how big the source is and how many workers are needed to bring it back to the colony. This is done by using their behavioral, communicative dancing. All lazy workers are dragged outside of the colony. If they return, they are killed.

King Solomon was right when he said we can learn a lot from these lowly creatures by being dedicated to our specific assignments in the body of Christ.

**James Thomas**

# DAY 284

# CHURCHLESS

> *Ye therefore, beloved, seeing ye know these things before, beware lest ye also, being led away with the error of the wicked, fall from your own steadfastness. II Peter 3:17*

The rising cost of living has caused many families to cut expenses drastically. Some have been forced into survival mode. Still, others have been thrust into homelessness. Makeshift tents in city parks, alleys, and under bridges are becoming homes for the homeless. Some live in their cars and often move from one city park to another. Although there have been legislative actions in an attempt to resolve the problem, the situation has become dire for many. Oddly enough, there are some that have learned to enjoy the spirit of *wandering*. Only compassionate leaders could help devise plans to combat the growing problem of homelessness in our nation and around the world.

Just as homelessness has increased in our cities, so has "*churchlessness.*" Easy access to social media devices has led many believers to conclude that there is no longer a need for in-person fellowship. Many feel that it is too risky. Many tune into their local church's televised or live streamed services. However, there is an increasing need for believers to enjoy face-to-face fellowship with one another. It is in fellowship that believers generate growth, strength, and spiritual maturity to endure life's challenges in the body of Christ, the Church. Have you become "churchless?"

**Geraldine Russell**

## DAY 285

# WHAT IS IT THAT YOU SEE?

> *Wherefore seeing we also are compassed about with so great a cloud of witnesses, let us lay aside every weight, and the sin which doth so easily beset us, and let us run with patience the race that is set before us, Looking unto Jesus the author and finisher of our faith; who for the joy that was set before him endured the cross, despising the shame, and is set down at the right hand of the throne of God. For consider him that endured such contradiction of sinners against himself, lest ye be wearied and faint in your mind. Hebrews 12:1-3*

Have you noticed what we see when we are afraid? Generally, we see all the negative possibilities. We see what could go wrong. We see the obstacles we may have to face. We sometimes see the obstacles that are really there. We even sometimes see the things that actually do go wrong.

But what do we often not see? God. While we are so busy "seeing" what could, might, and even what did go wrong, we generally are not focused on the only One who promised victory and can make the wrongs right.

We are busy watching problems and possible hindrances, and we are not watching Jesus. We are not attuned to His frequency giving us directions on where to move next, how to fix the problem that did occur, and how to dismiss those anxious, nagging worries of what could occur.

When we take our eyes off of our Creator, we too like Peter, just see the boisterous, tempestuous waves. But here is the irony. Fixing our gaze on the waves doesn't assist us. It stagnates our progress. However, fixing our gaze on the One always assures us victory and moves us from faith to faith and glory to glory.

We must stop wasting our time seeing the problem and instead spend our time seeing and seeking the Savior. When we fix our eyes on Him, we are assured victory every time.

**Cheryl L. Thomas**

## DAY 286

# 96 MINUTES TO ETERNITY!

> *O satisfy us early with thy mercy, that we may rejoice and be glad all our days Make us glad according to the days wherein thou hast afflicted us, and the years wherein we have seen evil. Let thy work appear unto thy servants, and thy glory unto their children. And let the beauty of the Lord our God be upon us: …. Psalm 90: 14-17*

A lesson learned from a sleepless night. In the late-night hours of the morning, I was awakened and could not get back to sleep. While trying to find sleep, I began to listen to my heartbeat as it went thump - thump, thump - thump in continuous rhythm. It suddenly dawned on me how important the heart was to existence. Doctors have long believed that if a person is without a heartbeat for more than 20 minutes, that the brain suffers irreparable damage.

The longest time on record of a human surviving without a heartbeat is 96 minutes. I began to meditate on my own mortality, this heart of mine has been beating continuously for eighty plus years, never taking a day off for rest or vacation (great is thy faithfulness). If my heart decided to quit, at best I am only 96 minutes away from my eternal destination. That is a sobering thought! How then shall we live?

**Lord, teach us to number our days, that we may apply our hearts to wisdom. Psalm 90: 12, KJV**

**James Thomas**

# DAY 287

# SPIRITUAL GROWTH

> *But grow in grace, and in the knowledge of our Lord and Savior Jesus Christ. To him be glory both now and forever. Amen. II Peter 3:18*

Physical growth is contingent upon many factors - DNA, nutrition, healthy/unhealthy habits and so many more. Observing those who society calls *dwarfs* draws attention to the challenges they may face. Some have their vehicles modified so that all controls can be navigated by hand. Some have their homes modified so that they will be able to attend to their household responsibilities. Even so, life can be challenging when they go into communities where everything is *standard* size.

How many times have you experienced the feeling of being a *"spiritual dwarf"*? Have you ever desired the gift of being able to quote entire chapters of the Bible? Have you ever listened to a message and wished you could put together an eloquent message like the one you heard? Have you ever desired to "pray the scriptures"? Feeling like a spiritual dwarf can be challenging. However, that feeling can be conquered by simply asking the Creator for wisdom, knowledge, understanding, and retention of His Word. When believers ask Him earnestly, He sends forth all that is needed for spiritual growth. That growth continues for a lifetime. Therefore, we must continue to grow in grace and the knowledge of our Lord and Savior Jesus Christ! "Spiritual dwarfism" is by choice and so is becoming a spiritual giant!

**Geraldine Russell**

## DAY 288

# SOMETHING THAT YOU NEED TO KNOW!

> *This know also, that in the last days perilous times shall come. II Timothy 3:1-5*

This world is aflame and overshadowed with darkness. The writer of the book of Ecclesiastes says that in all thy getting, get an understanding. Apostle Paul in these passages of scripture, forewarns the believers of his day to be alert and be vigilant: Do not be caught off guard for the world tomorrow will surely test your spiritual resolve. Get knowledge, get wisdom and all that pertains to life and prosperity; but this you need to know also, that in the last days dangerous times will come.

All the institutions and things that you have come to trust in will be shaken to the core. It will happen and it is even now upon us, so let us prepare for the battle ahead: the battle for the soul of the nation and for the soul of our families. Just as Noah prepared an ark for the saving of his family, so must we make like preparations. The apostle gives us a list of things to be aware of: men would be truce breakers, the times would be perilous, traitors, heady, high minded, despisers of those that are good, unholy, false accusers, lovers of pleasure more than lovers of God, having a form of godliness, but denying the power of God… from such turn away.

**Lord keep me day by day in a pure and perfect way!**

**James Thomas**

# DAY 289

# SANCTUARY DESECRATION

> *Observe my Sabbaths and have reverence for my sanctuary. I am the LORD. Leviticus 26:2 NIV*

"The way we build a church reflects the way we worship God." The way we behave in a church dedicated to the worship of God reflects our understanding of God.

During the early stages of twentieth-century church history, there was a deep sense of reverence and respect for the church building and for those who professed holiness. People readily accepted the belief that God met His people at church. As decades passed and political pressures mounted, religious leaders began to compromise principles that were once held dear.

Eventually, sanctuaries became gathering places for various activities. Some activities caused a shift in acceptance. Once that shift accelerated, there was no turning back to basic principles rooted in *holiness*. As the world began to embrace more deviant behaviors, the church seemed to feel a need to become more inclusive. That attempt to be more inclusive caused a shift in the foundation of many houses of worship.

Today, the Gospel has been *garnished* with hints of prosperity and an abundance of entertainment that has little to no power to transform the lives of congregants. Consequently, many churches are fighting for survival. Contrariwise, returning to the *great commission* has a guarantee that is underwritten by Jesus Christ. Isn't it time for *reverent worship* to return to the sanctuary?

**Geraldine Russell**

## DAY 290

# GOOD MORNING, HOLY SPIRIT!

> O God, thou art my God, early will I seek thee: my soul thirsteth for thee, my flesh longeth for thee in a dry and thirsty land, where no water is; to see thy power and thy glory, so as I have seen thee in the sanctuary, Because thy loving kindness is better than life, my lips shall praise thee. Psalm 63: 1-3

Pleasant greetings are a natural inclination for those that we love and honor. Since I believe that God is my Friend and Father, the first thing that I do in the morning is to greet and thank him for another day. To love God is to be in hot pursuit of his companionship. In many ways, our relationship with God mirrors the relationship that we cultivate with our significant other and it requires daily nurturing to keep it fresh and alive.

The writer of Psalm 63 expresses his human emotions regarding his adoration for God's presence in his life. We too will find great joy in making Him a living companion that we consult for advice and guidance in directing our daily affairs. Relationships work better when there is a mutual understanding and benefit. The writer emphasizes that his soul (mental appetite) thirsteth for daily face-time with God; my flesh longeth for thee, early will I seek thee. He cries out to see the power of God.

**James Thomas**

## DAY 291

# MY HOUSE!

> *Even them will I bring to my holy mountain, and make them joyful in my house of prayer: their burnt offerings and their sacrifices shall be accepted upon mine altar; for mine house shall be called an house of prayer for all people. Isaiah 56:7*

When God dictated the laws to Moses, He explicitly stated what was mandatory to maintain His presence among the Hebrew people. If the priests or the people violated the laws, they had to face the consequences. Sometimes they were immediate and sometimes severe.

Although the consequences were severe, some people took it upon themselves to take the law into their own hands and had to face additional consequences. Returning to the dictates of the law was the only thing that could save lives.

Centuries after the law was given, God's people found themselves on the receiving end of the consequences for violating the law. They were taken into exile and remained until they humbled themselves and recommitted to obeying God and His laws. Nearing the return of the exiles, Isaiah prophesied that God would call people from the four corners of the world and invite them into His house.

Obedient ones would be showered with abundant blessings! He would honor, exalt, and supply all of their needs. Today, believers are no longer required to present burnt offerings. However, they are required to present their bodies as living sacrifices before God. It's HIS House!

**Geraldine Russell**

# DAY 292

# GOD'S ENABLING GRACE!

> *Now unto him that is able to keep you from falling, and to present you faultless before the presence of his glory with exceeding joy, to the only wise God our Savior, be glory and majesty, dominion, and power, both now and ever... Amen. Jude 1: 24-25*

Apostle Paul writes in the book of Ephesians, that we are saved by faith, and that it is the gift of God, lest any should boast. He further states that we are created for good works, which God has ordained that we should walk in them. Many Christians do not understand and appreciate the full measure of the gift of God's amazing grace. It is a full coverage policy that is irrevocable; and coverage extends from the day of acceptance to eternity.

Many Christians have a misconception of the gift of salvation by grace. Since it is by faith, some have come to believe that they can receive this gift and continue living as they once did. God's grace is the foundation for our behavior as Christians. There is saving grace, and there is also enabling grace; the grace to keep us from falling, and to present us faultless before the presence of his glory...This gift of enabling grace provides us with dominion and power to sustain us in the time of temptation. When the enemy comes in like a flood, the spirit of the Lord will lift a standard against it and help us to live our lives according to God's will.

**James Thomas**

## DAY 293

# THE RIPPLE EFFECT

> *Let the words of my mouth and the meditation of my heart, be acceptable in thy sight, O LORD, my strength, and my redeemer.*
> Psalm 19:14

As children, it brought excitement to see the rippling of water when a rock was thrown into a canal, pond, or lake. The waves would start at the impact and ripple outward for several yards. Large or small, each rock would have a ripple effect when it was tossed into calm waters. Sometimes, observing the ripples would have a calming effect, especially upon those that were upset.

Unlike the calming effect of rippling water on a canal or lake, tossing a stone-of-offense into a fellowship could have an adverse effect upon its members. To prevent this from happening, believers should use three basic principles before "sharing" information. 1) Is it true? 2) Is it good? 3) Is it helpful? If a controversial statement has the potential of impacting a fellowship negatively, it's best to table it until later. It may be expedient to discuss the issue with a small group or one-on-one before it is shared with a larger group. Too many ministries have been impacted by statements that seemed harmless. However, once a stone is tossed, it can't be retrieved before causing a ripple effect.

**Prayer: Lord, help me to be motivated only by love and grace so my words will have a positive effect upon all that are touched by their ripples.**

**Geraldine Russell**

# DAY 294

## A COURAGEOUS REFUSAL!

> *By faith Moses, when he was come to years, refused to be called the son of Pharaoh's daughter; choosing rather to suffer affliction with the people of God, than to enjoy the pleasures of sin for a season; esteeming the reproach of Christ greater riches than the treasures in Egypt: for he had respect unto the recompense of the reward.*
> Hebrews 11:24-26

As we live this life of faith in an ungodly world; it often requires us to make some hard choices about success and the future. We may be faced with a wide range of hard decisions, such as a choice of career, choice of marriage and lifelong partner, morality, and integrity to name a few. Moses, by faith, and because of his faith, chose to suffer with the people of God, rather than enjoy the pleasure of sin for a season.

In walking out our life of faith, we too will at some point have to make such a decision. What will be our guiding principle? Will our faith rule our choice or will fame, and fortune be our priority? We have heard of the saying that opportunity only knocks once, and when it does you have to make the decision of a lifetime; one that may determine your destiny.

**Prayer: Lord grant me the wisdom to look beyond the pleasures of this life, and to esteem the riches of Christ of greater reward.**

**James Thomas**

# DAY 295

# THE MOON SHINE EFFECT

> *The LORD is my light and my salvation; whom shall I fear? The LORD is the strength of my life; of whom shall I be afraid?*
> *Psalm 27:1*

Although a full moon shines brightly in the sky during the night, it cannot generate light on its own. It only reflects the light produced by the sun. The gravitational powers in the solar system keep every planetary and non-planetary body in its own orbit with needle-point precision. The sun was created to control the life of everything in its trajectory.

Just as the moon reflects the self-generating light of the sun and remains within its trajectory, believers reflect the light of the SON and stay within HIS trajectory. He controls believers' orbits-of influence. He alone determines the amount of gravitational power each believer needs to maintain righteous precision – holiness - in the body of Christ. Therefore, life in the body of Christ is controlled by Jesus. When believers stay in their ministry orbits, they will always reflect the "full moon" effect of the SON. Non-believers will be able to see the full effect of the self-generating power of the SON being reflected in the lives of believers day and night, and around the world.

**Prayer: Lord, help me to stay in my ministry orbit so that all may see** Your self- generating light **being reflected upon my life day and night. In Jesus' name. Amen.**

Geraldine Russell

## DAY 296

# GOD'S EYES ARE WATCHING YOU!

> *For the eyes of the Lord run to and fro throughout the whole earth, to show himself strong in the behalf of those whose heart is perfect toward him. II Chronicles 16:9*

I think that most of us are comfortable in knowing that our day-to-day activities are personal and private; shielded from the public eye; however, it becomes a bit more unsettling to know that there are unseen eyes that never sleep nor slumber, beholding our every action. God sees the righteous as the bride of Christ and has chosen to exercise the unique privileges to create in us, vessels unto honor and worthy to worship the bride.

The Bible declares that the eyes of the Lord are upon the righteous and his ears are open to their cry. Psalm 34, KJV. The Bible also declares that the eyes of the Lord go to and fro through the whole earth searching for a heart that is perfect toward him. God wants to show his strength and power in you, through you and on your behalf. When our ways please the Lord he will make our enemies to be at peace, and no weapon formed against you shall be able to prosper, glory to God!

**Father, I thank you that you love us enough to keep your watchful eyes upon us. Keep me day by day in a pure and perfect heart to bring glory to your name, Amen!**

**James Thomas**

# DAY 297

# AN UNANSWERABLE PRAYER

> *And he cried and said, Father Abraham, have mercy on me, and send Lazarus that he may dip the tip of his finger in water, and cool my tongue; for I am tormented in this flame. Luke 16:24*

The sobering story of Lazarus and the rich man is still being dismissed as fallacy. Many people refuse to believe that a loving God could confine an individual to eternal torment in a place called hell. Therefore, they seek acceptance and fellowship among people that believe as they believe. They continue for a lifetime rejecting the "truth" that is revealed in many different ways – the heavens, the fearfully made human body, the endless evidence in nature, etc. Like the rich man, many will continue in unbelief until it is too late.

Though poor, Lazarus believed in the God of Abraham. The rich man put his trust in his riches. No doubt, he knew about the teachings of Moses and the prophets during his lifetime of affluence. However, he waited until it was too late to pray and seek an answer from God. His sincere prayer was "unanswerable" in the way he desired. His lifetime of rejecting truth led him to an eternity of rejection. From the moment of his death, his prayers were discarded as *unanswerable*.

When we confess our sins, Jesus is faithful and just and will forgive us of all our sins and iniquities. However, prayers of confession must be made while we live. *After-death- confessions* can never be appealed. Now is the time to pray while our prayers can be answered and not discarded as unanswerable.

**Geraldine Russell**

# DAY 298

# MORNING GLORY!

> *For which cause we faint not; but though our outward man perish, yet the inward man is renewed day by day. II Corinthians 4:16*

Growing up as a child, I remember my mother's flourishing flower garden. She had what is often referred to as a green thumb; everything that she planted survived and thrived. Among the many varieties of plants, was a vine called the Morning Glory. This vine produced the most beautiful blue-purplish blossoms that attracted bees and butterflies to enjoy the fruit of its brilliance and beauty. The blooms would only show their full beauty, during the early morning hours of the day. When the harsh and stressful noonday sun would beat down, the flowers would wither away.

The amazing thing is that this plant would rejuvenate itself overnight and bounce back the next morning with the same displayed brilliance of blooms as the day before. The Apostle Paul seems to suggest that for the cause of Christ and our abiding faith, we too have the power to rejuvenate our spirit man day by day. We do not faint or give up. We have a God to glorify. By displaying His brilliance we produce the fruit of His spirit that will attract men and women of all cultures to admire the beauty as we continue to blossom everyday all day.

**This little light of mine, I am going to let it shine, shine, shine!**

**James Thomas**

# DAY 299

# SHELF YOURSELF!

> *Then said Jesus unto his disciples, If any man will come after me, let him deny himself, and take up his cross, and follow me. Matthew 16:24*

As social, economic, political, and emotional challenges increase, self-preservation seems to be on the rise among believers. Sadly, instead of believers coming to the rescue of other struggling believers, many hoard resources for fear of not having enough for a rainy day. Trusting God to *supply all of our needs* has been revamped. Many feel that the resources they have are for their own enjoyment.

Consequently, many needy families are being neglected; just as it was at the beginning of the Gospel Age. Believers were eating, drinking, and enjoying life while others remained needy. Denying oneself has been readjusted to ease one's willingness to suffer. It's becoming much harder to *shelf oneself* because our desires have changed.

The Church is *one* body in Christ. If one part suffers, all suffer together. If one part is honored, the entire body is honored. If one part rejoices, the whole body should rejoice. When one part has a need, the body should feel it. When the body gets to the point where it does not feel the needs of its members, it's generally because self-denial is being ignored. Isn't it time to *shelf yourself* so that the whole-body can be in health and prosper?

**May God restore our sensitivity to the needs of others in the body of Christ. In Jesus name. Amen.**

**Geraldine Russell**

**DAY 300**

# IT AIN'T OVER TILL IT IS OVER!

> *In those days was Hezekiah sick unto death. And the prophet Isaiah the son of Amoz came unto him, and said unto him, thus saith the Lord, set thine house in order, for thou shalt die, and not live. Then he turned his face to the wall, and prayed… And I will add fifteen years: and I will deliver thee and this city… II Kings 20:1-6*

When trouble comes and storms begin to rise, hold on asnd learn to stretch out on God's Word. These are the words of a hymn from our past experiences. The Bible says that Jesus told Peter that Satan desires to have him and to sift him like wheat. The devil is the enemy of your faith, he comes to steal every ounce of faith that you may possess.

So, we must keep on fasting, keep on praying, hold on and learn to stretch out on his Word. Stay in the fight, even when it looks like you are losing. When the dream killers have pronounced your demise, turn your face to the wall and keep your focus on God's Word. It is He that will cause you to triumph and turn your midnight into a glorious new day.

For I know the thoughts that I think toward you, saith the Lord, thoughts of peace, and not of evil, to give you an expected end. Jeremiah 29:11

**James Thomas**

# DAY 301

# SPIRITUAL "GREEN FINGERS"

*Go out into the highways and hedges, and compel them to come in, that my house may be filled. Luke 14:23*

Throughout my childhood and teen years, my father managed to grow huge gardens. Some plants grew during the summer, some during the winter. During harvest time he would gather and store an abundance of vegetables for his big family and other families in our close-knit community. Afterwards, he would load his pickup with sacks of vegetables and take them into town and distribute them. Dad was known as the man with the big family and with a big heart. Each year he was blessed with an abundant harvest. Truly, he had *green fingers*.

Just as Jesus used parables to reveal the mysteries of heaven, believers must use the gifts, talents and skills God has given them to compel men, women, boys, and girls to come into the house of the Lord before the harvest season ends. To do so, they must use the *spiritual green fingers* God has given them. Not only has He given believers green fingers, He has also assigned each believer a plot of souls to harvest.

When believers sit on their fingers, souls are not harvested for the kingdom. He simply asks believers to plant and water the seeds of the gospel. He ensures the growth. When the growing season is complete, He wants all believers to report to their plots to harvest souls, whether spring, summer, fall or winter, because harvest time is year-round for *spiritual green fingers*.

**Geraldine Russell**

## DAY 302

# THE GREAT PRETENDER!

> *Woe unto you scribes and Pharisees, hypocrites! For ye are like unto whited sepulchers, which indeed appear beautiful outwardly, but are within full of dead men's bones and of all uncleanness. Even so, ye also outwardly appear righteous unto men, but within ye are full of hypocrisy and iniquity.*
> *Matthew 23:27-28*

"Oh-oh yes, I am the great pretender, pretending that I am doing well, my need is such that I pretend too much. I am lonely, but no one can tell. Oh-oh, yes, I am the great pretender, adrift in a world of my own. I played the game, but to my real shame."

These are a few of the lyrics from a song that the R&B group The Platters recorded in the 1950's. As I view the religious landscape, I have some concerns. Will the real saints please stand up! It is becoming harder to tell who is real and who is not real nowadays. We are living in changing times. What used to be considered right is now wrong, evil is called good and good is now evil, fake news is now put forth as the real thing.

The Bible speaks of the time when men would heap to themselves teachers, having itching ears, believing a lie rather than the truth. The scriptures warn us to be alert, that the time would come when, if it were possible, even the elect would be deceived. Let us hold fast to the thing that we have been taught and assured of which is biblical truth.

**James Thomas**

## DAY 303

# EXPUNGED!

> *Verily, verily, I say unto thee, the cock shall not crow, till thou hast denied me thrice. John 13:38b*
>
> *...Peter was grieved because he said unto him the third time, "Lovest thou me?" and he said unto him, "Lord, thou knowest that I love thee." Jesus saith unto him, "Feed my sheep." John 21:17b*

Peter became a vital spokesperson during the initial stages in the growth of the Church. However, he was not always proud of his behavior, especially during Jesus' final days before his crucifixion. Peter boldly stated that he would follow Jesus, even unto death. When it was time for him to come to Jesus' defense, he denied Him. He ran away filled with remorse and condemnation. After the death, burial, and resurrection of Jesus, Peter's denial was *expunged* from his records. Subsequently, he became the post Pentecostal leader of the early church. His first message caused 3000 souls to come to Jesus. From the day of Pentecost until his upside-down-death on the cross, he continued to lead souls to Jesus. The spread of the gospel has continued unto this day. What an expungement!

Fellow believers, is there anything that troubles your mind that you need to have expunged? Just as Jesus forgave Peter for each of his denials, He will do the same for all believers. Jesus will never reject a contrite and grieving heart. He still expunges! Have your denials been expunged?

**Geraldine Russell**

## DAY 304

# WHAT MUST I DO!

> *Whatsoever thy hand findeth to do, do it with thy might; for there is no work, nor device, nor knowledge, nor wisdom, in the grave, whither thou goest. Ecclesiastes 9:10*

If Satan prefers idle hands, God does not. If the scriptures are anything to go by, God's calling comes to those who are busy, already achieving things, not idle. Moses, David, Peter, Paul, and Matthew were all engaged in some meaningful work when the call of God came to them. God is seeking workers not loafers in his vineyard. Whatever the task, we must see it as a gift and opportunity from the Lord; and enter the challenge with the awareness that God will hold us accountable for its completion.

If we are to hear the welcome voice saying, "Thy good and faithful servant," we must work while it is day. When our days on earth are over, and our spirit goes upward, there is no more opportunity for making up for work left undone. Jesus understood and taught His followers by saying, "I must work the works of him that sent me while it is day, the night cometh when no man can work" (John 9:4).

Lord, teach me to hear Your voice when you call. Grant me clarity in all my assignments in the earth's realm. Let me not hesitate nor procrastinate in performing my assignments, for there is a crown of life waiting for all who will do Your will.

James Thomas

# DAY 305

# A CRY FROM THE DEEP

> *From inside the fish Jonah prayed to the LORD his God. He said: In my distress I called to the LORD, and he answered me. From deep in the realm of the dead I called for help, and you listened to my cry.*
> *Jonah 2:1-2 (NIV)*

God commissioned Jonah to go to the wicked city of Nineveh and cry out against it, and to declare that destruction would ensue if corrective measures were not taken. Instead of obeying God, Jonah ran away in the opposite direction. During his attempt to escape God's voice, he was captured and cast into a watery jail. While in that stockade of a whale's belly, deep in the Mediterranean Sea, he cried out to the LORD. The LORD heard his cry of repentance and released him from his watery stockade. Afterward, he completed his commission in haste. When God had mercy upon the Ninevites, Jonah fell into the *deep-sea-of-depression*. Once again, God reprimanded him for the way he responded.

As our world begins to accelerate toward the last days, many of God's people are running away from their commission to share the unadulterated truth of the gospel in this "*wicked*" world. Consequently, *repentance* is becoming a foreign word to many in the Gen-Z citizenry. Parents are weeping; crying out from the depths of their souls, seeking deliverance for a loved one that is hopelessly caught up in evil. They are sending up *cries from the deep*.

**Geraldine Russell**

# DAY 306

## DECISIONS THAT COULD ALTER YOUR DESTINY!

> *But the people took of the spoil, sheep and oxen, the chief of the things that should have been destroyed, to sacrifice unto the Lord thy God in Gilgal. And Samuel said, Hath the Lord as great delight in burnt offerings and sacrifices, as in obeying the voice of the Lord? Behold, to obey is better than sacrifice…Because thou hast rejected the Word of the Lord, he hath rejected thee from being King.*
> I Samuel 15:21-23

As believers we make decisions every day, all day; little decisions, big decisions, and sometimes they are life altering decisions. When Ruth made the decision to cling to her mother-in-law Naomi, she probably had no idea that this choice would one day gain her favor with the God of the Hebrews, and lead to becoming the wife of Boaz: a mighty man of great wealth.

King Saul, on the other hand, probably did not realize the tremendous impact his decision to disobey the voice of the Lord, regarding the battle plan and the spoils of war, would have. To some of us, this may seem to be a small thing, but following God's instruction is everything. As we observe the fate of King Saul, it should encourage us to make sound and prayerful decisions. Modifying God's Word to suit our personal taste and fleshly desires is a dangerous position to be in. Such decisions could cost you the favor of God, which is priceless.

**James Thomas**

## DAY 307

# NEVER AN EXPIRATION DATE – PRAYER

> *Pray without ceasing. 1 Thessalonians 5:17*

Abraham prayed and God granted him his desire for the son of promise, Isaac. Jacob prayed and God gave him courage to face his fears. Jehoshaphat prayed and God gave his army victory without a battle. Hezekiah prayed and God extended his life fifteen more years.

Elijah prayed and God rained fire from heaven upon the altar and his enemies. Daniel prayed and it infuriated his enemies. However, God shielded him from the fiery furnace, the lion's den, and the schemes of his jealous rivals.

Jesus prayed and the dead revived. He prayed and withered hands regenerated. He prayed for the disciples of his day and those in the future, which included *me*; well over two thousand years later! My parents prayed for me. I am praying for my sons. My sons are praying for their children. Prayer has continued from one generation to another for many millennia. Yes, prayer will never have an expiration date if there is seedtime and harvest, day and night, spring, summer, winter, and autumn. Prayer will continue until believers behold the face of the One to whom we pray. He's JESUS!

Have your prayers expired? If so, ask Jesus to add you to His list of prayer warriors where prayer ascends perpetually; never becoming outdated nor expired. Pray on, saints! Pass the *prayer torch* on to the next generation and pray on, without ceasing.

**Geraldine Russell**

# DAY 308

# HE IS ALSO GOD OF THE VALLEY!

> *And there came a man of God, and spake unto the King of Israel, and said, thus saith the Lord, because the Syrians have said, the Lord is God of the hills, but he is not God of the valley, therefore will I deliver all this great multitude into your hand, and ye shall know that I am Lord. I Kings 20:28*

King David declared, yea though I walk through the valley of death, thou art with me! Apparently, he had concluded that God would never desert him in battle or any conflict: even though he was fully aware of his own personal failures. David's enemies had defined the scope of David's ability to deliver him only when he fought in the hills, but that he would be on his own when fighting in the valley, therefore he could be defeated.

How do you see God's ability to handle your personal challenges? Never let your enemies tell you when, where, and how God will deliver you and give you a miraculous victory. Remember, he is God of your highs and your lows; he is not limited by altitude or attitude. His eyes are not so dim that he cannot see; his ears are not so heavy that he cannot hear your cry; his hand is not so short that he cannot reach you when you find yourself in the lowest valley.

**James Thomas**

# DAY 309

# SPIRITUAL RECALIBRATION

> *Not forsaking the assembling of ourselves together, as the manner of some is but exhorting one another; and so much the more, as ye see the day approaching. Hebrews 10:25*

During the start of the 2019 global pandemic, people around the world had to radically adjust to new norms. Some had to work from home. Some had to facilitate their children's homeschooling. Many had to adjust to living without loved ones that were lost to the pandemic. In many cases, the extended shutdown was the catalyst for an increase in the suicide rate. Leaders scrambled to enact emergency plans that would assist people in surviving the worldwide crisis. There was a worldwide *recalibration* of priorities. During the early stages of the pandemic, churches were prohibited from holding large gatherings so that mitigation measures could be more effective.

When mitigation efforts began to crumble, many leaders made radical changes to the way they facilitated services. Many moved away from in-person gatherings to virtual services. Although the pandemic has been tempered, many parishioners have recalibrated their lives permanently. Many are enjoying the luxury of virtual attendance. Their commitment to ministry was recalibrated. Now, churches are experiencing firsthand what the writer of Hebrews admonished believers to resist, *forsaking the assembling of ourselves together…*

**Lord, help us to become more** spiritually recalibrated **with You and our churches. Amen.**

**Geraldine Russell**

# DAY 310

# SUPPRESSING THE FLESH!

> *For they that are after the flesh do mind the things of the flesh; but they that are after the spirit the things of the spirit. For to be carnally minded is death; but to be spiritually minded is life and peace. Romans 8:5-6*

The Holy Spirit is the source of power in the Christian's life and should be considered as the only secure lifeline. He plays a major role; for by Him we move and have our being. To be a successful Christian, we must yield to His control. The natural man's first impulse is to exercise his carnal mind. At the moment of conversion, the Holy Spirit begins its work of regeneration.

We are the Temple of the Holy Spirit, and He desires to dwell in us. This does not depend on whether we feel like or not; the fact is that God said so, and so it is! The evidence is not our experience alone, but we trust the Word of God.

**Food for thought: We are indeed the temple of the Holy Spirit's dwelling; however, he does require daily maintenance. His holiness will not allow him to dwell in unclean Temples.**

**James Thomas**

# DAY 311

# LOVE GIFTS

> *I have manifested thy name unto the men which thou gavest me out of the world: thine they were, and thou gavest them me; and they have kept thy word. John 17:6*

Several times during the year, couples, children, parents, and friends give gifts to show their love and appreciation for those in their families and inner circles. Some gifts are expensive, and some are deeply sentimental. On rare occasions, some gifts are returned in exchange for something more meaningful. Either way, most people enjoy giving gifts to those they love.

During the Godhead's conference on the Redemption of Mankind, it was decided that Jesus would enter time, space, and the earth to fulfill each phase of the plan. Included in the plan was for God to give Jesus individual *love gifts* that would be instrumental in achieving God's demonstration of His love for the world. Therefore, God gave Jesus friends and followers that he could disciple into becoming lovers of God the Father. He gave Jesus those that He knew would surrender to his leadership and become *love beacons* to the world. Today, God is still giving Jesus *love gifts*. He will continue to do so until He calls all His *love gifts* unto Himself. Are you a *love gift* of God to Jesus?

**Lord, help us to love and appreciate You by loving those You have given us to disciple for your kingdom.
In Jesus name. Amen.**

**Geraldine Russell**

## DAY 312

# SEARCHING FOR A PLACE CALLED HOPE!

> *As it is written, I have made thee a father of many nations, before him whom he believed, even God, who quickeneth the dead, and call those things that be not as though they were. Who against hope believed in hope, that he might become the father of many nations -according to that which was spoken, so shall thy seed be.*
> *Romans: 4:17-18*

The beauty of hope is that it is a fundamental companion to our faith walk. Hope can never separate or divorce itself from faith; they are forever joined at the hip. We have Abraham as our model describing how faith and hope met together and kissed each other. Hope and faith are the intangibles in this Christian journey; however, they provide the access key to all the promises of God if we faint not.

Abraham left his home looking for a place that God would later reveal, sight yet unseen. He staggered not at the promises of God, hoping against hope that what God had promised he was able to perform. He found that place I call hope.

Hope is believing that your tomorrow will be better than your yesterday; hope brightens your outlook for the future. The place called hope is open 24/7 to all wayfaring believers. The place called hope is attainable to those who are seeking to embrace all that it has to offer.

**James Thomas**

# DAY 313

# REMEMBER

> *But Abraham replied, Son, remember that in your lifetime you received your good things. Luke 16:25a NIV*

*Righteous grief* continues to overtake believers who can discern the times. They see the eternal consequences of those who continue to ignore the evidence that *time is winding up*. Many of those who are classified as wealthy feel that their record of giving to charitable causes will be credited to them as deeds of righteousness. Many fail to understand that life is far more than material possessions and prestige. Many feel that amassing wealth is all they need. Spiritual needs are often drowned by material abundance. Jesus reminded the Pharisees that life consisted of more than material possessions.

Life has an intangible component that requires intangible access. That access comes only through having a relationship with the intangible God that became tangible in the person of Jesus Christ. All who fail to establish that relationship with him will face the same eternal consequences the rich man received in Luke 15. Just as it was in his day, so it is today. Jesus does not discourage *gaining wealth*. However, he does warn against wealth-gaining *individuals*. Rich, poor, or comfortable, all must *remember* that someday this tangible life will end. When it ends, what then?! *Remember* the rich man!!

**Geraldine Russell**

## DAY 314

# NEVER MORE THAN YOU CAN BEAR

> *There hath no temptation taken you but such as is common to man: But God is faithful, who will not suffer you to be tempted above that ye are able to; but will with the temptation also make a way to escape, that ye may be able to bear it. Therefore, my dearly beloved, flee from idolatry. I Corinthians 10:13-14*

Apostle Paul offers the believer a stark warning of the results of succumbing to lustful temptations. He gives us a history lesson of the forefathers, who fell by reason of lust and temptations. The Bible says that every man is tempted when he is drawn away of his own lust. However, Paul offers a way to avoid and overcome this fatal attraction.

The Hymn, "Farther Along," has lyrics that are resounding; "Tempted and tried we're oft made to wonder why it should thus all the day long." It seems like allurement is lurking on every side.

But, remember the word of Paul, all these temptations are common to man; you are not the lone sufferer. The Bible says resist the devil and he will flee from you; however, you must put up a fight. God will never allow you to be tempted above your spiritual capacity to withstand. You are more than a conqueror in Christ Jesus.

**Food for thought: Yield not to temptation, for yielding is sin, fight manfully onward, each victory will help you, some others to win.**

**James Thomas**

## DAY 315

# REMEMBERED

> *And said, Cornelius, God has heard your prayer and remembered your gifts to the poor. Acts 10:31 NIV*

Although Cornelius was classified as a Gentile, he embodied attributes of a righteous believer. He reverenced God. He took care of his family. He treated his subjects respectfully. He had great compassion for the poor and needy. He sensed that there was something unique about the Jewish Prophet he had heard about. He longed to hear more about the One called Jesus of Nazareth. This *attitude of righteousness* was rewarded when God told Peter to go and open Cornelius' understanding of the mystery about Jesus.

When Peter arrived at Cornelius' house, he was reminded of his Jewish heritage, however, he obeyed God. As he began to speak and yield to the leading of the Holy Ghost, he realized that God was no respecter of persons. All who came to Jesus in faith would be received into the kingdom of heaven. As a Gentile with authority, Cornelius used his position to help those in need.

Subsequently, God *remembered* his righteous services and rewarded him, along with all those that were gathered in his house. They were all filled with the Holy Spirit. God had taken note of Cornelius' heart of compassion and generosity and gave him an inheritance in His eternal kingdom. When God sees you, what does He *remember* most?

**Geraldine Russell**

## DAY 316

# STAY IN YOUR LANE!

*Watch and pray, that ye enter not into temptation; the spirit indeed is willing, but the flesh is weak. Matthew 26:41*

Keep your eyes wide open! Vigilance and prayer are necessary if we are to escape the evil of the last days. Sometimes we are very anxious that God hears us when we pray, but we are quite indifferent as to what He has to say in reply. Apostle Paul warned New Testament believers, lest any have unbelief in his heart, and then depart from God, he exhorts us to admonish one another daily with the truths that will strengthen our faith in Christ. "Let us not be weary in well-doing."

Keep doing what is good and you will reap if you do not give up. "Be strong in the Lord and in the power of His might". None of us can take full credit for our spiritual victories. It is the mercy of God that we are not all consumed. So be steadfast and unshakable in the Lord's Grace. Do not be moved by the evil craftiness and misinformation of this age, always abounding in the works of the Lord, knowing that your labor is not in vain in the Lord.

**Lord, help me to maintain clear eyes about the prophecies of this book. Let me not be confused by what I see, but firm in what I believe.**

James Thomas

## DAY 317

## REMEMBERS

> *And his affection for you is all the greater when he remembers that you were all obedient, receiving him with fear and trembling.*
> II Corinthians 7:15 NIV

After Paul's letter to the Corinthian church, which reprimanded leaders for not handling a conflict properly, he later commended them for *"biting the bullet"*. Initially, they were offended. Later, they chose to obey the instructions Paul had delineated in his letter. Their obedience caused them to be reinvigorated and empowered to endure affliction and to grow gracefully in the knowledge of Jesus Christ. Paul had informed Titus of the rich, spiritual blessings God had showered upon the believers at Corinth.

When Titus delivered Paul's follow-up message, everyone was filled with joy and the courage to live righteous lives during persecution. The reciprocal effect of *obedience* and *joy* was evident when Titus delivered Paul's letter of commendation to the Corinthian believers.

Wouldn't it be wonderful if believers responded to reprimands just as appropriately as they respond to commendations? Would there be evidence of growing gracefully in Christ?

Would the affections of leaders today increase as each one *remembers* the response of believers in their local congregations? What emotions are generated when your leader *remembers*? Is it strength, joy, affection, or sorrow?

**Geraldine Russell**

## DAY 318

# EMPOWERED TO PROSPER!

> *Blessed is the man that walketh not in the counsel of the ungodly, nor standeth in the way of sinners, nor sitteth in the seat of the scornful. But his delight is in the law of the Lord; and in his law doeth he meditates day and night. And he shall be like a tree planted by the rivers of water, that bringeth forth his fruit in his season; his leaf also shall not wither; and whatsoever he doeth shall prosper. Psalm 1:1-3*

I consider Psalm 1 to be a road map for a happy life. It provides us with some foundational principles which produce a good and healthy way of living. The instructions begin with "Blessed is the man", which can be understood to mean happy is the man or empowered is the man that embraces these instructions. Empowered will be the man or woman who does not order his steps according to the way and counsel of those that have an ungodly lifestyle. He is not a constant companion for those that are scornful and unproductive but chooses to mark the perfect man.

He finds delight and pleasure in doing it God's way, which is lawful and right. He meditates on God's Law day and night. This gives him deep roots, allowing him to be creative and industrious so that whatsoever he does will be successful. This recipe, when used consistently, will yield consistent results.

**James Thomas**

# DAY 319

# REMEMBERING

> *For this reason, ever since I heard about your faith in the Lord Jesus and your love for all God's people, I have not stopped giving thanks for you, remembering you in my prayers. Ephesians 1:15-16 NIV*

Maturing in Christ can be challenging when a new believer is not surrounded by sound, mature, and faithful believers who *know the way*. Lifelong experiences have taught them how to persevere through disappointments, trials, and hardships. As a result, they can share their experiences with babes in Christ and teach them how to endure hardness as a good soldier of Christ. When they see new believers growing in the grace, love, and knowledge of Jesus Christ, it gives them great joy and gladness. There is a feeling of confidence and the assurance that the "*church*" will be in good hands when they (mature believers) come to the end of their earthly pilgrimage.

They know that the ministry will continue to flourish. As in Paul's letter to the Ephesian believers, he expressed his joy in knowing that his labor among them had not been in vain. He assured them that he would be *remembering* them always in his prayers with thanksgiving.

**Heavenly Father, may the assurance of our leaders continue to grow as they observe the emerging leaders from Gen-Z. Amen.**

**Geraldine Russell**

## DAY 320

# IN TIMES LIKE THESE!

> *Put on therefore as the elect of God, holy and beloved bowels of mercies, kindness, humbleness of mind, meekness, long suffering; forbearing one another... and above all these things put on charity, which is the bond of perfectness. And let the peace of God rule in your hearts to the which also ye are called in one body; and be ye thankful. Colossians 3:12-15*

"These are the times that try men's souls" is a quote from the poem Common Sense, by Thomas Paine. In the writings, he refers to summer soldiers and sunshine patriot. They were men who were willing to fight for the cause of the country before the war began and those who shrank back once the war started. Today's world and our country are in a moral crisis, but we are called to fight the good fight of Faith.

In the hymn Solid Rock, a treasured part of the lyrics says, "in times like these we need an anchor... on Christ the solid rock I stand all other ground is sinking sand... I dare not trust the sweetest frame but wholly lean on Jesus' name... When darkness veils its lovely face, I rest on his unchanging grace". Let us not shrink back from the fight. We are not summer soldiers but sunshine patriots, willing to fight the good fight of faith and to finish our course. There is a crown of life waiting for the victors in Christ Jesus.

**James Thomas**

# DAY 321

# ONE-WAY TICKET

> *Blessed are they that do his commandments, that they may have right to the tree of life and may enter in through the gates into the city. Revelation 22:14*

In an attempt to redirect her son's waywardness, one mother bought her thirty-year-old son a one-way plane ticket to Atlanta in pursuit of a job working with his cousin. He was extremely nervous because he had never flown on an airplane. The first thing he learned was never to eat a meal before boarding! He got sick upon takeoff. His stomach did not settle until the pilot announced that they had arrived safely.

After working his way through the terminal and baggage claim, he followed his cousin's explicit instructions on how to get from the airport to where they would connect. When he finally saw his cousin, all his fears vanished. He had arrived at his new hometown! Two days later, he called his mother to thank her for helping him see the wonder of stepping outside of his destructive, comfort zone. Now, he is enjoying a new lease on life in a beautiful new community.

Jesus offers all humanity a "one-way ticket" to the pristine shores of Heaven. There will be times when some may feel sick or nervous about the travel experience. However, the Word of God reassures believers that when they arrive, all their destructive, earthly experiences will vanish. They will be replaced by eternal joy and the unending wonders of Heaven! *Tickets are still available for the asking! Do you have yours?*

Prayer: Lord, thank You for giving me my one-way ticket to Heaven. Help me to trust You for safe travels and a heavenly landing. In Jesus' name. Amen.

Geraldine Russell

# DAY 322

# THE WELL DRESSED CHRISTIAN

> *Wherefore take unto you the whole armour of God, that ye may be able to withstand in the evil day, and having done all, to stand. Stand therefore, having your loins girt about with truth, and having on the breastplate of righteousness; and your feet shod with the preparation of the gospel of peace; above all, take the shield of faith, wherewith ye shall be able to quench all the fiery darts of the wicked. And take the helmet of salvation, and the sword of the spirit, which is the Word of God. Ephesians 6:13-17*

Apostle Paul seems to be using battlefield language to drive home to the believer that we are engaged in warfare, and the battle is for our souls. This warfare is spiritual and cannot be fought with carnal and non-spiritual weaponry. "For we wrestle not against flesh and blood, but against spiritual wickedness in high places" etc…. For this cause, he recommends a special class of body armor designed for us to always be in an attack position and never in retreat.

Nothing is suggested to protect the rear end. All our weapons are offensive in nature. Satan has enjoined the battle, but God has given us sufficient armor and weaponry. Therefore, let us go forth in the power of His might to the conquest. System upgrades and enhancements are available with daily prayer and consultation with the System Provider.

**James Thomas**

# DAY 323

# FLESH, RELEASE YOUR WILL!

> *Watch and pray, that ye enter not into temptation: the spirit indeed is willing, but the flesh is weak. Matthew 26:41*

As Jesus faced the final phase of redemption's price, his humanity fought to find a less excruciating pathway to victory. During the night of his betrayal, he went into the Garden of Gethsemane to pray. Jesus, the Son of Man, cried out to the Father to permit "this cup" to pass from him. After his third labor in prayer, the angels came and ministered to the needs of his flesh. His flesh became subservient to the will of the Father.

He had to endure the wrath of God in his flesh to redeem mankind from the curse of sin. After he prayed, he released his flesh into the hands of the executioners. He was led before Pilate and condemned to die as a criminal, although no one could find a single fault. He gave his back to the smites, his cheeks to them that snatched off his beard, and his face to them that spat on him.

He truly released his flesh into the hands of his abusers. He would not permit the sufferings of his flesh to hinder him from fulfilling the "perfect will" of his Father. He took upon himself the sins and iniquities of the entire human race. He did it all in the flesh. That flesh released its will to the will of God so that whosoever believed the work that Jesus did in the flesh would have eternal life.

Prayer: Heavenly Father, I thank You for sending your Son, Jesus, to die in my place. He endured your wrath for me. Now, I am free to worship You in the beauty of holiness. Help me to release my flesh to your will at all times. In Jesus name, I pray. Amen.

Geraldine Russell

# DAY 324

# A BIBLICAL FORMULA FOR SUCCESS!

> *This book of the law shall not depart out of thy mouth, but thou shalt meditate therein day and night, that thou mayest observe to do according to all that is written therein; for then thou shalt make thy way prosperous, and then thou shalt have good success. Joshua 1:8*

How do we define success? How do I chart my course? What does the pathway look like? In the earth realm, there are many counselors. Many books have been written on success. However, there is one book that is available to us which is a sure method for long term success. "This book of the law" has the promise of the law giver Himself as the guarantor. So then, what great wisdom can I extract from this book of the law?

Well, here is my take on some key points to ponder. Be strong and very courageous, never afraid to face new challenges and opportunities head on, knowing that God is with you. Cast your bread upon the waters, for it shall return after many days with some butter on it.

Consult the Lord in all that you seek to do and allow Him to direct your pathway. Be diligent to know the state of your affairs and lean not unto your own understanding. No one has ever followed God's advice and ended up broke or destitute. King David said, "I have been young and now I am old, and I have never seen the righteous forsaken nor his seed begging for bread." Is there anything too hard for God?

**James Thomas**

# DAY 325

## A LIVING TEMPLE

> *What? Know ye not that your body is the temple of the Holy Ghost, which is in you, which ye have of God, and ye are not your own? 1 Corinthians 6:19*

While David stood in awe of the blessings God had bestowed upon him, he long to show God how much he appreciated Him by building a magnificent temple in which He could dwell. However, David's "war-time" experiences disqualified him from building the temple of God during his lifetime. Subsequently, God told him that his son, Solomon, could build it. Therefore, during David's final years, he gathered all the laborers and materials Solomon would need to build God a magnificent temple.

Sadly, because of the cumulative sins of God's people, that beautiful temple was destroyed by a Babylonian invasion. Years later a second temple was built. It stood for many years, as well. However, it too, was destroyed 70 years after Jesus died on the cross for the sins of the world. Jesus predicted that the temple would be destroyed because, during the Gospel Age, believers would become the *living temples* of God.

Today, God lives in believers through the Holy Spirit. Through faith in the finished work of Jesus Christ, He makes them *temples* of the living God. Are you a living temple of God? If not, He is still building *living temples* where He will dwell forever.

**Geraldine Russell**

## DAY 326

# PRAY LIKE A KING!

> *In those days was Hezekiah sick unto death, and the prophet Isaiah the son of Amoz came to him, and said unto him, thus saith the Lord, set thine house in order, for thou shalt die, and not live. Then he turned his face to the wall, and prayed unto the Lord, saying in truth, I beseech thee, O Lord, remember now how I have walked before thee in truth and with a perfect heart, and have done that which is good in thy sight. And Hezekiah wept sore. And it came to pass…That the Word of the Lord came unto him saying I will heal thee… II Kings 20:1-6*

Hezekiah offers us a notable example of how to pray prayers that prevail, prayers that move God to act in our favor quickly. What do we observe in the actions and reactions of Hezekiah when the bad news came? He did not become hysterical and said woe is me. He did not allow himself to sink into the house of depression.

He immediately turned his face and attention to the God of heaven and began to plead his case of worship, obedience, and servanthood. He put God in remembrance of his perfect heart and walk before the Lord. When a man's ways please the Lord, the Bible declares the Lord will make even his enemies to be at peace with him. When we walk before the Lord in truth, honor, and integrity, God will honor our prayers.

**James Thomas**

## DAY 327

# CHANGE HAS CHANGED!

> *Remember now thy Creator in the days of thy youth, while the evil days come not, nor the years draw nigh, when thou shalt say, I have no pleasure in them; Ecclesiastes 12:1*

In 1992 the smartphone made its way into the marketplace of innovative products that would solve many of the world's problems. Little did the inventors know that it would solve one problem and generate a myriad of new ones. Thirty years of changes have come and gone; however, new changes are needed to correct issues that arise with each new innovative idea. Within a few months of change, other changes must be made to insure viability and durability of each new product that hits the marketplace. One thing is for sure that *change* will *change*.

As years begin to slip away into our past, we see that change continues to occur. Beautiful, firm skin begins to loosen. Hair begins to change texture and color. Keen vision begins to require assistance. Vibrant walks become laborious. Life changes as each new day slips away into history. Our earthly changes are certain. However, there are some things that have been established forever.

The Word of God promises that our bodies will be changed from mortal to immortal, from corruptible bodies to incorruptible, and from temporal bodies to eternal. As we behold ourselves in the reflective mirror of life, it may seem like changes occur overnight. However, all things will be made new and unchanging when God welcomes His children into the new heaven and new earth. Where will you be when change ceases to change?

**Geraldine Russell**

# DAY 328

# MY NORTH STAR!

> *Thy word is a lamp unto my feet, and a light unto my path.*
> Psalm 119:105

The Bible says that the wise men followed the star in search of the Christ child that was to be born in Bethlehem. Today wise men still follow His star. The North Star is said to be the brightest star in the Western Hemisphere. Why is the North Star so special? Unlike all other stars in the sky, it is located in the same place every night (a constant, dependable, and unchanging star) from dust to dawn.

Likewise, the Word of God is my compass and my North Star; it is unchanging and can be found in the same place every night from dust to dawn and beyond. It is the constant light of my life. It serves as my onboard /On-star resource. It's the red, yellow, and green traffic signal that tells me when to stop, when to be cautious, when, and how to proceed carefully. The North Star symbolizes a beacon of hope and inspiration to millions around the world.

The word of God is the principle guiding light, that orders the steps of a Godly man who wishes to please God in all things.

**Wise men will always follow the brightest star, Jesus is the bright and the Morning Star. He will be a lamp unto our feet and the light that shines before us in the darkness.**

**James Thomas**

## DAY 329

# THE TRANSLATOR

> *Beloved, believe not every spirit, but try the spirits whether they are of God: because many false prophets are gone out into the world. I John 4:1*

As we near the end of the Gospel Age, many people are seeking various means to prepare themselves for what they know is on the horizon: imminent destruction. Some people look to transcendental meditation. Others look to various translations of the bible that will affirm their self-centered behaviors. Still, others find solace in reading translations of the Bible that will cause them to feel better about their misguided convictions.

Amid all the cultural wars and ideologies, those who are truly seeking a relationship with the Creator must develop a relationship with the *"Translator"* of truth. He is the Holy Spirit. He teaches, leads, and guides all those who are truly seeking God. The Holy Spirit will lead an individual into the path of righteousness. He will show him/her the translation of the scriptures that will lead to a deeper relationship with the only true and living God.

Many denominations have their translation of the Bible which has led many people away from the God of creation. Some have been deceived into thinking that their translation is the only way to the god they serve. However, like the rich man in Lazarus' day, they will not accept the truth until it is too late to trust the true *Translator*, the Holy Spirit.

**Geraldine Russell**

## DAY 330

# SURVIVING ON BROKEN PIECES!

> *But the centurion, willing to save Paul, kept them from their purpose; and commanded that they which could swim should cast themselves first into the sea, and get to land: and the rest, some on boards, and some on broken pieces of the ship. And so it came to pass, that they escaped all safe to land. Acts 27:43-44*

In the verses above, Apostle Paul shares a time of tragedy and shipwreck in his own life and ministry. This story can be helpful to us as we face times of shipwreck. Life has a way of taking us through mountain top as well as valley experiences. It is the pressure over time that makes a diamond in the rough, however, a good jeweler can bring out its brilliance.

There may be a time in your life when you find yourself experiencing a personal shipwreck, a time when all your visions and dreams are shattered. Paul shares a way to handle such situations. His advice is to stick with the ship. Surviving a shipwreck required a plan. Paul instructed them to take hold of the broken pieces of the ship to be used as flotation devices that would transport them to land safely. So, when life breaks you into pieces, take hold of its broken pieces and give them to the master jeweler and He will reconstruct those broken pieces into the vessel He so desires you to become.

**James Thomas**

# DAY 331

# THE NAVIGATOR

> *Howbeit, when he, the Spirit of truth is come, he will guide you into all truth... John 16:13a*

Paper maps have become obsolete. They have been replaced by the Global Positioning System (GPS). When a person wants to travel from one place to another, they may be assisted by GPS. Their ground receivers are guided by one of the satellites that orbit the Earth. When the receiver functions properly, a person can navigate through terrain or planes to arrive at their destination. It may be a challenge for many in the Gen-Z generation to find their way through unknown territory by following a paper map. Many depend on the navigation system (GPS) on their phone or vehicle to arrive safely.

When Jesus was in the process of preparing the disciples for His heavenly departure, He told them that He would send them a *Navigator* that would lead and guide them in all the ways of truth; through rugged spiritual terrain and leveled planes. He would lead them all the way from earth into the eternal presence of God. That *Navigator* was sent from heaven and He knows how to bring all believers safely to their destination – Heaven.

**Heavenly Father, thank You for sending your** Navigator **to guide us through the rugged terrains of this life. Help us to keep our eyes on Him as He leads us onward into glory. In Jesus' name. Amen.**

Geraldine Russell

## DAY 332

# LORD, FAST TRACK MY BLESSING!

> *Hide not thy face from me in the day when I am in trouble; incline thine ear unto me: in the day when I call answer me speedily. Psalm 102:2*

In the early years of my Christian experience, I would often hear the saints say or repeat the phrases that say, "You can't hurry God. He is a God that you just can't hurry. He may not come when you want him, but he is always on time." I have come to believe that there is some truth to the old saying, but it is not exactly how God operates. He can be moved to accelerate our pain for disobediences, and our pleasure and bounty for our obedience. I once thought that it was wrong to question or seek to rush God!

However, when I read how God has engaged himself with mankind in the Bible, I see a God who can be touched by the feeling of our infirmity. The woman with the issue of blood did not have to wait, nor did the woman at the well, nor did Peter's mother-in-law. The ten lepers did not have to wait. King David prays in Psalms, I am poor and needy, make haste unto me; make haste to deliver me, make no tarrying. Faith and obedience give us the privilege to ask God to fast-track our blessing.

**James Thomas**

## DAY 333

# GUILTY AS CHARGED!

> *If we confess our sins, he is faithful and just to forgive us our sins, and to cleanse us from all unrighteousness. 1 John 1:9*

It is customary in America that when a president prepares to leave office, he issues "pardons" for those who have been convicted of federal crimes. When that convicted felon is released, he can never be charged again for the crime he was convicted of and pardoned. He is free to live the remainder of his life without fear of being arrested again for that crime.

Although all people have sinned and come short of the glory of God, He made provisions for all of our sins to be pardoned. Not only are they pardoned, they are cleansed; washed away forever. Yes, we were all *"guilty as charged"* from our mother's womb. However, when believers come to Jesus and surrender their lives to Him, He pardons them and frees them to live the remainder of their lives justified. They are free from sin and condemnation.

When believers feel condemned for sins they have committed before being cleansed, they must realize it is a trick of the enemy. He desires to retry and convict all believers for the sins they have committed in the past. Believers must hold on to the fact that once Jesus pardons them, it is irrevocable; never again to be *"guilty as charged."*

**Geraldine Russell**

# DAY 334

# POLLUTED BREAD!

> *A son honoureth his father, and a servant his master, if then I be a father, where is mine honor?...Ye offer polluted bread upon mine altar...and ye offer blind sacrifice, is it not evil... offer it now unto thy governor; will he be pleased with thee, or accept thy person?... Neither will I accept an offering at your hand.*
> *Malachi 1:6...10*

What shall I render unto God for all his mercies? Levitical animal sacrifices are no longer required; all I can render is my body and soul. The Bible says that our bodies are the Temple of the Holy Ghost; therefore, my whole duty is to fear God and keep His commandments.

My temple must be kept clean and pure for His continued dwelling, for He cannot dwell in an unclean vessel. God has demonstrated through the Bible that he will not accept halfhearted offerings of worship sacrifices, lifestyle or otherwise. He is the God of all creation and deserves our best, for he gave us his best to redeem us. I will offer unto Him the sacrifice of praise, the fruit of my lips.

**Lord let my worship come up before thee as a sweet-smelling savor, that I will always be able to dwell under an open heaven where no good thing is withheld from me.**

James Thomas

# DAY 335

# TIME IS TEMPORAL

> *The world and its desires pass away, but whoever does the will of God lives forever. 1 John 2:17*

School is out! Families are hitting the road! Vacation time has arrived. Families desire to take every opportunity to get away from the busyness of everyday life and make memorable moments. Year after year, vacations come and go. Videos and pictures capture some of those memorable times. However, those moments eventually come to an end. Then, the cycle of life starts again with hopes of enjoying another family getaway someday.

Each vacation comes to an end because *time is temporal*. Just as vacations come and go, life on earth comes and passes away. Each person is allotted a beginning date and an ending date. After that ending date comes only eternity; no beginning, no end! Our response to the temporal, yet eternal life of Jesus will determine our eternal destiny. Believers will be in the eternal presence of God. Unbelievers will be separated from the presence of God forever.

*Time* will never come and go because it is only for the earth. It is *temporal*, not eternal.

**Lord, when time is no more, I look forward to spending eternity in your presence. Thank You for revealing the truth to me in** temporal time. **Amen.**

**Geraldine Russell**

## DAY 336

# GET READY FOR THE BATTLE!

> *And he said, hearken ye, all Judah, and ye inhabitants of Jerusalem, and thou King Jehoshaphat, thus saith the Lord unto you, be not afraid nor dismayed by reason of this great multitude; for the battle is not yours, but God's. 11 Chronicles 20:15*

It is said that a general was asked about the secret to winning battles. He replied, "Make a good ready." Another was asked when battles were won. He replied, "The night before they are fought." Both answers emphasize the importance of being equipped. Ephesians 4:12 recommends that we arm ourselves likewise with the same mind. Arm means to "equip" or "outfit" as one would outfit an army with the best possible weapons for a battle.

You can supply a soldier with clothing and weaponry, but it is up to the soldier to furnish the courage to fight with a heart to win the victory. We must put on the whole armor of God in this fight for spiritual survival. The best "weapons" here would be the mind of Christ concerning victory. Our mindset and attitude will make all the difference in the outcome when conflict comes into our lives. No weapon formed against us will be able to overcome us. God will supply all the ammunition and the strategy for the battle.

**James Thomas**

# DAY 337

# A GOOD LIE?!

> *So, God was kind to the midwives... And because the midwives feared God, he gave them families of their own. Exodus 1: 20a; 21*

In an attempt to control the Hebrew population in Egypt, Pharaoh commanded the midwives of the Hebrew women to kill all the male infants that were delivered. However, two of those midwives feared God more than Pharaoh and refused to obey his commands. When he interrogated them, they lied. Subsequently, the king ordered all Hebrew male infants to be thrown into the crocodile infested Nile River; all in an attempt to keep God's people from multiplying. Ultimately, God used Shiphrah and Puah's *lie* to solidify His Plan of Deliverance for His covenant people through an infant that survived...Moses.

Has anyone ever lied to you? Have you ever told a *"good lie"* to avoid trouble? What was the result?

Yes, lying is a sin, but God can use it for our good and to His glory. He is sovereign over all things. Glory, honor, dominion and power are HIS! Persevering through the effects of a lie produces a new level of understanding and maturity in believers. Resisting the temptation to lie when you are guilty, increases one's trust in God's grace, His unmerited favor. Because of our propensity to embellish, God's grace comes to our rescue when we are afraid to speak truth. Ultimately, truth will be revealed, no matter how good a lie sounds. Taxes, tithes, offerings, favoritism, greed, or taking an innocent life...truth will be revealed. Therefore, believers must trust God when they are tempted to tell *a good lie* to avoid trouble. *All* power is in His hands, and His grace is sufficient! Just trust Him!

**Geraldine Russell**

## DAY 338

# HOW TO MAKE IT, AND NOT FAKE IT

> *For they are after the flesh do mind the things of the flesh; but they that are after the Spirit the things of the Spirit. For to be carnally minded is death; but to be Spiritually minded is life and peace.*
> Romans 8:6

The Holy Spirit plays a major role in the life of a Christian. By Him, we move and have our being. Who we are and who we are becoming is a reflection of his indwelling presence. For if indeed he is dwelling within us, then all that comes out of us should reflect His Holiness, if he is allowed to rule in our hearts. A carnal mind will not allow him to rule. To be successful at living a Godly lifestyle, the Spirit must be the dominant force that controls our minds.

At the moment of conversion, the Holy Spirit begins its work regenerating our carnal thinking to bring every thought into captivity to the will of God. We are the temple of the Holy Spirit and the Spirit dwells within us. We can then put our lives on autopilot. So, to be spiritually minded is your key to a life of peace. You no longer need to fake it. He will ensure that you make it.

**James Thomas**

# DAY 339

# DYSFUNCTION WITH A PURPOSE

> *Then God remembered Rachel… She became pregnant and gave birth to a son (Joseph) and said, God has taken away my disgrace.*
> Genesis 30:22-24a

When Adam and Eve sinned, Pandora's Box-of-sin opened to mankind. Just when you think things can't get any worse, it happens.

Jacob's *dysfunctional* family was used to bring forth God's covenant people. Sibling rivalry, polygamy, incest, murder, jealousy and hatred were all used as *steppingstones* to God's ultimate plan and *purpose*, the redemption of evil men. Therefore, no matter how evil a person seems, redemption reaches out to him/her.

Sometimes, a church family may become dysfunctional. Spiritual sibling rivalry, jealousy, envy and bitterness may become evident in a congregation. Instead of allowing the dysfunction to destroy a congregation, it can be used as a stepping stone to *purpose* and to fortify believers. Through fervent prayer, training, conflict resolution and actively embracing the power of forgiveness, a dysfunctional church can become destined for "*relevance.*"

When addressed properly, dysfunction in a congregation can be transformed into a powerful ministry opportunity with a *purpose*. That purpose is to reap the harvest of sinners, no matter how ungodly they may appear to be. They understand that God's grace and mercy reach far beyond our "salvation-boundaries." They reach to the ends of evil and into the depth of sin to save sinful man. If you are in the midst of a dysfunctional situation, embrace God's *purpose*, whatever it may be, because in God, there is no *dysfunction*, only *purpose*.

**Geraldine Russell**

## DAY 340

# THE ENEMY WITHIN!

> *But I see another law in my members, warring against the law of my mind, and bringing me into captivity to the law of sin which is in my members. Romans 7:23*

Apostle Paul here describes what I believe is every Christian's common fight, the battle of the flesh and the spirit man. Unless we come face to face with this reality, we may find ourselves captured by the enemy of our souls. Temptations are common to man, however, let no man say when he is tempted, that it is of God, for He cannot be tempted to do evil. Paul confesses that there is a war going on within our minds.

We desire to be controlled by the law of God, but because of our selfish desires for fleshly gratification, we yield to the law of sin. The misery of the struggle should cause us to cry out as Paul did, oh wretched man that I am, who will rescue me from this body that is doomed to die if left unchecked? Paul provides us with the answer: thank God! Jesus Christ will rescue me, even though the law of sin presses me on every side. He makes a way to escape. Yield not to temptation, for yielding is sin. Jesus will help you, the victory to win.

**James Thomas**

## DAY 341

# ETERNAL VETTING

> *And before him shall be gathered all nations: and he shall separate them one from another, as a shepherd divideth his sheep from the goats: Matthew 25:32*

When people apply for various security positions, they must pass a rigorous screening process to insure their qualification. If a person is determined to be *dishonest* or *sticky-fingered* the chance of him/her being selected will diminish. Contrariwise, if an individual is known for being trustworthy, he/she will likely be chosen for the position. Some people are masters of deception and can appear to be above reproach, until their true identity is unveiled. When that happens, how will the company be impacted? Will it recover from the deception?

Matthew 25:32 is a stern reminder that there will be another vetting (careful examination) process. This mandatory process will determine whether an individual will end on the left side of the judgment seat of Christ, or the right side. Those on the left will go into everlasting punishment. Those on the right will reign with God eternally. Today, every individual is in that *vetting* process. Whether or not a person is placed on the right or left is contingent upon their relationship with Jesus Christ. Those that are faithful and genuinely love Him will reign with Him. Those that reject Jesus will not. When *vetting* processes are finished, where will you be *eternally*?

**Geraldine Russell**

## DAY 342

# MOUNTAIN RAILROAD!

> *Be ye steadfast, unmovable always abounding in the work of the Lord, knowing that your labor is not in vain in the Lord.*
> *1 Corinthians 15:58*

"Life is like a mountain railroad, with a brave engineer. You can make the run successful, from the cradle to the grave. Watch the curves that are in the tunnel, keep your hands upon the throttle and your eyes upon the rail." These are some of the lyrics of an old hymn, which describes the ups and downs of life and the creativity necessary to navigate its peaks and valleys. The imagery is of early American Folk culture with a train engineer driving a train through the dangerous mountain terrain.

It demands his full and constant attention to the road ahead. He's always looking for potential rock slides and dead animals that have fallen on the tracks which can cause possible derailment and loss of its cargo. He must keep his hand on the throttle, knowing when to slow down or to speed up to carry the heavy load up the mountain range. He cannot allow himself to become distracted by the beauty of the wildflowers along the way. He must keep his eyes dedicated to the task at hand. The goal is to reach his destination safely.

**James Thomas**

# DAY 343

# LET IT GO AND GROW!

> *Ye therefore, beloved, seeing ye know these things before, beware lest ye also, being led away with the error of the wicked, fall from your own steadfastness. But grow in grace, and in the knowledge of our Lord and Savior Jesus Christ. II Peter 3:17-18a*

The impact of social media and celebrity status has influenced the way some believers see and understand worldviews. The twenty-four hours, seven days a week barrage of information increasingly pulls and clinches the attention of many of God's people. Too many are being *led away into the error of the wicked*. Some are beginning to embrace the misguided beliefs of politicians because the war between absolute truth and relativity is intensifying. The thin line between good and evil is disintegrating.

Therefore, in order to become transformational believers in today's society, we must *let go* of those ideals that are at the periphery of the *truth* and pursue the unchanging principles of God's word. His Word will stand the test of time. It will last forever. In other words, believers must return to the full gospel which has the power to grow and transform any congregation, any society, and any person. Believers, *let it go* so that our ministries may *grow* in the knowledge of God!

**Geraldine Russell**

## DAY 344

# YOUR FUTURE IS STILL UNWRITTEN!

> *I know the thoughts that I have for you, thoughts of good and not evil to bring you to an expected end. Jeremiah 29:11*

My life is not my own, it belongs to Jesus. He is the writer of my life story, from beginning to end. By His grace, he has given all of us the free will to make choices and decisions to chart the direction of our lives. However, in the end, it is His handwriting that is on the wall. He has the final say. Many said I would not make it, but God was still writing my future, and I am still here today.

We can do all diligence to prepare for our future, but the bible says that it is God who puts one up and takes another one down. We do not know what our future holds, but we do know who holds our future. I am willing to allow him to write the script for my future. Early will I seek his advice in all my decision-making. I will lean not to my understanding so that He alone can direct my path. I declare that I have a bright future. I am in good hands. He will guide me with His own eyes.

**James Thomas**

# DAY 345

# GLOBAL WARMING

> *But the day of the Lord will come as a thief in the night; in the which the heavens shall pass away with a great noise, and the elements shall melt with fervent heat, the earth also and the works that are therein shall be burned up. II Peter 3:10*

The "*global warming* fault line" between scientific researchers and unbelieving conspiracy theorists is widening. Many believe that recent reports about melting glaciers and shrinking shorelines are being used to score political points or to secure massive funding for additional research. Whatever the reasoning behind one's conviction, the fact is that there will come a day when *global warming* will be realized and acknowledged by *all*.

What we are experiencing in "real-time" is a shift in natural phenomena that will continue to increase as we see the *day of the Lord* approaching. Just as we are witnessing deception today, it will continue until *all* hear that *sound* from heaven. For some, it will be too late! For others, it will be welcomed.

Believers, nothing in this tangible world is worth rejecting the truth about the *state* of the world. It is slated for destruction! In God's timing, a "new" heaven and a "new" earth will descend from God. When that descent occurs, where will you stand?

**Lord, help me to keep standing on your Word.**

**Geraldine Russell**

## DAY 346

# A CLEAN HEART!

> *Create in me a clean heart, O God; and renew a right spirit within me. Cast me not away from thy presence; and take not thy holy Spirit from me. Psalm 51:10-11*

Lord, keep me day by day purely and perfectly in Your sight. This is my prayer each day. The Bible says that David was a man after God's own heart, even though he had many character flaws and secret sins. He acknowledges that his heart is not right and pleads to God to create in Him a new and right spirit. A clean heart requires that we come clean with God in confession of our iniquities and secret sins, also.

God promised his people that he would take away the old stony heart and replace it with a heart of flesh. A clean heart will require a daily emptying. The Holy Spirit will dwell comfortably in a clean heart. As David was, so must we become God-chasers, desiring His continual Presence in our daily lives and business.

He will make you a great business partner and confidant. Our iniquities can separate us from God's best. Though He will not leave us nor forsake us, He will also not dwell in an unclean vessel. It is a good thing to ask God for a spiritual cleansing regularly, for we dwell among a world of iniquity and contaminants, and He alone is our safety shield.

**James Thomas**

# DAY 347

# GRACE FOR THE GRIEVING

> *Now Jesus loved Martha and her sister, and Lazarus. Jesus said unto her, I am the resurrection and the life: he that believeth in me, though he were dead, yet shall he live. John 11:5, 25*

One of Jesus' closest friends (who wasn't a disciple) was Lazarus. When Lazarus died, mourners from all around gathered to comfort his sisters. Their grief was real and intense. During the days before Lazarus' death, they wondered if Jesus would arrive in time to heal him. However, he delayed his arrival to demonstrate *"grace for the grieving"*. When he got there, he raised Lazarus from the dead. Their mourning turned into a great celebration.

There are many people grieving the loss of loved ones. Some of them died as friends of Jesus; others did not. Those who died as friends are comforted in knowing that Jesus is the *resurrection* and the *life*. When He returns to receive His people, He will bring *all* those who died in the Lord. In that resurrection morning, there will be joy unspeakable that's full of glory! Until then, let's be encouraged to demonstrate the same kind of *"passion"* Jesus demonstrated when He wept with Mary and Martha as they grieved the loss of their only brother. Grace coupled with compassion, helps those who are grieving to emerge in faith; knowing that in God's timing, the dead will *rise to die no more*. Therefore, let's offer greater *grace for the grieving*.

**Geraldine Russell**

# DAY 348

## UNDER HIS WINGS!

> *He shall cover thee with his feathers, and under his wings shalt thou trust: His truth shall be thy shield and buckler. Thou shalt not be afraid for the terror by night, nor for the arrow that flieth by day; Nor for the pestilence that walketh in darkness; Nor for the destruction that wasted at noonday. Psalm 91:4-6*

I often read the prayers of the psalmist and meditate on its core meaning. I find myself searching for contemporary examples of God's mercies that are relevant to my life experiences.

This passage of Psalm 91 reminds me of a time long ago when many of our neighbors had chickens roaming loose in their yards. Occasionally, the hens would have little chicklets, trailing and feeding beside the mother hen. I recall on several occasions observing the Hawk (which we referred to as the chicken hawk), the mother hen could sense the presence of the dangerous hawk, circling above.

The mother hen would sound her alarm by making a special clucking sound that alerted the baby chicks to run for her protection. The mother hen would raise both wings and spread them wide so that the baby chick could get under her wings. She would close her wings down and prepare to defend her chick with her own life, if necessary. I am persuaded to think that this is what God offers us as present-day protection from our spiritual hawks today.

**James Thomas**

## DAY 349

# LIGHTHOUSES

> *That ye may be blameless and harmless, the sons of God, without rebuke, in the midst of a crooked and perverse nation, among whom ye shine as lights in the world. Philippians 2:15*

Nestled among beautiful, evergreen shrubs in Florida's Jupiter Inlet, sits a 108-foot, red lighthouse that has guided ships, yachts, and boats since its first illumination in July of 1860. Today, it is still used as a beacon of light for maritime travelers along the coastline of Central Florida.

As our world becomes increasingly darker, we are reminded of Paul's instructions in his letter to the Philippian believers. Many of them suffered darkness through intense persecution. Some had become discouraged and were looking back into the world for relief and greater comfort. Paul encouraged them to hold on to the faith and promises of God. He would give them strength to become beacons of light (lighthouses) to those who needed perseverance. Furthermore, he reminded them that what they were enduring caused the gospel to spread further among unbelievers; even among those that lived in the king's royal palace.

Fellow believers, continue to be a beacon of light and hope so that those in darkness may be guided to the *Light of the World*! Like the Jupiter Lighthouse, you are still a light shining in darkness! Shine on!

**Geraldine Russell**

## DAY 350

# RUN LIKE A DEER

> *The Lord God is my strength, and he will make my feet like hinds' feet, and he will make me to walk upon mine high places.*
> Habakkuk 3:19

Apostle Paul encourages the believer to run with patience, the race that is set before us. Every individual will have his own unique race to run, however, you are built to handle the turf.

Life is filled with swift transitions, none on earth unmoved can change it, you ought to hold on to God's unchanging hand. Great advice from songs of old. The mountain goat and the deer are animals that are uniquely suited for a fast getaway from predators, escaping by virtue of their fleet-footed speed and agility. Their feet are designed to be both offensive and defensive weapons when necessary. Being sure-footed is a survival skill. They can handle the rough and rocky mountain terrain.

The deer must consume enough daily nourishment to be energized to go from 0 mph to maximum speed on a moment's notice to survive. Likewise, we must stay fully charged on the word of God, so we too can make our quick escapes when necessary. In a similar fashion, you have been uniquely empowered by God to handle the rough and rocky roads that you may be called to travel, He maketh my feet like hinds' feet that will not slip. You have been endowed with the speed and tenacity to endure the race.

**James Thomas**

## DAY 351

# THE END TIME DRAGNET

> *And he said unto them, Cast the net on the right side of the ship, and ye shall find. They cast therefore, and now they were not able to draw it for the multitude of fishes. John 21:6*

As a child, I watched my father and uncles catch fish from the St. Lucie River. They caught many different kinds, shapes, and sizes. After each catch, they would toss or bring the fish to shore where their wives would clean and fry them over an open fire. They used poles and nets to catch mullets, brims, catfish, bass, turtles, and more. As the men fished, the children would play around the edge of the water until they were summoned to a hearty meal of freshly caught, fried fish. Memories of those days have been engraved in the recesses of my mind since childhood. Those were fun days!

After Jesus' death, his disciples returned to fishing. They had not fully understood the new occupation to which they had been called. One day, after fruitlessly toiling for fish, Jesus told them to cast their net on the *"right"* side of the ship. When they obeyed, they caught many fish. That was a preview of their *new* occupation. Before Jesus ascended, he commissioned them to go into the world and catch men in the *dragnet of the gospel*. When all fishing is done, Jesus will send forth his angels to separate the good catch from the bad. When that separation is complete, Jesus will call his children to a hearty meal in heaven.

Have you been caught in the *end-time dragnet* of the gospel? It's still being cast.

**Geraldine Russell**

# DAY 352

# ANGELS ON ASSIGNMENT!

> *For he shall give his angels charge over thee, to keep thee in all thy ways. They shall bear thee up in their hands, lest thy dash thy foot against a stone. Psalm 91:11-12*

*All day, all night, the angels are watching over me.* This gospel song was of great comfort to me as a little child. At the time, I certainly did not understand the full implication of what this really meant. Now that I am more aware of the watchful eyes of God for his children, as we read Psalm 91 in its fullness, I believe that God has assigned every one of his children a special host of angels to watch, guard, and protect them day or night. They have to protect us from self-inflicted wounds.

Those who will accept their angelic presence and guidance will eat the good of the land, But, if they resist and rebel, they may risk losing their protection. Their divine assignment is to keep you in all your ways, day and night, spring, summer, or fall. The Bible also declares that the Lord is mindful of us. He will bless us more and more, and our children (Psalm 115).

**Father, I thank you for the angels that you have assigned to cover me and my household, knowing that we are prone to follow our own way that is sometimes not in our best interest and will lead us astray!**

**James Thomas**

# DAY 353

# GOD DOES FACIALS

> *For the LORD taketh pleasure in his people: he will beautify the meek with salvation. Psalm 149:4*

The beauty industry racks in billions of dollars from the sale of beauty products. Famous celebrities spend millions of dollars trying to maintain a vibrant, youthful look. When nature can no longer be manipulated, many dwarfs go into seclusion to hide their appearance. One famous artist explored cryogenics in a futile attempt to prevent aging. All of his attempts failed when his life ended with an overdose of prescription medication. One is left to wonder how his life could have ended if he had surrendered with meekness to the call of God.

The Greek word *meek* means *"strength under control."* The English term means *"gentle and submissive."* The biblical term means *"a person that is willing to accept and submit to someone else without resistance."* People who are characterized by meekness are made *attractive/beautiful* by God Himself. He beautifies them with the meekness of *salvation*.

This beautification lasts a lifetime. It's guaranteed by the One who sculpted *"beauty"* from the *rib* of a man and sealed His creation with a stunning *facial* that mesmerized God's image bearer, Adam.

**Heavenly Father, thank You for the high cost of salvation and the low cost of obtaining its beauty.**

Geraldine Russell

## DAY 354

# THE FAITH OF OUR FATHERS!

> *We have heard with our ears, O God, our fathers have told us, what works thou didst in their days, in the times of old. How thou didst drive out the heathen with thy hand, and plantedst them how thou didst afflict the people, and cast them out...Because thou hadst a favor unto them. Psalm 44:1-3*

One of the legacies of our spiritual fathers was their living faith. Oh, how I long to be like them!

The hymn written by William Faber feeds the longing heart for days gone by, *when the faith of men moved God to action. Faith of our fathers living still, in spite of dungeons, fire, and sword: Oh, how our hearts beat high with joy, whenever we hear glorious word.*

Oh, how our lives would be different if we could now embrace the faith of our fathers. The possession of a deep and abiding faith, that honors God and is fully persuaded that He can sustain us in all of life's adversities. He will perform his Word concerning us. Faith of our fathers, Holy faith, we will be true to thee til death.

**Prayer: Lord, if I have found favor in Thy sight, revive me again to trust your Word, knowing that you will watch over your Word to perform it and that none of it shall fall to the ground unfulfilled.**

**James Thomas**

## DAY 355

# THE SEAL OF APPROVAL

> *Then the LORD said, "Rise and anoint him; this is the one." So Samuel took the horn of oil and anointed him in the presence of his brothers, and from that day on the Spirit of the LORD came powerfully upon David... 1 Samuel 16:12b-13b*

After Saul was stripped of his kingship, God sent Samuel to Jesse's house to anoint David as Saul's successor. After God revealed His choice to Samuel, he anointed him with oil. The Spirit of God came upon David and empowered him to do the job as king of Israel. In spite of all the opposition David faced from his anointing to the start of his official duties as king, he endured all of the challenges and attempts on his life. He wore the *seal of God's approval* until his death. When his reign ended, the entire world knew that David had been appointed and anointed by God to do his work.

In our world of increasing competitiveness, many people are resorting to crafty schemes and character assassinations to get ahead in society. However, there is a principle that was instituted by God which remains true throughout all generations: *"Your gift will make room for you."* It doesn't matter what schemes are formed against God's people, He is the One that works the will and the ability within His people to complete the work He has assigned. Even if He has to remove a Goliath, nothing can stop the forward movement of God's plans for His people. His kingdom has come to earth, and He's still handing out *Seals of Approval – His anointing.*

**Geraldine Russell**

## DAY 356

# THE HIJACKING OF YOUR FAITH!

> *The thief cometh not, but for to steal, and to kill, and to destroy. I am come that you might have life, and that they might have it more abundantly. John 10:10*

Hijacking is a term we rarely mention in the religious faith arena. Many of us have deluded ourselves to think that faith is rigidly fixed and off-limits. We read where Christ told Peter that Satan desires to have you and sift you like wheat. We may become convinced that we are untouchable.

The term hijack means to unlawfully seize another property for your advantage. We walk around with our heads in the air, unaware of our surroundings, our spiritual guardrail down, leaving ourselves open and exposed. But, thanks be to God, he knows our frame, that we are weak. He will build a hedge around our faith because he knows that Satan desires to sift us like wheat. His goal is to sift every ounce of faith you have while offering you a counterfeit alternative to serving a lesser god. Eternal life is your intended destination.

Satan wants to hijack your plans for a long and bountiful life here in the now. Whatsoever God has promised He is able to perform. He will perform all things concerning you. Firm faith is the vehicle that will also get you the abundant life here on this side. So, lock your doors, close the windows, and have safe and happy travels.

**James Thomas**

## DAY 357

# "A FLASHBACK PRAISE"

> *Remember the wonders he has done, his miracles, and the judgments he pronounced, you children of his servants... Psalm 105:5*

There is a song saints used to sing with fervor and conviction entitled, "*When I Think of the Goodness of Jesus.*" It goes on to say, "*...and all He has done for me, my soul cries out, 'Hallelujah', I thank God for saving me!*" During those early days, many of God's people did not have funds or insurance to go to doctors. They had to depend on God for healing.

When they prayed, they believed God. There were times when God shielded His people from the dangers of racism. He protected them from diseases that destroyed many. He gave them jobs they were deemed unqualified to receive.

When they assembled for service, they came with praises in their hearts. They arrived early and sat with considerable expectations of a move from God. There were spontaneous songs extolling God for His goodness. Worship flowed from heart to heart. Sinners were delivered from the shackles of sin. Children reverenced the presence of God. Preachers preached as God led and empowered them. There was no artificial prompting or invoking of God's power to reign among the assembly. They lived in the presence of God daily. Praise and worship were a constant companion of the early saints.

When was the last time you had *a flashback praise*? When you think of the goodness of Jesus, how do you respond?

**Geraldine Russell**

# DAY 358

# THE WORLD, THE FLESH, AND THE DEVIL!

> *Put on the whole armour of God, that you may be able to stand against the wiles of the devil. For we wrestle not against flesh and blood, but against principalities, against powers, against the rulers of the darkness of this world, against spiritual wickedness in high places. Ephesians 6:11-12*

Being a Christian does not exempt us from trouble and hard times in this life. This is a common experience of all mankind. As you journey through this land, you will have the Holy Spirit as a Comforter and Supporter at all times. He will never desert you or leave you defenseless. You will always have the supreme Problem Solver to guide your thoughts. The difficulties that you will face as a Christian will come from one of four sources:

The natural consequences of foolish and amoral activities, the lust of the eyes and the pride of life – Hosea 8:7, KJV

The temptations of Satan – 1 John 2:15-16, KJV

The discipline of God, as a consequence of sin – Hebrews 12:5-15, KJV d, The testing of God, designed to cause spiritual growth – John 12:27, KJV

And having spoiled principalities and powers, he made a shew of them openly, triumphing over them in it… -Col. 2:15

So, let us stand fast and be still for the battle is not ours, but the Lord's.

**James Thomas**

# DAY 359

# HE BROUGHT HOPE

> *Glory to God in the highest, and on earth peace, good will toward men. Luke 2:14*

I would like to share a Christmas lyric that always blesses my heart and this time, I want to share the song, "O Holy Night". I imagine that, although the stars were "brightly shining", the night our Savior was born had to be one of the darkest nights ever because the world lay wallowing in sin and error, simply awaiting the coming of the Messiah. Sounds like our lives, right?

However, His coming made it also the holiest night ever, and OH when He came! I remember when He was born in my life. My soul truly felt the weight and worth of His birth and His coming brought so much joy and hope. HOPE. That is a word that the world is sorely lacking these days and it is the very reason that Jesus came. It is also the reason we should have no problem falling on our knees before Him and worshiping with the angels as they cry, "Holy", to our God. While others are in despair, we as the people of God, STILL have a reason to hope!

**Think About It:** What situation do you need to look at again through the lens of hope?

**Domonique Brunson**

# DAY 360

## FILL MY CUP!

> *Know ye not that are the Temple of God, and that the Spirit of God dwells in you? 1 Corinthians 3:16*

The Holy Spirit is the major source of power in the life of the Christian and should be considered the only secure lifeline. The Holy Spirit is our energy supply, by Him we move and have our being. To be a successful Christian, one must yield to his control. At the moment of conversion, the Holy Spirit begins his work of regeneration. We are now the temple where He dwells.

He will fill us to overflowing with His Holy Spirit, If we yield to his control, the work of regeneration is a lifelong process. So, allow the Lord to finish the work that He has begun in you. **For they that are after the flesh do mind the things of the flesh, but they that are after the Spirit do mind the things of the Spirit. For to be carnally minded is death, but to be spiritual minded is life and peace (Romans 8:5, KJV.)**

**Prayer:** Lord, fill my cup with your Holy Spirit until it overflows in my life reflects your glory and in my actions that others may see your glory revealed in me.

James Thomas

# DAY 361

# WHO, ME?!

> *Pardon me, my lord, Gideon replied, but how can I save Israel? My clan is the weakest in Manasseh, and I am the least in my family.*
> Judges 6:15

After the children of Israel rebelled against God, He allowed the Midianites to raid their land for seven years. When they cried out to God, He commissioned Gideon as Israel's deliverer. While in hiding, the angel of the Lord delivered the message to Gideon. As with Moses, he felt that he was not qualified to complete the task of becoming a deliverer. He tried to reason his way out of the angel's directives. However, after a series of tests and the assurance that God would be with him, Gideon finally agreed to obey his commission. He was victorious over the Midianites because he trusted God's plan of deliverance. In the end he boldly proclaimed, "*Yes, me!*"

Has God nudged you to venture out of *hiding* into the marketplace of world views to fight against the enemies of God's people? Do you feel timid and unqualified to affect changes in a difficult and seemingly hopeless situation? Are you asking God a "*Who, me?*" question because you feel inadequate? If you answered "Yes" to any of these inquiries, then you are just right for God to enlist you as a "*mighty warrior*" for His kingdom. All He needs is your willingness to come out of *hiding*. He will do the rest. He's still able to turn the least into the best and the weakest into the strongest to save His people from the *raiders* that are leaving them famished. Yes, He wants you! *Who, me?* "Yes, you," says the Lord!

**Lord, grant me boldness to come out of** hiding. **Amen.**

**Geraldine Russell**

## DAY 362

# BLOWN BY THE WINDS OF CHANGE!

> *And then the rains descended, and the floods came, and the winds blew, and beat upon that house; and it fell not: for it was founded upon a rock. Matthew 7:25*

In what direction are we being blown by the shifting winds of change of this modern church age? There is a song that says, "The times of time, ring out the news, another day is through, someone slipped and fell, was that someone you…" Our modern culture is ever-evolving and drifting away from the religious standard once held by Christians to be sound doctrine. God said in the Bible, that I am the Lord your God and I change not.

Well, did he change his mind for this present age, or are we becoming his undesignated change agents? We are witnessing sweeping changes in the way Christians are being led to understand and to interpret scripture, which are seemingly designed to fit the times we now live. It seems that all our sacred institutions are being shaken by the winds of cultural change, proposed by a people who no longer believe in the God of Moses, Abraham, Isaac, and Jacob.

What then should be our plan of resistance? Be steadfast, unmovable… always abounding in the work and Word of the Lord, no man to take away your crown, for we will reap if we faint not, the crown goes to the finisher in the race; so, run well, finish strong!

**James Thomas**

## DAY 363

# THE PROSPERITY GOSPEL

> *Keep this Book of the Law always on your lips; meditate on it day and night, so that you may be careful to do everything written in it. Then you will be prosperous and successful. Joshua 1:8*

In recent years, there has been a shift in preaching. That shift has been disguised as *Prosperity Gospel*. It teaches that if believers elevate their minds, they will be able to acquire the possessions they desire. Many no longer believe that the *pure gospel* has the attraction needed to produce a faithful following. Therefore, many feel that it has become necessary to embellish the Gospel with promises of material abundance. That popular ideology is called *Prosperity Gospel*. When material blessings do not materialize, many say that it's because of an individual's lack of faith. This trend has resulted in many people rejecting the truth that says, "*Those that live godly in this present world will suffer...internal or external opposition or persecution.*"

In God's initial chat with Joshua, He stated that *prosperity* and success would come only through unwavering adherence to the Book of the Law. Since the Book of the Law was fulfilled in Jesus Christ, believers must adhere to Jesus' instructions in order to experience true *prosperity*. That prosperity may not include an earthly mansion or a Maserati, but it does include a mansion built by Jesus, and it's prepared for *move-in*. It will never lose its market value, and it's guaranteed by its Builder, Jesus! That *prosperity* comes only through believing in *and* adhering to the full *Gospel* of Jesus Christ. How prosperous are you?

**Geraldine Russell**

## DAY 364

# LORD, HELP MY UNBELIEF!

> *Jesus said unto him, if thou canst believe, all thin are possible unto him that believeth. And straightway the father of the child cried out and said with tears, Lord I believe; help thou mine unbelief.*
> Mark 9:23-24

There have been many times I, too, have needed divine intervention in my faith walk. The story here in the Bible is one of a man who had watched Jesus perform a miracle and yet he struggled to exercise sufficient faith to deliver his son from this disease. Sometimes, issues will arise in our lives, and attack our bodies to the point, that if God doesn't do it, it just will not get done, We often exercise all our faith muscles; we honor God with the tithe and offerings, we attend all the church events, pray unceasingly, receive the laying on of hands by the Elders, and yet our breakthrough is delayed.

I think that these verses speak volumes to us about spiritual surrender and submission. We must come to grips with the fact that we cannot do life without God's divine intervention. Admit to yourself that this problem that I have is too big for me, and Lord if you do not do it; it will not get done. I need you to help my unbelief. Bridge the gap, supply the missing link in my faith muscle. Just as Jesus told Mary, at the tomb of Lazarus, if *you will only believe, you will see the glory of God!*

**James Thomas**

# DAY 365

# SOW WELL, REAP WELL

> *The King will reply, Truly, I tell you, whatever you did for one of the least of these brothers and sisters of mine, you did for me.*
> Matthew 25:40

Sorrow, suffering, and challenging times are evident in many of our communities. Untold numbers of families are enduring hardships like never before. Some are on the brink of hopelessness. They are in need of simple acts of compassion. Some need shelters. Others need clothing to protect them from the looming winter. Still others are orphaned and long to hear a word of comfort and reassurance that better days will come. There are some that are fleeing from imminent danger in their home countries. Global missions are critical to addressing the needs of suffering people. Therefore, believers must increase their desires to *sow* into the lives of those in dire need. One seed sown in good soil will produce a much greater return. Too many resources are earmarked for those that already have more than enough, while the needy continue to suffer.

Matthew 25 informs believers that it matters how we *sow* into the kingdom of God because *reaping* days are sure to come. Therefore, we must resolve to *sow* into ministry endeavors that have eternal benefits for both the contributors and the recipients. Subsequently, all who *sow well* in God's kingdom on earth will *reap well* on that great day when God sends forth His angels to separate those who *sow* in righteousness *from* those who *sow* with unrighteous motives.

Believers, if we *sow well* today, we will *reap well* in that great day of separation. The reward? Eternal life!

**Geraldine Russell**

# CONTRIBUTING WRITERS

Bishop James E. McKnight, Sr.
Leading Lady Delois McKnight
Ruling Elder James Williams
Leading Lady Lillie Williams
Ruling Elder HN Turner
Leading Lady Precious Turner
Leading Lady Gwendolyn Ware
Ruling Elder Reginald Daymon
Leading Lady Veronica Daymon
The Late Evangelist Nathaniel Scippio (Edited Writings)
Dr. Deloris Y. McBride
James Thomas
Geraldine Russell
Mary Calhoun
Dr. Leticia Hardy
Walter Booth
Mary Smith
Lynette Whitfield
Domonique Brunson
Cheryl L. Thomas
Jessica Lucas
Elder Garry Shelton
Lesley Thomas
Felicia C. Parker
Venetta Law
Helen V. Tate
Brittany Rudolph Montgomery
Sharon Smith
Evelyn Beachem
Sheila F. Jones

www.ingramcontent.com/pod-product-compliance
Lightning Source LLC
Chambersburg PA
CBHW051031160426
43193CB00010B/908